POLITICS AND PEOPLE

The Ordeal of Self-Government in America

Politics and People

The Ordeal of Self-Government in America

Fighting the Spoilsmen

By

William Dudley Foulke

ARNO PRESS

A New York Times Company

New York — 1974

Reprint Edition 1974 by Arno Press Inc.

Reprinted from a copy in The University
  of Illinois Library

POLITICS AND PEOPLE: The Ordeal
of Self-Government in America
ISBN for complete set: 0-405-05850-0
See last pages of this volume for titles.

Manufactured in the United States of America

Library of Congress Cataloging in Publication Data

Foulke, William Dudley, 1848-1935.
   Fighting the spoilsmen.

   (Politics and people: the ordeal of self-govern-
ment in America)
   Reprint of the 1919 ed. published by Putnam, New
York.
   1. Foulke, William Dudley, 1848-1935. 2. Civil
service reform. I. Title. II. Series.
JK693.F6A3 1974   353.006 [B]   73-19146
ISBN 0-405-05870-5

Fighting the Spoilsmen

Reminiscences of
The Civil Service Reform Movement

By

William Dudley Foulke, LL.D.

Author of "Slav and Saxon," "Maya," "Life of O. P. Morton,"
"Protean Papers," "History of the Langobards," "Dorothy Day,"
"Masterpieces of the Masters of Fiction," "Some Love Songs
of Petrarch," "Lyrics of War and Peace," etc.

G. P. Putnam's Sons
New York and London
The Knickerbocker Press
1919

The Knickerbocker Press, New York

To the Memory

OF

GEORGE WILLIAM CURTIS

" We have laid our hands on the barbaric palace of patronage and have written 'Mene, mene,' upon its walls, nor will it be long, as I believe, until they are laid in the dust."

A kingly spirit and a vision clear,
　A prophet's prescience and a statesman's mind,
A face to win us and a smile to cheer,
　A heart that glowed with love of humankind!
His voice was music and his words were song,
　His ways were gentle but his reason just,
Quick to discern the right and scourge the wrong,
　And him we followed with unfaltering trust.
He wrote his "Mene, mene," on the wall,
　Then passed, and lo! before our eager eyes
The spoilsman's palace crumbles to its fall
　And on the ruins goodlier mansions rise.
Too soon his voice grew silent, yet its thrill
Along the cliffs of memory echoes still!

ERRATUM

Page 51, third line from foot, *for* Mahone of West Virginia *read* Mahone of Virginia.

CONTENTS

Fighting the Spoilsmen

Fighting the Spoilsmen

CHAPTER I

EARLY EFFORTS FOR REFORM

AMONG the voluntary associations which have existed in this country for the propagation of various political and social movements there are two which have fairly won an honorable place in history: the Anti-Slavery Society which played an important part in the movement for the abolition of human bondage, and the National Civil Service Reform League which, with its constituent local and State associations, has done much to bring about the establishment of the competitive system in the civil service.

The history of such organizations ought to be preserved, not only on account of the things they did, but as an illustration of the power of comparatively small groups of men, when properly organized and skillfully led, to accomplish by long and persistent efforts great public reforms. It shows what immense possibilities there are in voluntary association with self-sacrificing devotion to a cherished cause.

The work of the Anti-Slavery Society has long since been completed and that of the National Civil Service Reform League has passed the most important crises of the issue which it represents and has accomplished a great part of what it was striving for in the federal service, yet its continued existence will still be necessary for many years not only in extending the reform into the States and municipalities of our country but also in preventing a retrograde movement to the spoils system from which we are not entirely secure. It is therefore not yet time to write an account of the National Civil Service Reform League or of the movement which it led, as a completed chapter in the history of our institutions. But the men who were active in the most stirring periods of this movement are now rapidly passing away and the advancing age of those who remain reminds us that it is quite time that the materials for such an account should be collected and preserved if we are to keep for future chroniclers the facts from which this chapter of history shall at last be written.

I should much like to write in full the whole story of the reform movement, but the small fraction of life which still remains to me will not allow so extensive an undertaking. I can, however, contribute some of the materials for the future history of that movement by recording the activities of the League and of my own Indiana Association so far as they have come under my personal observation.

The League was organized in Newport in 1881 and within four years thereafter I was actively participating in its efforts, attending most of its meetings and later taking part in the deliberations of the executive committee and the council and in charge of many of its important investigations. In this work I have been in touch with a great part of all that has been done and have been familiarly associated with the leaders of the movement.

The National Civil Service Reform League has been singularly fortunate in its leadership. Just as the Anti-Slavery Society has become historic largely through its association with such names as William Lloyd Garrison, Wendell Phillips, and Henry Ward Beecher, so the National Civil Service Reform League has been distinguished by the names of George William Curtis, Carl Schurz, Dorman B. Eaton, and Theodore Roosevelt.

The number of those engaged in the movement was never very large, but under such leadership it could not fail to be an important factor in American political life.

My interest in Civil Service Reform was first aroused in

1884. It was at this time that the work of Dorman B. Eaton on the Civil Service in Great Britain fell into my hands. It is still the standard work on the subject and although unnecessarily diffuse it presents a wonderful argument in favor of the abolition of patronage and the substitution of competitive methods. Indeed I thought then, and I think still, that no other public issue since the agitation against slavery has been so clearly and incontestably proved as Civil Service Reform. Every other question has two sides and a conclusion must be formed by balancing the advantages and disadvantages of each. There is much to be said in favor of a high tariff or a low tariff, a pacific or a military policy; in support of woman's suffrage or against it; in favor of direct legislation by the people or in opposition to it, and so with other issues, and although I have convictions in regard to these things I think I can understand the views of those who take the other side. But the necessity of abolishing the evils which have accompanied the spoils system seems so clear and the methods proposed so perfectly adapted to the purpose that I find it hard to understand how any unprejudiced mind, after careful study of the subject, can oppose the competitive system.

It is hard for us to-day to appreciate the condition of American political life prior to the passage of the Pendleton law. The spoils system which came in with Andrew Jackson had been growing worse and worse. Many civil service reformers trace its origin to the violent partisanship of that narrow-minded and strong-willed President or to the politicians who at a still earlier period introduced it into New York. But in my view it was rather a necessary outgrowth of the political conditions which preceded its birth, as much so indeed as the feudalism of the Middle Ages or the balance-of-power statesmanship of modern Europe.

ORIGIN AND DEVELOPMENT OF THE SPOILS SYSTEM

In a popular government political parties are a necessity. The men who think alike will vote together. They will establish organizations to give effect to their collective desires and, once established, these parties will struggle hard and persistently. Washington deprecated party spirit and foresaw its evils but he could no more stay its progress than he could check the tides.

Two great parties were organized at an early day, and under different names and with changing issues they have ever since struggled with each other for mastery. The makers of our government saw this probable result, but possibly they did not clearly see all the consequences which were to flow from it, for they placed the appointment of important offices —department heads, foreign ministers, judges, and the like— in the hands of the President, subject to the "advice and consent" of the Senate, and then provided that Congress might vest appointments to subordinate places in the President, the heads of the departments, or the courts of law. Congress was to pass the act and then these officials were to choose subordinates at their discretion. When the Constitution was adopted and for many years afterward that proved to be a workable plan. The civil service was then comparatively small. Parties had sprung into being, but their organization was rudimentary. Their control over the Executive was far less absolute than it afterwards became, and during the adminstrations of the earlier Presidents appointments, and, still more, removals from office, were dictated more by public considerations than by mere party or personal interest, though under Jefferson there were a good many political changes. But the germ of the spoils system even then lay sleeping under the existing conditions.

Given party government on the one hand with the hunger of partisans for power, and on the other hand discretionary appointments under the control of a President selected by party agencies, and the spoils system was sure to follow. It was certain that some President would be chosen at some time who would use his arbitrary power to reward his supporters and to strengthen the organization to which he owed his election and when Andrew Jackson became President, that hour arrived. It would have come if Jackson had never lived. The politics of the State of New York had led the way in this sinister development, which, once established could not be uprooted so long as appointments remained discretionary.

An outgrowth of the new patronage system, equally logical and inevitable, soon followed. As soon as the offices came to be considered the property, not of the state but of the successful party—as soon as there were spoils to distribute—there must be some method in the distribution of these spoils.

The civil service had grown so large that it became impossible for the President and heads of departments to make selections upon their personal knowledge. How should they know the character and qualifications of the applicants from all parts of this great country? As to their own districts Congressmen were generally better informed. Moreover the President was dependent on Congress for appropriations and for all other legislation which he desired. He was specially dependent upon the members of Congress who belonged to his own party. Upon these he must rely. Whenever he asked a favor he must be willing to grant a favor and the offices at his disposal were the readiest fund out of which to pay his political debts.

"Rotation in office" was encouraged, for by this means there were more offices to be bestowed. So these were distributed among the supporters of the administration in Congress. Gradually the distribution of these largesses came to be made according to a sort of rule. The member of the House of Representatives belonging to the party in power controlled the places in his district, the Senator from this party controlled the appointments in the State at large, and all had an "equitable share" in general appointments from the nation, from consulships and foreign missions to clerkships in the departments. Bear in mind, these appointments were not given to all Congressmen, it was only the adherents of the party in power who were thus favored, and even among these adherents those who were refractory and would not conform to the wishes of the administration were often excluded.

In districts where the Representative was in opposition, there the Senator controlled the patronage, and where there was neither Senator nor Representative, some influential party manager, perhaps the defeated candidate for Senator or Representative, had the selection. The primary question was, how much political or personal service could the man render who controlled or who received the appointment.

This involved both bad men and bad discipline as well as the paralysis of Congress and of the higher executive officers in the performance of their really important duties.

But the most disastrous effect of the spoils system was not upon the civil service itself but upon the people. Such is the vitality of republican institutions that they could live and thrive if the service were twice as bad as it then was and cost twice as much but they could not live and thrive if either popular elections or the nominations which led to these elections were controlled by the personal and venal motives which the spoils system directly encouraged.

Lincoln in the crisis of a great war had no time to devote to its overthrow, but he realized very clearly the disasters it portended. Once pointing out to a friend the eager multitude of office-seekers which thronged the White House he said: "There you see something which in course of time will become a greater danger to the Republic than the rebellion itself." And once to Carl Schurz he observed: "I am afraid this thing is going to ruin republican government."

Under Andrew Johnson the "bread and butter brigade" of officeholders who held a separate convention to sustain his administration was the object of general ridicule and the proscription of all those who would not support the President in his struggle with Congress brought the civil service of the country to the lowest depths of degradation. But it was in the midst of this degradation that the first systematic effort for reform was made. The national movement in favor of appointments by means of competitive examinations was begun by a bill introduced in the Senate by Charles Sumner, in 1864, followed by another by Mr. Thomas Allen Jenckes, a member of the House of Representatives, in 1867, and an elaborate report discussing the civil service systems of other countries. Early in the administration of President Grant an attempt was made to remedy the evil of patronage. By a law passed March 3, 1871, the President was authorized to prescribe such regulations for admission into the civil service as would best promote the efficiency thereof and ascertain the fitness of each candidate and he might employ suitable persons to conduct such enquiries and prescribe their duties and establish regulations for the conduct of the appointees. He appointed an advisory board of seven persons with George Wm. Curtis at its head[1] which undertook to establish rules for competitive examinations, but Congress refused an appropriation, the enterprise broke down, and the distribution of spoils under President Grant was as great as under any of his predecessors.

Under President Hayes, Mr. Carl Schurz, Secretary of the Interior, instituted competitive examinations in his department, and similar examinations were established in the New York Custom House and Post Office. It was also during this administration that Dorman B. Eaton, by the President's authority, went to England, and investigated the Civil Service of Great Britain, making a report which was afterward published as a treatise and became the standard work upon the subject as above stated.

The assassination of President Garfield, in 1881, by a disappointed office seeker, was an impressive object lesson of the need for the overthrow of the spoils system.

In 1880, George H. Pendleton, a Democratic senator from Ohio, had introduced a bill for the reform of the civil service. The bill was in many respects incomplete, and a committee of the New York Civil Service Reform Association set to work to prepare a substitute. Dorman B. Eaton drafted it, George Wm. Curtis, Silas W. Burt, Orlando B. Potter, and Everett P. Wheeler revised it, while Carl Schurz and Wayne McVeagh aided by their counsels. The substitute was introduced by Mr. Pendleton in January, 1881. A general con-

---

[1] Mr. Curtis was succeeded by Dorman B. Eaton in 1873.

ference of civil service associations assembled at Newport on August 11th of that year, formed the National Civil Service Reform League, and earnestly advocated the measure. It was again introduced December 6, 1881, and on the reform wave which then swept over Congress it passed both houses, a majority of members of both parties voting for it, and it was approved by President Arthur, January 16, 1883. It created a federal Civil Service Commission and introduced competitive examinations. Dorman B. Eaton was appointed President of the first Commission.

Mr. George Wm. Curtis thus accurately described the conditions which prevailed prior to the passage of this law.

Every four years [he said] the whole machinery of the government is pulled to pieces. The country presents a most ridiculous, revolting, and disheartening spectacle. The business of the nation and the legislation of Congress are subordinated to the distribution of plunder among eager partisans. President, secretaries, senators, representatives are dogged, hunted, besieged, besought, denounced, and they become mere office brokers. . . . The country seethes with intrigue and corruption. . . . Economy, patriotism, honesty, honor, seem to have become words of no meaning.

NATURE OF THE COMPETITIVE SYSTEM

It may be interesting to consider for the moment the essential character of the system introduced by the Pendleton law. To what class of reforms did it belong? The remedies against corruption may appropriately be divided into three principal classes. We have first, penal legislation, second, appeals to the moral sense of the people or the creation of a sound public sentiment, third, devices for the removal of temptation.

1st. Penal legislation is necessary to correct certain flagrant crimes of the graver sort, but it is rarely useful anywhere else; there is little certainty of punishment, and to be effective it must be sustained by the moral power of the community. Where public sentiment condones an offense, punishment is rarely possible. We see this in the failure of the laws regulating the liquor traffic. It is only the most flagrant cases of bribery, embezzlement, or fraud which we can hope to reach by means of punishment.

2d. An appeal to the moral sense of the community for the upbuilding of character, the development of civic virtue, and the creation of a healthy public sentiment is certainly the most desirable, final, and effective remedy, but this is too often immediately unattainable. For nearly two thousand years, the churches have been exhorting men to be good, unselfish, patriotic, to lead purer lives, to perform their duties to the State as well as to their Maker, and yet to-day in spite of these appeals, crime is prevalent and the seeds of vice are still sown broadcast over the land.

3d. To take away the incentive to corruption, to remove the jewels from the sight of those who covet them, wherever that can be done, is more effective than punishment or exhortation. It is the application to our political institutions of the words of the Lord's Prayer, "Lead us not into temptation." Where temptation has begotten corruption the withdrawal of temptation will lessen or perhaps eliminate it.

Any contrivance which will accomplish this is sure to be more or less effective. Take for instance the Australian ballot law. The evil to be remedied was twofold: 1st, the purchase of votes, and 2d, coercion such as that exercised by the employers of labor over the men employed. Where the purchaser or employer could not tell how the vote was cast for which he had paid his money, or which he sought to coerce, the temptation to buy or to force men to vote in any given way was largely removed, and so far as the Australian ballot is really a secret ballot, it has measurably accomplished its purpose. There are subterfuges by which it may still be evaded; the machinery is not perfect, but the principle upon which the law is founded is unquestionably sound.

Now this is the principle which underlies civil service reform, and the competitive system furnishes, in my judgment, a far more effective kind of machinery than the Australian ballot law. What is the object of this reform? The great purpose of it is not so much to provide an efficient civil service (although it does this) as to remove the temptation to use the offices of the government for personal or party ends, in other words, to remove the incentive to that kind of political corruption which is nourished by the hope of office. It does this by something akin to a mechanical contrivance, making it automatically impossible for the politician seeking the control of patronage to appoint the particular man he wants. It was the concurrence of personal discretion with party government which brought in the spoils system, and rules requiring appointments by competitive examinations destroy this personal discretion. The Pendleton bill provided the appropriate machinery for this purpose and the development of the system was left largely to the President and to the Civil Service Commissioners who were his advisers in regard to the application of the law.

THE BLAINE CAMPAIGN

The year after the Pendleton bill became a law, Mr. Blaine was nominated by the Republicans for the Presidency. Serious scandals had been connected with his name. The Democrats, on the other hand, had nominated Grover Cleveland, who had made a creditable record as the reform governor of New York.

At this time I represented the county of Wayne in the Indiana State Senate, having been elected in 1882 for a term of four years. I was a Republican and had taken an active part in the previous session of the legislature, but I was deeply impressed with the charges made against Mr. Blaine, supported apparently by his own letters and by his evasive explanations and denials. I was, therefore, unwilling to vote for him or to take any part in the campaign, but I was still too strong a Republican to support the Democratic candidate, and thus break all my associations with a party to which I had been devoted and which I was then representing in the State Senate.

The Republican platform promised all that could be desired on behalf of the competitive system and Mr. Blaine expressed himself in the clearest manner as favoring this reform. But he was deeply distrusted while Mr. Cleveland, whose platform and promises were less explicit, had made an excellent record as governor of New York and was supported by perhaps the greater number of the advocates of the reform.

My refusal to vote for Mr. Blaine aroused intense indignation. I was represented as seizing the ballot from the election officer, throwing it upon the floor, stamping on it, and uttering furious maledictions on the party which had honored me by electing me to the Senate. I was hooted and jeered at as I rode through the streets to my office and on one occasion a crowd of men and boys assembled with the intention of marching out to my house east of town, breaking the windows, defacing the walls, and making unseemly observations regarding the occupant of the premises. From this, however, they were dissuaded through the counsels of an old friend of mine whose stalwart Republicanism could not be suspected by anyone in this patriotic gathering. A petition was started asking for my resignation as senator and I believe a good many signatures were attached to it, but somehow the project fell still-born and the petition was never presented. By the time the Legislature had convened much of this effervescence of wrath had passed away and I found myself welcomed by my old associates as well as by the new Republican members of the Senate with cordiality.

There were only seventeen Republicans all told in the Senate of 1885, barely more than one third.

This Republican minority was a pretty creditable body of men. There was not one of them whom I ever suspected of personal corruption. We worked together in great harmony on nearly every subject and in entire good will in everything.

The Democratic members were also cordial, especially so because I had not voted for Blaine. They placed me upon important committees and even singled me out for a chairmanship, but I did not care to be the only Republican thus honored and I therefore declined.

THE INDIANA CIVIL SERVICE BILL

I introduced as the first measure of the session and on the very first day "A Bill to Regulate and Improve the Civil Service of the State of Indiana," a measure similar to the federal civil service law, although I knew that my bill had very little chance of passing.

The judiciary committee reported against it and the bill was made a special order. I addressed the Senate on the subject at length, setting forth as fully as possible the advantages of the competitive system and urging its adoption. Quite a large audience had gathered in the Senate chamber on this occasion as the subject excited general interest.[1]

Among the auditors was the Vice-President elect, Hon. Thomas A. Hendricks, who had been chosen on the same ticket with Mr. Cleveland but who was not at all in favor of this "schoolmaster's plan" as he called it, and who probably came out of curiosity to see what could be said in favor of such an impracticable scheme. The Democrats in the Senate never intended to allow the bill to pass but some of them were willing to give me the compliment of supporting it upon the second reading and it was ordered engrossed by a vote of twenty-four to eighteen. A week later when it came up for final passage a number of these votes were changed and it failed. One of its opponents declared that he was in favor of civil service reform but desired it to be made applicable to Democrats only! Another declared that it was only Republicans who needed such reform and that inasmuch as the Democrats were in control it was quite useless. Such was the variegated wisdom of those who enacted the laws of Indiana.

LUCIUS B. SWIFT

It was during this session that I made the acquaintance of Lucius B. Swift. He was present with his wife when I spoke in favor of this civil service law. He was a few years my elder, a sturdy, rugged man who had been a private in the Civil

[1] This address appears in Appendix I.

War (of which fact he so seldom spoke that hardly anyone knew of it). He was at this time practicing law in Indianapolis. The close friendship which we formed has continued uninterrupted ever since. Our political views have been remarkably similar. We were both mugwumps, but were so dissatisfied with Cleveland's removal of officeholders upon secret charges and his partisan administration of the civil service in Indiana that we supported Harrison at the next election. But Harrison disappointed us still more. He too made removals upon secret charges and delivered the unclassified service almost bodily into the hands of spoilsmen, so after four years of Harrison we decided that Cleveland was the better man of the two.

It was during this period that the New York *Sun* gave a humorous description of what it called a convention of the mugwump party in Indiana which was held when Swift called up Foulke over the telephone and they decided upon the resolutions and candidates. In point of fact it was a good deal that way. There were hardly more than a dozen of us all told but we made as much noise as the two wolves described by General Grant in his memoirs whom he compared with dissatisfied politicians. Yet we were very far from being politicians, and our dissatisfaction was based upon shortcomings which still appear to me in retrospect to have had a sound basis.

We both supported McKinley against Bryan, yet we protested earnestly when McKinley removed several thousand places from the protection of the civil service rules. We have both always been devoted friends of Mr. Roosevelt and his policies. We were both in favor of the nomination and election of Taft yet greatly disappointed at what seemed to us his failure to carry out the policies of his predecessor. We were both afterwards active in the Progressive party in the convention of 1912, Mr. Swift as chairman of the Indiana delegation and I as member of the resolutions committee, and four years later we both belonged to that branch of the remnant of the Progressive party which supported Mr. Hughes. In looking back upon this somewhat variegated assortment of political views our concurrence has seemed to me the more remarkable since neither of us was much inclined to be guided by the opinions of anybody else and each of us was perhaps a little obstinate in maintaining his own peculiar notions.

NATIONAL CIVIL SERVICE REFORM LEAGUE AND INDIANA ASSOCIATION

It was in 1885 that I began to attend the meetings of the National Civil Service Reform League which at this time were held in the summer at Newport and at which George William Curtis, the president, delivered the annual addresses. I can recall very vividly some of these early meetings, especially one where Mr. Curtis called upon the Maryland Association for a report of its doings and a young man whom I had not known before but who bore the not unfamiliar name of Bonaparte rose to reply. The Maryland Association, he said, had been eminently successful in only one thing, and that was in making a great nuisance of itself to pretty much everybody. I have no doubt that was true, especially to those politicians, Gorman, Rasin, and the other worthies of Baltimore, who formed the ruling dynasty. It was on that occasion that my acquaintance and friendship with Mr. Bonaparte began. The civil service reformers of Indiana and Maryland were companions in tribulation, and, at that period, to make a nuisance of ourselves was our first duty to mankind. We did our best at it in Indiana though for a long time our outcries fell upon deaf ears. These were seasons of great famine in the crop of converts. The sentiment in favor of the merit system found scanty nutriment in the public opinion of a community violently partisan and thoroughly committed to spoils, a community where a mugwump was as rare as a dodo and a reformer as unpopular as a Chinaman.

Now how different it all is! Hardly anyone says he is against civil service reform. It would be like saying he was against the Rule of Three or the Copernican System or that he was opposed to religious liberty. He has to keep such obsolete doctrines to himself. But many a man is in favor of the law but greatly opposed to its application. He doesn't want to see a good thing run into the ground. There ought to be exceptions and his case is one of them, etc., etc.

In 1885, the Indiana Civil Service Reform Association was organized, very largely through the efforts of Mr. Swift and myself together with Oliver T. Morton, the son of the war governor of Indiana, and Louis Howland, then the editor of a low tariff and civil service reform periodical called *The Freeman* and now editor of the *Indianapolis News*.

I was made the president of the new organization and continued to hold that office for four or five years when I was succeeded by Mr. Swift who has ever since remained its head. Our numbers were not large; we held our annual meetings in one of the rooms of Plymouth Church in Indianapolis and our work was mainly done through the executive committee and special committees appointed to make investigations. But there was finally developed a widespread public interest in the result of our work and abundant space was soon accorded to us in the newspapers of the State. The most important investigations made by our association were: first, into the abuses at the Indiana Hospital for the Insane at Indianapolis; second, into the system of removal of postmasters upon secret charges under Mr. Cleveland; and third, into the administration of the civil service in the post offices and other federal places in Indiana.

In considering the investigation of the Indiana Hospital I must go back two years in my story.

CHAPTER II

As I sat in the State Senate at the opening of the session of 1883 the first bill introduced for our consideration was for the regulation of the three principal benevolent institutions of the State: the Hospital for the Insane, the Asylum for the Blind, and the Asylum for the Deaf and Dumb. This bill provided for a board of trustees of three members for each of these institutions, one man to act as president of all three of the boards. The members were to be elected by the General Assembly in joint session.

I was at that time entirely inexperienced in legislative work and I could not quite see the drift of this proposed legislation nor understand the intense feeling on both sides of the Senate Chamber when the bill was read. The Democrats were in a large majority and the bill was introduced by the Democratic leader, Senator Jason Brown (or as he was generally called "Bazoo Brown"). He was a party boss, a man with a resolute and rather brutal face—a man of singular eloquence and really fine diction, one of the most successful criminal lawyers in the State, unscrupulous and supposed to be even venal in his political transactions but genial and popular among his friends; a man of loose life and often intemperate. The bill was named after him "The Brown Bill."

It was explained to me by those better intitiated that its object was to turn over the benevolent institutions to Democratic politicians to be administered for the benefit of the party rather than of the inmates or the public. I belonged to the Republican minority and was not in the inner circle of those who knew the details of the scheme but we could see two men of sinister omen constantly in the lobbies and in the aisles of the Senate who were doing a lot of work in buttonholing the Democratic members and holding whispered consultations with them. One of these was a big burly vulgar looking man whom I afterwards learned was Dr. Thomas H. Harrison of Boone County. The other was a thin, pale, cadaverous person more nearly of the Uriah Heep variety, whom I ascertained was Philip M. Gapen. These men with a number of confederates of lesser note kept up a constant agitation in the lobby on behalf of the bill.

We Republicans did our best to oppose it, but of course it passed, and in joint session of the two houses of the Legislature Dr. Harrison was elected president of the three boards while Gapen and one B. H. Burrell were elected the remaining trustees for the Indiana Hospital for the Insane, an institution containing 1566 patients and employing some 336 caretakers.

The Board of Trustees were to elect a superintendent of the hospital and they chose Dr. Wm. B. Fletcher, a well-known physician of Indianapolis, who had also been a prominent Democrat. He was a member of the State Senate in the following session of 1885 where I served with him. Although a strong partisan he was a man of humane disposition and of high professional attainments.

In 1885 and 1886 there were rumors of very serious abuses at the hospital but nothing very definite was known until sometime during the spring or summer of the latter year. Dr. Fletcher, in view of my interest in civil service reform, came to me and asked if something could not be done to remedy the deplorable conditions in that institution. He was not in a position, he said, to take the initiative himself, being a subordinate of the trustees who were administering the hospital as a vast political machine for the benefit of themselves and their political associates.

I was at that time president of the Indiana Civil Service Reform Association and suggested that an investigation by that body might reveal these abuses to the public. Accordingly our executive committee appointed Oliver T. Morton,

Louis Howland, and myself as a committee of investigation, and we soon went to work with a will. Legally we had no powers at all beyond those of ordinary citizens. We had no right to subpœna witnesses or administer oaths or require the production of documents, but we believed that a good deal could be found out even without authority and the event proved that we were right. We put in considerable time during the hottest part of the summer in our enquiries. I remember trudging out with Mr. Morton to the hospital one broiling day in August to inspect the books and the supplies. We were unwelcome visitors to everybody except Dr. Fletcher and he was not in a position to disclose his sympathy with our proceedings.

We examined the minute books of the Board, the bids for supplies and other accounts, and we talked with a number of employees, who, however, were extremely reticent. We also interviewed a number of discharged patients, visitors, and others who had seen various acts of cruelty. We also conferred with contractors and bidders for supplies and by these means we finally unearthed a mass of testimony showing a shocking condition of affairs. Places were given entirely for political reasons. Democrats only received appointments and votes for the Brown Bill had been obtained by promises to appoint great numbers of friends of the legislators to positions in the hospital. One senator alone secured places for a daughter, a nephew, three nieces, and a number of friends and henchmen. Letters were written by direction of the Board to various members of the Legislature asking them to send persons to the asylum for appointment. Boone County, the residence of Dr. Harrison, had many employees.

There were no examinations or tests of any kind to ascertain the fitness of those employed nor apparently were any enquiries made upon that subject. But the employees were active political workers. Subscriptions were circulated among them and funds collected for campaign and other political purposes. Thus money was raised to prosecute the Democratic campaign in Dr. Harrison's county of Boone.

The politics of the township where the institution was

situated was controlled almost wholly by these employees and on the day of a Congressional convention in Indianapolis the hospital was almost deserted. Additional places were made for political workers until it took two or three men to do the work of one. Most of the men who furnished supplies were also prominent Democratic politicians.

The results were such as might have been expected. Careless and unbusinesslike methods prevailed with corruption, inefficiency, and constantly recurring cases of neglect and cruelty toward the unfortunate patients. The minutes showed that Trustee Gapen had been absent nearly a year, running a sawmill in Arkansas but still drawing his salary. No by-laws were adopted for nearly three years after the Board began its work. Of the 336 employees more than four fifths were changed. A certain few among the bidders were always successful. J. E. Sullivan, Democratic candidate for clerk of Marion County, was the principal furnisher of supplies for the tables. Sullivan had presented a bill for butter to a former board of trustees but $476.25 was disallowed, because the alleged butter was found to be oleomargarine, whereupon Sullivan waged political war upon the old board, lobbied for the Brown Bill, gave a dinner to his friends in honor of its passage, presented his claim again, and it was allowed.

He had made a bid to furnish creamery butter at twenty-five cents a pound, and had furnished an article which could be bought at six and eight cents a pound, which, however, was accepted. When winter came he began to supply butterine, which was also received by the storekeeper, who said he did not care "so long as they did not kick in the wards."

In May, 1885, the superintendent reported to the Board that he had bought produce elsewhere at nearly one half less than the lowest bid offered and that the eggs and poultry were better than any ever used in the hospital, yet the Board continued to give Sullivan the contracts and he was paid at his own price. As a consequence other bidders refused to compete.

On one occasion, when our committee visited the hospital, butter infested with maggots was concealed in the sewer beneath the storeroom to avoid inspection.

Mr. Hall, the book and store keeper, an active politician who had lobbied for the Brown Bill, did not keep the books at all but others kept them for him and as storekeeper he did not receive and inspect the goods purchased. A protest against this, made by a former trustee, was disregarded and the trustee who made it soon ceased to be a member of the Board.

It further appeared that a rebate of $64.77 which had been sent to Mr. Gapen, one of the trustees, was never accounted for.

Of over six hundred hogs purchased, more than half died. One lot was apparently "death stricken" when delivered at the hospital. The animals began to die rapidly and at the same time slaughtering went on for the tables. "It was neck-and-neck between disease and the butcher's knife."

The character of the attendants procured by this political system was so bad that acts of neglect and cruelty were frequent. Visitors to the asylum saw patients slapped severely, struck with the fist, shaken, kicked, dragged by the neck, and teased both by attendants and by their fellow patients in the presence of attendants who did not interfere. The superintendent, Dr. Fletcher, wrote to the Board that owing to the large number of complaints of cruelty he had introduced the system of having upon each ward a man and his wife.

We reported the foregoing facts to our Association on September 10, 1886, and the report was published. It thus concluded:

The mismanagement of the asylum—a peculiarly great evil, considering the character of the institution—lies in that abominable system by which the welfare of the unfortunate beings for whom the benevolence was created, is made a secondary consideration to some supposed party advantage or political necessity, and no permanent improvement can be looked for while this continues to be the case.

The obvious remedy for abuses connected with this institution is the enactment of a law by the General Assembly providing for competitive tests of fitness, to be applied to all persons seeking employment in the asylum, followed by a suitable probation, prohibiting appointments or removals for political reasons, and placing the administration of this hospital, as well as the other benevolent institutions of this State, in the hands of non-partisan boards of trustees.

This report was called by the *Sentinel*, the Democratic organ, "a batch of old campaign charges revived." It was at first declared to be a tissue of lies to which no attention need be paid. But from every quarter of the State came anxious enquiries and angry remonstrances and it was found that something more had to be done. Dr. Harrison accordingly prepared an answer which was published in the *Sentinel* on September 23d, under the headlines: "A Complete Defense. President Harrison of the Benevolent Institutions Refutes the Republican Slanders." After insisting that our report had been made for political purposes, he said:

They say the management is partisan, to which charge we plead guilty. *If there is a Republican voter in the employ of the hospital the Board of Trustees does not know it.* We know there are competent Democrats in the State who can perform the duties required and so long as they can be found we want no other. Upon that proposition we have no compromise measures. We are responsible to the people for the internal management and we want our friends, and not our enemies on guard. As *long as this management continues it will be strictly partisan. . . .* It is true that some of the hogs died of cholera but it is maliciously false to say that one ounce of diseased meat was ever used on the tables and the Superintendent will testify under oath that such a charge is wholly untrue.

Here followed tables showing a reduction in cost under Democratic management. He thus continued:

To say that the food given to the patients is not first class in every particular is contradicted by more than ten thousand personal witnesses and could only be spoken by the foul tongue of the slanderer.

Will this committee tell the public why the Republican party never thought of a non-partisan management of the benevolent institutions during twenty years under their control? Will they state why they began to whine like hungry spaniels for a divide of the offices immediately on losing them? Will they state that they have attempted to make 1600 unhappy homes among the people of this great commonwealth in order to benefit the Republican party? . . .

It is strange that so fair a committee could spend seven days in an institution and find so much evil and no good. No, the truth is they were sent by the Republican managers in the interest of Senator Harrison

covered all over with hypocrisy, to attack the great charitable institution of the State—the one nearest the hearts of the people—with the
hope of producing alarm and dissatisfaction. The Chairman of this
committee, William D. Foulke, was the acknowledged leader of the Republican side of the Senate and lately telegraphed from Rhode Island that
"he was ready to do anything he could for the Republican party." They
would not even trust a "Mugmump" on that committee. Only true
Republicans were permitted in the scheme, and then with tallow-faced
hypocrisy they disclaimed that it has any partisan relations. . . .

Now to conclude, this management invites every interested person in
the State to investigate the affairs of the hospital. The doors will be
thrown wide open to every ward and department of the great institution. The books and papers are ready for inspection, even the butter
and meats will be shown to a Republican Committee for party purposes.
We live in no glass house in the management of that institution, and
join Mr. Foulke in asking that on the first day of the meeting of the next
General Assembly a committee be appointed for an impartial investigation, composed of men who are honest in their purpose and truthful in
their report.

After this answer had been published, we did not allow
either the hospital authorities or the public much breathing
time, for Mr. Howland, Mr. Morton, and myself met that
very day and drew up a reply in the shape of an open letter
to Dr. Harrison which was submitted that evening both to
the *Sentinel* and the *Journal* for publication. It contained
the following:

It is not true that our charge is maliciously false when we say that
diseased meat was used upon the tables. It is not true that the superintendent will testify under oath to the falsity of such charge. We challenge the production of such an affidavit. . . .

It is not true that any member of this committee was sent to investigate
the hospital by any Republican managers.

It is not true that every member of the committee is a Republican. . . .
At the meeting of the executive committee, at which this report was
unanimously adopted and ordered printed, only two of the four members
present and voting were Republicans. . . .

You say that your books and papers are ready for inspection, yet you
refused to let us see the correspondence of the asylum. Did not Dr.
Fletcher, under your direction, send from St. Paul a telegram directing
that the minutes of the board should not be shown to us? Do you not
know that we were refused access to these minutes by no less than three
persons at the asylum and that they were only shown to us after the

Attorney General had given an opinion that we had the right to see them? Does not your present candor and liberality come a little late? We are much pleased, however, at your changed attitude, and that you desire that a committee should be appointed by the next General Assembly for an impartial investigation. We promise you our cordial coöperation in making such an examination thorough and exhaustive. . . .

You have not denied that additional places have been made for political workers. . . .

You have not denied that prominent politicians of your party, Messrs. Landers, Cooper, Sullivan, and others, are prominent in furnishing supplies.

You have not denied that Mr. Gapen, one of your co-trustees, has been regularly receiving his salary, although he is managing a sawmill in Arkansas and was not present at more than one meeting between October, 1885, and July, 1886. . . .

You have not denied that wholesale discharges of employees are frequent. . . .

You have not denied that the very morning our committee were at the asylum, butter infested with maggots had been concealed in the sewe to avoid our inspection. . . .

You have not denied that of over six hundred hogs purchased, more than one half died, and you cannot deny that killing for the table went on out of the dying drove.

You have not denied a single act of cruelty to the patients in the asylum. . . .

You have not denied the dissatisfaction of Dr. Fletcher with the present system and his proposal to secure a higher degree of efficiency among the attendants by a regular system of training; nor have you anywhere claimed that such suggestions have been acted upon by you.

All these things are admitted by your silence. You cannot justify nor defend your administration by showing the shortcomings of your Republican or Democratic predecessors. If you are content to go before the people of Indiana upon such a record as that presented in your communication you may rest assured that your conduct will be approved only by those whose partisanship is paramount to their humanity.

The *Journal* published this reply but the *Sentinel* refused to do so in an editorial which said: "To print it would be to give further currency to the charges made by Republicans for the benefit of the Republican party in this campaign."

The *Journal* answered on the following day that this was the first time it ever knew a paper to announce that it was afraid to print a reply to an article to which it had previously given currency on the avowed ground that if its readers should see the reply, the result would be detrimental to the party of which it was an organ. On which the *Sentinel* exploded as follows:

A contemptible lie in every syllable. You, you hypocrite, prate of fairness? Your issue of Saturday reeks with blackguardism. You have printed both the screeds of this Foulke committee, headed as it is by a man who has not even the common sympathies of humanity to commend him and you have neither the grace nor the courage to print President Harrison's refutation of the detestable slander conceived and perpetuated by this slimy Republican reptile. You stand upon a housetop and, with the whites of your eyes turned to the sky, spit venom on honorable men in the name of heaven and the Republican party

In other articles in the *Sentinel*, our committee were "Buzzards," "Hungry Hawks," "Political Pharisees," and "A Trinity of Counterfeiters." But the facts appearing in the records of the asylum were not to be smothered by these endearments. The more the *Sentinel* shrieked and sputtered the worse things got to be. Even the old mossbacks, who never saw any other paper, began to think that there must be something the matter to give rise to such convulsions. Dr. Harrison now made a second reply dated September 26th, under the headlines: "No Diseased Meat and no Cruelty." It contained some curious things, for instance the following answer to our charge that butter infested with maggots had been concealed in the sewer to avoid our inspection: "Then it was not put upon the table for the patients to eat; therefore your statement that they ate maggoty butter was a lie."

As a matter of defense this was overwhelming! It was subsequently shown in the Senate investigation however, by the testimony of the assistant storekeeper, that this butter *was* taken out of the sewer after we left and sent up to the table for the patients.

In this answer Dr. Harrison incorporated a letter from Superintendent Fletcher in which he said: "While a large number of hogs died upon our hands, in no instance was diseased pork ever slaughtered or put upon the tables."

We were now compelled to disclose the authority for our statements, which was no less than Superintendent Fletcher himself, to whom these statements had been read before publication and pronounced correct. The subject was now becoming too dangerous to handle in the public press so there was no more direct discussion of our report. The trustees, however, thought that a flank movement might safely be made, so they got the State Board of Health to go to the asylum and report that everything was in good condition. The columns of the *Journal* were open to me and I wrote an article satirizing the logical character of this answer to our charges.

Charge: Merithew Thayer, Mrs. Anglemeyer, and others saw patients beaten, teased, and inhumanly used. Answer: On October 6, 1886, when the Board of Health visited the asylum for a few hours, not a single act of cruelty was committed.

Charge: In December, 1884, and July, 1885, hogs died of cholera and slaughtering went on out of the dying drove. Answer: On October 6, 1886, when the State Board went to the asylum, no diseased meat was observed by them.

Charge: John E. Sullivan was found by the records of the Board to have supplied the asylum with oleomargarine. Answer: On October 6, 1886, the asylum authorities provided a supply of good butter. . . .

Charge: Political favorites are awarded most of the bids, and double prices are paid. Answer: "The drainage is good."[1]

By this time the campaign for the election of members of the Legislature was in full swing and those of us who had taken part in this investigation improved our opportunity to speak in various parts of the State. For this we were ubjected to much animadversion.

I remember going to Lafayette and meeting an old Democratic colleague in the Senate, Mr. Francis Johnson, who kept a little bookstore in that town. He was an honest, simple-minded German with whom I had served on committees and a warm personal friendship had sprung up between us. When I greeted him, he said: "Ah, Mr. Foulke, I am ashamed to see you." I asked him why, and he answered: "Because

[1] It was about this time (October 6, 1886) that our Indiana Civil Service Association held its second annual meeting. I delivered the President's address discussing our investigation of the Insane Hospital as well as of the federal service in Indiana.

I presided not long ago at a Democratic meeting here in the court house, when Senator McDonald spoke and after him Mr. Myers, Secretary of State, and Myers said in his speech: 'Who made that report on the Insane Hospital? A fellow by the name of Dudley Foulke, a man who was drunk every day during the last session of the Legislature.' After the meeting was over I said to him: 'Why Mr. Myers, I sat next to Mr. Foulke in the Senate and he was not drunk *one* day and now you say he was drunk *every* day.' And what do you think Myers did? He just laughed. I am ashamed that I was presiding at the meeting."

The public indignation at the management of the hospital spread like wildfire. Nothing could be done to stem the tide, and in spite of the outrageous gerrymander of the State, the Republicans won the election and carried the lower House. In the Senate with its two-thirds Democratic majority half the members held over on their four years terms and prevented that body from becoming Republican also.

Things had gone desperately wrong with the politicians who had been mismanaging the hospital. The trustees had found out by this time that while speech might be silver, silence was eighteen-carat gold. So when the Legislature met nothing was said about the asylum. Maybe the Republicans, having won the election, would now turn their attention elsewhere.

LEGISLATIVE INVESTIGATION

But on the 31st of January, the House of Representatives appointed a committee to investigate the hospital. On February 8th, this committee began to take evidence. At first the *Sentinel* pretended to consider this inquiry amusing. The proceedings were entitled: "An Evening with the Mugwumps," into which, by this time, we had become transformed from base Republican politicians as hitherto portrayed in its columns. But as the investigation went on it was realized that the committee would in all probability present a damaging report. Something had to be done, so the Senate determined to make an investigation of its own to counteract that of the House. The inquiry was taken away from the regular Committee on Benevolent Institutions, of which Senator Rahm, a comparatively fair-minded man, was chairman, and Green Smith, the President of the Senate, who was a beneficiary of the spoils system and who had relatives and friends employed at the asylum, appointed certain other beneficiaries as members of a special committee to inquire (quoting his own words) "whether hog cholera and maggoty butter took any votes away from the Democrats."

It was easy to see from such a beginning what the end would be, yet we determined to present our evidence to this Senate committee as well as to the committee of the House and I asked leave to be present by attorney for the purpose of substantiating the charges. My wife had been very ill and I had to go with her to Fort Monroe and be with her during her convalescence so that I could not be personally present. Mr. Morton and Mr. Howland, however, the other members of our committee, were prepared to conduct the examination.

As the investigation proceeded, Dr. Fletcher himself testified to the political appointments, the wretched supplies furnished at the highest prices, the vile butter, the brutal attendants, the disagreements between himself and the Board. Then the *Sentinel* wheeled to the right about and for a day or two assumed the office of reformer-in-chief. In an article entitled, "Let the Light in," it said: "If villainy abides in that noble charity let it be unkenneled! The time has come for scrutiny, for exposure, and for justice! . . . The evidence for the prosecution has been extremely damaging. This must be admitted."

But this panic-stricken newspaper was soon reinvigorated on account of an incident quite outside of the merits of the controversy. Owing to a deadlock between the two houses all legislation came to a standstill and no election of trustees of the Insane Hospital at a joint meeting of House and Senate was possible. Hence it was believed that Harrison, Gapen, and Burrell would keep their places until the next session of the Legislature, which was two years away, and if this were so they must be sustained by the Democratic members and by the Democratic organ or else there would be two years of an administration which had been condemned by its own party.

So the Democrats on the Senate committee made up their minds to exonerate the hospital management no matter what the evidence might be. This evidence was indeed more damaging to the management than our own original report, for even after we had published that report and during the political campaign in which it was an issue, unscrupulous contractors had continued to furnish the same vile butter, while eight new boilers, worthless and dangerous, were placed in the asylum. They leaked when subjected to a hydrostatic test of one hundred pounds, and seven of them had to be patched within a short time. The trustees had been notified of the defects yet the boilers were accepted and paid for at a price far above their value.

Fights between patients were of frequent occurrence; escapes were numerous; one of the patients was never found, and another not until after she was dead; and the political prostitution of this vast charity and the incompetency of its employees were set forth in a striking manner.

But all this was nothing to the Senate committee. That committee employed as its own counsel the attorney of the trustees and thereby put him into the anomalous position of acting as a lawyer for the defense as well as adviser of the judges and they afterwards paid him out of the moneys of the State. It was easy to see what the result of such an investigation would be, and at its conclusion there was drawn up a report exonerating the administration and declaring that the hospital was "the best managed institution of its kind in the world."

This report seemed an appropriate object of ridicule and in the *Journal* I quoted the verses of Coleridge

The river Rhine, it is well known
Doth wash the city of Cologne
But tell us, Muse, what power divine
Shall henceforth wash the river Rhine?

At the same time that the Senate committee was making its investigation, the House committee was also taking testimony. The committee's report, which was adopted, confirmed all the charges we had made, added a number of other matters, recommended an action by the Attorney General for the removal of the trustees and that a non-partisan board should be substituted; that applicants for positions should pass rigid examinations to ascertain their fitness and that they should be forbidden to take part in politics.

The House also passed a general civil service bill which had been drawn up by our Association, but naturally such a bill did not receive the favorable consideration of the Senate and failed to become a law.

Tirades in the *Sentinel* against our Association continued from week to week and from month to month until they at last became a subject of amusement. The following which is found in the issue of August 24, 1887, is a fair specimen of the type of journalism which they represented.

The Indiana Civil Service Reform Association is composed (if indeed such a clique existed at all) of Republican moral lepers, who, if capable of distinguishing between the truth and a lie, always chose the lie, just as a buzzard prefers carrion to fresh meat. The representatives of this aggregation of Republican ulcers, warts, tumors, sties, and fistulas pretended to investigate affairs at the Insane Asylum. They did not investigate, they were incapable of investigating. Their purpose was to manufacture and publish a lying report. They constituted the dregs of partisan malice. Each one of them was a moving, crawling, breathing pestilence. There was not a cholera-cursed hog in Indiana which was not the perfection of robust health compared with any one of the representatives of the so-called "Indiana Civil Service Reform Association." There was not a maggot in any tub of butter anywhere that was not a superior creation to any one of the "Civil Service Reform Association" who pretended to investigate the Insane Hospital.

But the Democrats themselves by this time had become so thoroughly convinced that the management was a discredit to the party as well as the State that Governor Gray determined to get rid of Harrison and Gapen. Their terms of office expired on February 27, 1887, and the Governor, assuming that there were vacancies after that date on account of the failure of the General Assembly to hold an election, appointed successors to each. Harrison and Gapen, however, held on to their places; a suit was brought against Harrison for possession of the office. But the Supreme Court decided the Governor had no right to make the appointment.

One would have supposed that after so much criticism and investigation there would have been at least an attempt at improvement, but this was not the case. One of the patients, a paralytic, was scalded to death in a bathtub by the negligence of an attendant, a recent political appointee, and the cause of his death was concealed.

Gapen actually took a position at twenty-five dollars a week with John E. Sullivan, the purveyor of the vile and unwholesome supplies, and Sullivan was more than ever successful in securing his contracts and getting his goods accepted.

SUIT TO REMOVE THE TRUSTEES

The House of Representatives had recommended that a suit be instituted by the Attorney General for the removal of the guilty trustees. That had not been immediately done since Governor Gray had put other men in their places, and while the proceedings for the possession of the office still remained undecided, it was hoped that such a suit might be unnecessary. But after the Supreme Court had held that the removals made by the Governor were illegal, Attorney General Michener determined to file a complaint in the Superior Court of Indianapolis to remove the trustees for misfeasance in office. Our Reform Association tendered its services, the Attorney General accepted our offer, and Judge James E. Black and myself were appointed to act as counsel and assist him in the prosecution. Mr. Michener and I then began the work of preparing the complaint. It contained some twenty counts of a varied nature and was filed on the 23d of March, 1888. Among the counts there were two which raised the distinct question of the illegality of the spoils system itself.[1]

[1] On the 5th of April, an unexpected episode occurred. Two libel suits were brought, one by John E. Sullivan and the other by Harrison against

We insisted that the proceedings to remove the trustees were in the nature of impeachment and that officers were impeachable for a wanton abuse, even of discretionary authority, as in the case of judges, where the motives of their judicial acts were shown to be improper. It was claimed as a principle of common law that public office was a public trust; that the duty imposed in this case was to take proper care of the insane and to use all reasonable diligence in securing as caretakers those who were skilled in such work and who would properly perform it; that the removal of meritorious employees could be properly made only where the object was to secure those who were more meritorious; that the trust could not be made subordinate to any personal or political interest of the trustees; that the appointment of any employee because he was a person serviceable to the trustees without regard to the manner in which he should perform his duty, was as much a violation of the trust as a diversion of the trust fund, for personal or party use; that the best service obtainable could not be secured where any considerable class among those who were competent were excluded from the opportunity for appointment; that the trustees had no more right to say that none but Democrats should take care of the insane than they would have the right to say that none but red-headed men should take care of the insane; that by reason of these appointments and exclusions made for personal and political reasons without regard to fitness, many unfit, brutal, and vicious men were appointed to take charge of these wards of the State, to their great injury. There was, in the language of the statute, a failure "faithfully to perform the duties of their office" for which they should be removed.

In regard to the second paragraph the obligation was to

Mr. Michener, the Attorney General, and myself, each for $20,000 for damages to their respective reputations. Sullivan's suit was based upon a charge of bribery contained in our complaint which was alleged to be false and Harrison's suit upon this charge of bribery as well as the charge of the appropriation of hospital supplies, but neither complainant did anything to press these suits and in the following December they were dismissed.

see that the men selected should properly perform their duties. The trustees were bound to abstain from any act which would lead to the neglect of those duties. But they induced these men to abandon the care of the insane in order to perform political services. This was a direction to violate their duty, and was, of itself, a failure upon the part of the trustees to fulfil the trust which devolved upon them.[1]

After these paragraphs were prepared, they were submitted to several of the most eminent men of the Indiana bar, and the opinion among these gentlemen was unanimous that they alleged a violation of duty sufficient to justify the removal of the trustees. Mr. John T. Dye, one of the most

---

[1] Many precedents were cited, both in England and America, among the most important being the following: Comyn's Digest: Tit. Parliament, L. 35: "The Spencers were impeached for 'that they put good magistrates out of office and advanced bad,' citing 4 Coke's Institutes, 53."

Story on the Constitution, speaking of impeachments at Common Law, Section 800, says: "Others, again, were founded on the most salutary public justice, such as impeachments for malversations and neglect in office, for encouraging pirates, for official oppression, extortions, and deceits, and especially for putting good magistrates out of office and advancing bad."

In Rex *vs.* Williams (3 Burr, 1317) an opinion was granted by the Court against the defendants, as Justices of the Peace for the borough of Penryn, for refusing to grant licenses to those publicans who voted against their recommendation of candidates for members of Parliament for that borough. "It appeared that they had acted very grossly in this matter, having previously threatened to ruin these people, by not granting them licenses in case they should vote against those candidates whose interest the Justices themselves espoused, and afterwards actually refusing them licenses, upon this account only. And Lord Mansfield declared that the Court granted this information against the Justices not for the mere refusing to grant the licenses (which they had a discretion to grant or refuse as they should see to be right and proper) but for the corrupt motive of such refusal—for their oppressive and unjust refusing to grant them because the persons applying for them would not give their votes for Members of Parliament as the Justices would have had them." *See also* Rex *vs.* Hann., 3 Burr, 1716, 1786.

In 1789, Mr. Madison, in the debates on the Constitution, said: "The President is impeachable for the wanton removal of meritorious officers" (Elliott's *Debates*, vol. i., p. 350–404), 6 Am. Law Reg., 649, or for continuing bad men in office (*id.* 652, 4 Elliott's *Debates*, 38).

distinguished lawyers of Indianapolis, volunteered to assist us and took an active part in the oral argument of the demurrer which was filed by the trustees. Unfortunately the question had to be submitted to a tribunal which had been long accustomed to the methods of the spoilsmen. The judicial tendencies of the Court were shown by a brief colloquy during the argument of the demurrer, between the defendants' counsel and the presiding judge, Napoleon B. Taylor. Mr. Herod, who represented the trustees, began his argument as to one of our paragraphs with the remark, "The millennium of Civil Service Reform has not yet come." "No," answered the presiding judge, "nor will it come until the government provides an office for every citizen." The reasoning by which his Honor reached this conclusion was not disclosed. Indeed the argument was a running fire between the presiding judge and the counsel for the prosecution. "If these principles are law, they have been violated ever since the foundation of our government." And when his Honor was reminded that in the early administrations, from Washington to John Quincy Adams, they had been observed, he answered that since that time we had set aside such notions, and that the appointing power had a good right to remove a meritorious officer! It was suggested that a breach of duty or of law could not make a precedent, that no matter how many corporate directors violated their duties in the purchase of corporate property to their own advantage, this could never make it anything but an illegal act. But such analogies were listened to by most unwilling ears. Indeed, I could not help thinking of an old story in Indiana, of one of our backwoods lawyers in early times, who set up against an indictment for stealing hogs the plea that it was the custom of the country to steal hogs.

Not an authority was presented by the other side in answer to the considerations which we submitted. In a brief filed some ten days afterwards the only claim which I recollect was that if civil service reform principles were part of the common law, why was it that a civil service reform law was introduced into the Senate some years before? The

3

judges took the case under advisement, and afterward announced that they would sustain the demurrers to these paragraphs; but said they had decided not to give any opinion nor to state the grounds upon which the demurrers were sustained—a course which prudence manifestly dictated.

The case was set for trial in September, 1888. The prospect of succeeding in a tribunal which had made such an extraordinary decision was not flattering and in any event the defendants could by an appeal and other dilatory proceedings postpone their removal from office until after the General Assembly met whose duty it was to elect their successors. Our best course to obtain their removal was to secure the election of members of the Legislature who were pledged to the reform of the benevolent institutions. So we determined to press the matter in the coming campaign rather than in this suit and the case dragged on without any active proceedings on either side.

CAMPAIGN OF 1888

In the campaign of 1888 General Harrison had been nominated as the Republican candidate for the presidency. The Republican National and State platforms contained strong declarations in favor of civil service reform. I took an active part in the campaign. On one occasion, I addressed a meeting in the court house at Bloomington with Albert J. Beveridge, then quite a young man but one who had greatly distinguished himself upon the stump. I spoke first and related the abuses we had discovered, making, as it seemed to me, a pretty strong case. I had perhaps a better personal knowledge of the facts than any other person outside of the institution we investigated. After I closed, my companion rose. He walked backwards and forwards along the small open space reserved for the members of the bar and gave a burning description of the horrors inflicted upon the helpless victims of madness. You could smell the tainted meat and see the maggots in the butter; you could hear the blows of the brutal attendants upon the backs of the patients; and their screams as the scalding water was poured upon them in the bathtubs where they had been left by their caretakers. So vivid was the scene that the audience became hysterical with sympathy and indignation. To tell the truth, I never myself realized the enormity of the outrages I had taken so considerable a part in revealing until I heard them described by the eloquent young orator who knew nothing at all about them.

The campaign ended with a Republican victory. Benjamin Harrison was chosen President and carried Indiana. Alvin P. Hovey, the Republican candidate for Governor, was also elected, but owing to the gerrymander which had been passed by the Democratic Legislature of 1885, the State was again misrepresented in the General Assembly. The Democratic members had, however, at last become alive to the fact that the management of the Insane Hospital was an injury to their party so it was determined that the trustees who had aroused such criticism should no longer be retained. Moreover on the 29th of January, while the Legislature was in session, John E. Sullivan failed in business and made an assignment to Trustee Gapen. Two days later, Sullivan started for Canada. Governor Hovey asked for an investigation. A joint committee was appointed by the Senate and the House, which on the last day of the session presented a report finding all sorts of corruption and many defalcations.

REMOVAL OF TRUSTEES

The Legislature did not wait, however, until this report was made before superseding the guilty board of trustees. A bill was passed repealing the Brown Bill of 1883 and substituting an act providing that the three benevolent institutions should be governed by three separate boards of three members each to be elected by the Legislature, and on March 5th, Thomas Markey, Joseph L. Carson, and Zachariah H. Houser were elected trustees. Still the old board refused to turn over the hospital without certain "concessions" and it was not until April, 1889, that the new board actually took possession.

The new act did not do away with partisanship in the benevolent institutions. It simply removed the individuals who had been guilty of mismanagement. But by this time the new board, although it was a Democratic body, had become convinced that the graver abuses which had existed under its predecessors must not be continued and most of the scandals ceased.

It was not until 1895 that these benevolent institutions of Indiana, which by this time had increased in number, were removed from partisan management by the act of March 11th of that year. A Board of Control was then established and it was provided that the Governor should appoint on this board eighteen persons, three for each institution, and that not more than nine should be members of one party nor more than two in each particular institution, and that no employee should be selected or dismissed on account of his political affiliations. Two years later this Board of Control was abolished and boards of trustees of three each were provided for instead; not more than two in any one board were to be of the same party, and political appointments and removals were in like manner forbidden. Several other changes have occurred in the law. By an act of March 2, 1907, the boards were to be composed of four trustees each, two from each party, and all employees were to be appointed by the superintendent, regardless of political affiliations, on the basis of fitness only and after such examination as might be prescribed by the board of the particular institution. The trustees were forbidden to request appointments or discharges and campaign assessments were prohibited.

It is unnecessary to pursue the subject further. Indiana has not yet adopted any comprehensive or effective civil service law for her State institutions but public opinion is now so strong and universal that it is believed that any extensive manipulation of these institutions for party purposes is no longer to be feared.

CHAPTER III

THE investigation of the Hospital for the Insane was only one of the activities of our Indiana Civil Service Reform Association. Indeed even before that was undertaken I had made an inquiry into the system of removals upon secret charges adopted by President Cleveland early in his administration, an inquiry which was afterward considered by the Association.

REMOVALS UPON SECRET CHARGES

In December, 1884, shortly after Mr. Cleveland had been elected and before he had been inaugurated, he wrote to George Wm. Curtis, president of the National Civil Service Reform League, an open letter in regard to the civil service law. In this letter, after promising an earnest effort to enforce the act, he said:

There is a class of government positions which are not within the letter of the civil service statute, but which are so disconnected with the policy of an administration that the removal therefrom of present incumbents, in my opinion, should not be made during the terms for which they were appointed solely on partisan grounds and for the purpose of putting in their places those who are in political accord with the appointing power· But many now holding such positions have forfeited all just claims to retention, because they have used their places for party purposes without regard to their duty to the people, and because, instead of being decent public servants, they have proved themselves offensive partisans and unscrupulous manipulators of local party management. The lessons of the past should be unlearned, and such officials, as well as their successors, should be taught that efficiency, fitness, and devotion to public duty are the conditions of their continuance in public place.

When he became President, Mr. Cleveland appointed Mr. Wm. F. Vilas as his Postmaster General. The Post Office

Department controlled far more patronage than any other. The pressure for place was enormous and Mr. Vilas and the President attempted the impossible task of yielding to it and at the same time of trying to reconcile it with the principles announced in the letter to Mr. Curtis. Republican officials were to be dismissed for "offensive partisanship" and Democrats were to be put in their places.[1]

It was announced that removals from subordinate positions were only to be made upon charges either of such offensive partisanship or some other violation of duty.

Between the 1st and 20th of August, 1885, noticing that "suspensions" of postmasters were becoming very frequent, I addressed 193 letters to postmasters suspended in Indiana and 102 letters to Presidential postmasters elsewhere. I inquired of each the cause of the suspension, whether any charges had been made, and whether there had been any investigation or any opportunity for defense.

In only two instances, according to the answers, had there been any investigation. In every other case no notice of any charges had been given, no cause assigned, no opportunity afforded for defense, denial, or explanation. In a large number of cases the first information on the subject received by the postmaster removed was by newspaper report or upon presentation of the order of removal by the new appointee.

In fifteen cases in Indiana the change was attributed to the Congressman in the district, the successor in some instances having been promised the office in advance. Sometimes the

[1] The Postmaster General in a circular letter, dated April 29, 1885, laid down the following specifications of what constituted "offensive partisanship."

(1) Having been an active editor or proprietor of a Republican newspaper printing offensive articles.

(2) Having been a stump speaker.

(3) Having been a member of a political committee.

(4) Having been an officer of a campaign club.

(5) Having been an organizer of political meetings.

(6) Having made his office headquarters of political work.

(7) Having put his clerks to the performance of political duties.

(8) Possibly other acts of equal force.

parties learned by hearsay or street rumor that charges of "offensive partisanship" had been preferred. In twenty-one cases a request was made for information respecting the charges and for an opportunity for investigation but no such opportunity was given nor were the charges disclosed.

Knowing that this information was *ex parte* and not believing it possible that these removals had been thus made with the approval of the author of the letter to Mr. Curtis, I communicated to the President, personally, the results of my inquiries together with the names of the postmasters in question.

The President told me, however, that he approved of this course, that he considered it impracticable to inform the postmasters of charges against them; that this would be turning the question of their removal into a judicial investigation; that they were continually protesting, objecting, and asking for copies of the charges, but that these could not be furnished them. I suggested that there was little use of requiring that charges should be preferred, if the man to be removed was not permitted to see them; that charges were frequently made by persons utterly irresponsible and often by those who did not pretend to know the facts; that such charges were frequently false and that it was not possible to procure accurate information until both sides had at least a chance to be heard. He said *he regretted that I had made these inquiries;* that the Department had to get its information as best it could; that he had great difficulty in bringing many of his party friends up to his ideas of this reform and *that Indiana was a particularly bad State in that respect.*

This system of removals upon secret charges was evidently the joint offspring of the President's desire for civil service reform and the clamor of his party for the spoils, and, like many other hybrids, the progeny was inferior to either progenitor. It encouraged spies and informers; slander, falsehood, and suspicion. The political retainers all understood that they were to get the offices by some underhand method, while every man suspended carried with him the implication that he had been discharged for some breach of duty, of which he might have been wholly innocent.   Frequently the accuser was rewarded for his secret slander by appointment to the office.[1]

I gave the President many instances of such removals upon charges which were said to be entirely false. No doubt some of the denials by the suspended postmasters were themselves untrue. They were *ex parte* statements and necessarily so from the fact that neither the charge nor the accuser was known. Among so many removals there were no doubt some which were properly made. The objection was not to any particular case, but to a system which made it impossible for the Department to know whether the charge was proper and under which many acts of flagrant injustice were sure to be committed. Such a system would naturally be used by spoilsmen and even criminals to get places. Indeed the appointees appeared to be largely from that class.[2]

[1] The following cases are illustrations of this system of removals:

Louisa C. Canine stated that she was removed, without notice, upon the false charge, preferred by A. J. Kitt, her successor, that she was a non-resident.

E. R. Kirk, of Sioux City, Iowa, was removed through the agency of one Chase, an office broker, upon affidavits of partisanship, made by an ex-policeman and the son-in-law of his successor, Crawford.

S. A. Marine of Vinton, Iowa, heard that the specification against him was the delivery of a partisan address on Decoration Day, which was in fact delivered by his brother.

[2] Thus W. M. Hancock, postmaster at Meridian, Miss., was succeeded by Colonel J. J. Shannen, who was convicted January 2, 1872, in the United States District Court at Jackson, Miss., of criminally conspiring with others for the purpose of depriving negroes of equal rights under the Constitution.

One Crawford, successor of Kirk, of Sioux City, Iowa, had been sentenced to the penitentiary at Yankton, Dak.

James Dowling, appointed by the influence of Mr. Bynum, Democratic Congressman from Indianapolis, to a position in the railway mail service, boasted that he had bribed certain members of the Common Council of Indianapolis, of which body he was a member. For this he had been tried by the Council and found guilty, by a two thirds vote, of bribery. A majority voted to expel him, but the requisite two thirds was lacking for that purpose. Before the grand jury Dowling had refused to testify on the ground that his answer might incriminate him.

These facts were notorious in Indiana. The Postmaster General was

It was not until near the end of Mr. Cleveland's term, however, that the details of the system of removal upon secret charges were generally spread before the country. On March 27th, 1888, I called upon Mr. Eugene Hale, the chairman of the Senate Civil Service Committee, and told him the results of my inquiries. He asked me to appear before the committee on the following morning and to bring with me the correspondence and documents relating to my investigation. I did so and detailed what I had done. The account of this testimony was scattered broadcast by the Associated Press and other newspaper agencies and excited comment everywhere.

THE FEDERAL SERVICE IN INDIANA

At the time i related this story of removals upon secret charges, I also left with the committee the report of another investigation made by Mr. Lucius B. Swift, and approved by our Indiana Association. It was a general review of appointments and dismissals in the federal service in Indiana. It commenced with an account of the management of the Indianapolis post office, which was then the only classified office in the State. The report showed that Aquilla Jones, who had been appointed postmaster by Mr. Cleveland and took charge of the office April 19, 1885, began at once a clean sweep of the unclassified places.[1]

---

notified of them by Lucius B. Swift, but wrote to Mr. Swift that it would be fair for Mr. Dowling "to have notice of the accusation, because inquiry might put a different complexion on the case." The importance of investigation and of the old maxim *audi alteram partem* was thus recognized by the very man who refused to grant it in the cases above.

Mr. Dowling remained in the service until he suffered a mail train to go to Peoria and back without any attendant and the mail remained undistributed. Then he was discharged.

[1] He appointed as assistant postmaster John W. Dodd, an obscure and reduced politician. A worse selection could not have been made. He appointed as cashier his son, Ben. Jones, both Dodd and Jones taking the place of a single man. The other places were filled with untried men. In the sack repair department within a few weeks every man and woman was dismissed and succeeded by a Democrat. The janitors of the building, watchman, engineer, and elevator boy were changed in like

Next the classified service men were wantonly displaced
and Democrats selected for their positions.[1]   In order to do
this a new examination was held although there were many
eligibles remaining.   Mr. Jones said that no Republicans
passed this examination.   There was a sudden monopoly of
the ability to answer questions in the adherents of the party
in power.

After this examination removals began in good earnest.[2]

Sometimes instead of dismissing carriers, resignations were
forced.   In a number of cases charges were preferred.[3]

Sometimes these were manufactured out of whole cloth.[4]

---

manner.   Mr. Jones said: "I have made such removals for no other
reason than that the persons were Republicans."   The men appointed
were active political workers; their names and acts of partisanship were
specified in the report.

[1] Mr. Jones told Louis Howland and Lucius B. Swift that he would not
appoint Republicans even if they passed and no matter how high they
stood.

[2] Oscar P. Hoover had to go because, as Jones said, he was going to make
places for others; that it made no difference whether this was a violation
of the civil service law.   Mr. Jones told W. E. Tousey that he had no
complaint to make; that all he wanted was the place.

Jones told M. A. Lockwood: "You are all going anyway; I have kept
all of you longer than I have wanted to; summer has come now and you
can make a living and I want you all to get out of here."

To Gustav Schmedel, Jones said: "I have no complaint to make only
I have a Democrat whom I wish to put in your place," and later Dodd
told him that if he did not resign Jones would find some charges against
him.

Mr. Dodd said: "If we begin to make promises to keep carriers we
shall have no places for our political friends."   Dodd gave Levi S. Hand
as the reason for his dismissal: "I don't know anything more than we want
your place for a Democrat; we have got to begin somewhere so we begin
with you."   To Oliver P. McLeland he said: "It is better for the boys to
resign than to have us drum up charges against them."   And, "It almost
breaks Mr. Jones' heart to have to drum up charges against the boys."

[3] Charles P. Sample was discharged because he owed a debt of ten
dollars for a cloak for his sister, but Harry Crane, appointed by Jones,
who owed forty-seven dollars, was retained.   Jones told the widow to whom
he owed the money that he had no power to turn Crane off if he didn't
pay it.

[4] As in the case of Wilmington who was removed without cause, but
when an investigation was demanded, a charge was trumped up that he

There were many curious characters among the new appointees, for instance a negro, Alfred Harrison, whose autograph letter was shown, in which he promised to let a client's suit go by default in consideration of ten dollars to be paid in advance. Another was still warm in the service when he was detected stealing a registered letter, pleaded guilty, and was sentenced. Another carrier who passed the examination creditably could not read the superscriptions of his letters, and had to be removed from his route and set to collecting mail. He was a politician of long standing.

Another carrier was appointed who misdelivered a letter and when complaint was made answered: "I leave just such mail here as I like; if you don't like it you may go to hell." Yet the man was retained.

The recapitulation showed that in the unclassified service all were succeeded by Democrats; and in the classified service, of seventy-one former incumbents thirty-six were forced out, and forty-three Democrats appointed. The effect upon the service had been most injurious. Complaints of letters misdirected, engagements lost, and of important mail matter misdelivered were made almost every day.

Mr. Jones said publicly of the civil service law, "I despise it," and the inquiry naturally arose, "Why is he permitted to remain there to nullify it?"

But the administration of the Indianapolis post office, bad as it was, was better than that of the remaining federal service in Indiana. Here there had been a clean sweep everywhere, except in the railway mail service, where although some Republicans remained, the changes had been very numerous and the service had been thrown into disorder.

Page after page of Mr. Swift's report were filled with illus-

had acted as challenger at the last Presidential election. This was signed by six persons, one of whom afterwards stated that he did not know what he signed. The actual challenger proved that Wilmington was absent, and the books at Wilmington's office showed that he was there and not at the polls during election day. This was a charge against a Republican. Yet Henry R. Browning, one of the new appointees, worked actively at a primary, made motions and speeches, and had a fight with one Hennessey, yet still remained in office.

trations by the score of officeholders whose appointments were due to Congressmen and who took the most active and unscrupulous part in political movements for the renomination of the Congressmen by whom they were appointed.

Mr. Swift after contrasting the facts found with Mr. Cleveland's promises thus concluded his report.

It is not a pleasant task for those civil service reformers who had a steadfast faith that every promise would be kept, to examine the work done and report the truth; but their sincerity is on trial. Besides to stand silent now would impose silence when some other party succeeds to the national administration. The truth must be stated plainly. In Indiana civil service reform has been disgraced and made contemptible.

On September 13, 1888, Mr. Swift was examined and on the 10th of October, 1888, the committee reported. It found in a general way the truth of Mr. Swift's statements and declared that the system of secret charges flourished in Indiana.

Senator Blackburn, a Democratic member who had said in the Senate that what I had told the committee was "the unsworn statement of a tramp" now prepared and published a minority report, which said: "The only two persons, misnamed witnesses, who came to assist the committee and whose remarks and exhibits submitted to it comprehend the entire 'investigation' of the civil service in Indiana were William Dudley Foulke and L. B. Swift, neither of whom are connected with the service, neither of whom spoke from personal knowledge, and neither of whom could testify to the truth or falsity of the charges made."

I immediately addressed to Senator Blackburn who had prepared this minority report an open letter which was quite generally published, containing among other things the following observations.

You criticize the statements made by Lucius B. Swift and myself as being merely hearsay. . . .

I made a list of all the cases I examined, classifying them, and submitted it to the President personally and *learned from his own lips that he approved of this system of removals upon secret charges* preferred by unknown accusers, without any opportunity for defense or explanation.

The original correspondence was left in the hands of your committee for many weeks. The summary of the answers was placed in the hands of the President by me. Would you kindly point out to me any form of investigation less open to the imputation of being hearsay?

You say "rumors and suspicions may fittingly lead to preliminary investigations by grand juries, and other intermediate bodies may initiate proceedings upon them, but neither in judicial trials nor committee investigations have they ever been admissible as the foundation of judgment." If you believe this, what must be your opinion of the administration which you are supporting in requiring charges to be filed for the removal of officers upon the ground that they have been guilty of some violation of duty, and then regarding the mere charge, unsustained by proof and often hearsay in its character as well as false, as the sole foundation for the judgment of the administration in removing the persons accused?

This ended our experience with the Senate committee. But the abuses disclosed, together with those which had occurred in other States, had a very considerable influence on public opinion in the campaign for the Presidency, and were undoubtedly among the factors which led to Mr. Cleveland's defeat.[1]

[1] Our Indiana Civil Service Reform Association had very efficient support in the *Civil Service Chronicle*, a monthly periodical edited by Lucius B. Swift. This paper discussed the merit system from quite a different angle from that of investigations and reports. It contained (besides able editorials) extracts from the press all over the country of *spoils news*. A single item of such news will attract little observation but when a great number are brought together in mass from every side they present a concrete argument sometimes impressive, sometimes ridiculous, of monstrous abuses in the patronage system so that the dullest could realize what that system really means. "It was like a well placed machine gun on the enemy's flank." In this work Mr. Swift was ably assisted by Mrs. Swift, by whom indeed the greater part of the labor of collecting and classifying these data was performed. The paper had really a profound influence not only in Indiana but elsewhere. It was continued down to the end of the administration of President Harrison.

CHAPTER IV

THE CIVIL SERVICE UNDER HARRISON

As we have already seen the Independents of Indiana were greatly dissatisfied with the administration of Mr. Cleveland and they nearly all opposed him in the campaign of 1888. We regarded the question of the civil service as far more vital than the tariff and we were indignant at Mr. Cleveland for setting it aside and devoting his exclusive attention to this later born child of his political fancy, since he was elected, not as a tariff reformer, but as an administrative reformer. Moreover as chief executive he was responsible for the civil service while the tariff was a legislative question in which his responsibility was partial only and indirect.

In addition to our dissatisfaction with Mr. Cleveland we were led to support General Harrison by the strongest assurances on his part, both in public, as a member of the United States Senate, and personally, that he would support the competitive system. As early as 1885 while our Indiana Civil Service Reform Association was investigating the abuses at the Hospital for the Insane, and considering the system of secret removals by President Cleveland, I received from him the following autograph letter:

INDIANAPOLIS, Oct. 14, 1885.
Hon. W. D. Foulke, Richmond, Ind.
    My Dear Sir:
    I was sorry indeed not to see you when you called on the day of your Civil Service meeting. If it had been possible I would have attended the meeting in the evening, tho' knowing from our talk some of your plans, it was perhaps as well that I was not there to support your proposition to look into some of the removals in this State. Some of the gentlemen present were very sensitive. I am thoroughly in sympathy with civil

46

service reform and do not know any field that needs work more than our own State. It will give me great pleasure to aid in any way I can a movement to secure legislation upon that subject in our next Legislature. We ought to begin with the Benevolent Institutions and take advantage of the indignation that has been aroused by the low partisan management which the Democratic party has imposed upon some of them. I would not attempt too much at once for there is absolutely *no* civil service sentiment in the democracy of this State and not as much as there ought to be in our own party. . . .

Very truly yours,
BENJ. HARRISON.

There were a number of us who took a very active part in the campaign, detailing the abuses in both Federal and State administration, and our efforts were not without influence. But while our Indiana reformers generally supported Mr. Harrison, this was not true of the independents in the East. The most prominent of these, George William Curtis, Carl Schurz, and Dorman B. Eaton, as well as many others, still remained faithful to Mr. Cleveland. I wrote to Mr. Curtis on the subject and received the following answer:

WEST NEW BRIGHTON, STATEN ISLAND, N. Y.
June 28, 1888.

MY DEAR MR. FOULKE:

I have your note and I thought of you when I saw that Harrison was nominated. But the evident tone of the Convention, the present leadership and spirit of the Republican party, and its outrageous platform, will prevent me from supporting General Harrison.

McKinley put in my plank, as he did four years ago, to catch reformers. Then they put Blaine upon it to show their sincerity. Now they sneer at those of us who did not keep our pledges to reform by voting for Blaine and say that, nevertheless, they will keep theirs. And this in a Convention where there was no more mention or purpose of reform, than of temperance legislation. That is the measure of the party pressure upon General Harrison and as I do not suppose he has any stronger convictions upon the subject than the President or firmer will to enforce them, I could not swallow the platform upon the shadowy chance of Harrison's improvement upon Cleveland. I should not be surprised if he were elected, to see Blaine Secretary of State and Sherman of the Treasury, or at least the offer, to both.

After my address, Seth Low wrote me hoping that we could pull together for a good Republican upon a good platform. But he has promptly announced that he shall support Cleveland. One of my best Republi-

can neighbors told me last evening of the general Republican dissatisfaction with the platform and the party management and of his friends
who declare for Cleveland and I know other such.

I am very sorry that we take different views of the campaign, but I
console myself with thinking that our purpose is the same.

Please give my kindest regards to Mr. Swift when you see him and believe
me always

Very truly yours,
GEORGE WILLIAM CURTIS.

I afterwards visited Mr. Curtis at his home in New Brighton
and reminded him of Mr. Cleveland's failures and of the
abominable system of removals on secret charges he had instituted. I called his attention to the fact that the platform
he had criticized contained in respect to civil service the very
words that he himself had written, that Harrison had made
the promises his own, and that he had always been a man
of his word. Yet I could not convince Mr. Curtis. He evidently distrusted Harrison and he added that the extreme
high tariff plank of the Republican platform also made it
impossible for him to support that party.

After a strenuous campaign, in which Mr. Cleveland's
shortcomings were well ventilated, General Harrison succeeded in carrying his own State as well as the country at
large. He was to be our next President. What then was to
be the attitude of the civil service reformers who had supported him? Evidently it was our duty to apply to his
administration the same standard of official action that we
had applied to the administration of Mr. Cleveland and in my
address as president of the Indiana Association at its annual
meeting January 3, 1889, I discussed in somewhat radical
terms the meaning of the promises of the Republican party and
insisted upon an administration in which not only should the
law be generally enforced and extended but in which merit and
fitness and not political considerations should be the determining motive in all appointments.

On the day this was delivered I met General Harrison on the
street and told him I intended to consider the meaning of the
civil service clauses of the platform upon which he said, "I
may want you for Civil Service Commissioner and I hope you

will not say anything to make that impossible." These words appeared to me of sinister omen and I answered that I did not know whether that appointment would be possible in any event. No modification of the address was made in consequence of the warning.[1]

Right at the beginning of Mr. Harrison's administration came his first significant defection. John Wanamaker, the distinguished merchant of Philadelphia, had been engaged in raising funds for the Republican campaign and had succeeded in securing several hundred thousand dollars. The place of Postmaster-General in the new Cabinet was now demanded on his behalf and it seemed evident that this place, if given to him, would be bestowed as a reward for securing these contributions since he had not previously been prominent in public life and would hardly have been thought of were it not for this financial service. Vigorous protests were made yet Mr. Wanamaker was appointed. His appointment caused scandal at the outset and his subsequent career justified the unfavorable opinion then formed of him.

President Harrison in his inaugural retreated a long way from the advanced position taken by the platform and in his letter of acceptance. He said that the heads of departments would be expected to enforce the law, a thing they were bound to do, and continued, "Beyond this obvious duty I hope to do something to extend the service. Retrospect will be a safer basis of judgment than promises." But the promises had been already made and it was not merely to do "something" but to do everything possible. "Some extensions of the classified list," he said, "are necessary and desirable." But it was not merely "some extensions" which he had promised to make but extensions to *every* office to which this system could

---

[1] One month after this annual meeting a conference of civil service reformers was held at Baltimore. In the evening at a public meeting at which Mr. Charles J. Bonaparte presided, Theodore Roosevelt, Richard Henry Dana, and I delivered addresses. I followed the same line of discussion as at the annual meeting of the Indiana Association. This address, entitled "What have Civil Reformers a Right to Expect from the Republican Party," will be found in Appendix II.

4

properly be applied as well as the observance of the spirit of reform in *all* executive appointments. Upon this latter promise the President had now become entirely silent.

A short time before the election, Mr. Elijah Halford (who afterwards became the President's secretary) said to me, "The occupant of the White House lives in a fool's paradise. He is surrounded by sycophants, flatterers, and office seekers, takes their opinions for the opinion of the country, and has no idea of the great public sentiment beyond." Only a month or two after Mr. Harrison's inauguration, when this gentleman had himself become a dweller in this charmed region, he gravely told me that public sentiment had recently gone back a long way in regard to civil service reform! I could not help thinking of the fool's paradise, of the herd of office seekers immediately around the President which shut out the view of the great people beyond. For the clamor of politicians gives no indication of public sentiment on the subject of patronage. On other questions they study the currents of popular opinion with much care. The average politician is a great adept in Huxley's coach-dog theory, which is "to find out first which way the coach is going and then run ahead and bark loud." But patronage is the mainspring of his political action. Office is what he is doing these things for, and in regard to the distribution of the offices it is his own cause he pleads and his own desires which he represents as the views of the people.

Another illustration of Republican backsliding after Harrison became President was in the railway mail service. After the election had gone against him, President Cleveland had made a really valuable extension to the classified system by including in it this branch of the service. It is never hard for an outgoing administration thus to classify additional positions and thus give greater permanency of tenure to those who have been appointed while that administration was in power. The inclusion in this case was made by executive order on January 4, 1889, and the classification was to take place March 15th, almost immediately after the inauguration of Mr. Harrison. But the Civil Service Commission was unable, with the limited force at its command, to make the classification in time, so President Harrison postponed the taking effect of the order until May 1st. In the meantime the Republicans who had now come into power improved the shining hours by removing Democrats and filling the places as rapidly as they could with men of their own faith and President Harrison did little to stop this loot of the service, which was widespread, although not complete, when the places were finally classified.

This was followed by other acts which gave great dissatisfaction to civil service reformers. Mr. H. G. Pearson, the postmaster of New York, who had administered the law with fidelity in that great office and who, although a Republican, had been reappointed by Mr. Cleveland on account of his eminent services, was displaced by Mr. Harrison, and Mr. Van Cott, a politician, was appointed in his stead.

Silas Burt, who had distinguished himself in like manner as Surveyor of the Port in New York and had enforced the law impartially, was also separated from the service to make way for another politician; and at a later time Mr. Leverett Saltonstall, Collector of Customs at Boston, who had maintained the merit system with signal ability, was removed in a similar manner.

Moreover President Harrison made a number of astonishingly bad appointments, for instance, that of Corporal Tanner as Commissioner of Pensions, who was so impossible that he soon had to leave and was succeeded by Greene B. Raum, under whom grave scandals also occurred.

J. S. Clarkson was appointed First Assistant Postmaster-General and commenced turning out Democratic Fourth Class Postmasters and putting in Republicans, at the rate of about thirty thousand a year, during the early part of Harrison's administration.

Moreover, the President seemed to be greatly under the influence of three of the most unscrupulous bosses in the Republican party, Platt of New York, Quay of Pennsylvania, and Mahone of West Virginia. All these things awakened lively criticism in the independent press.

In another respect, however, Mr. Harrison justified the

expectations of the reformers.   He appointed on the Civil Service Commission Theodore Roosevelt, one of our foremost protagonists and Governor Thompson of South Carolina, a high-minded Southern gentleman who was unflinching in support of the merit system.   These men with Charles Lyman (who held over from the preceding administration), now constituted the Commission and everything was done by Messrs. Roosevelt and Thompson which was humanly possible to enforce the law.   They insisted upon the utmost publicity and opened the eligible lists to general inspection.   In many places, particularly in the South, there was a general disbelief in the fairness of the examinations and they caused notices to be spread broadcast over the country that no discrimination would be made in favor of one party against the other.   By this means they secured such confidence that the examinations were well attended.   Where violations of the law were brought to their notice they were prompt to correct them, traveling over the country to New York, Indianapolis, Troy, Milwaukee, Boston, Atlanta, New Orleans, and elsewhere, investigating abuses.

I well remember the occasion when Mr. Roosevelt came to Indianapolis.   It was in June, 1889.   I had met him before in New York and at Baltimore but it was in Indianapolis that our real acquaintance began.   We took a drive together and discussed many things.   He had just completed one of his volumes of *The Winning of the West* which was at that time his *magnum opus* and we talked of this.   He also spoke of what he called the "Cleveland Cult" a sort of blind adoration by the eastern mugwumps which did not permit them to see the defects of his administration.   Mr. Roosevelt himself, although he had a good opinion of the ex-President, could not tolerate this excessive sycophancy on the part of his independent supporters.

The occasion of Mr. Roosevelt's visit to Indianapolis was this: President Harrison had appointed as postmaster to that city, Mr. Wm. Wallace, a man of excellent character but entirely inexperienced, who said he intended to obey the civil service law but frankly declared that Republicans would be given the preference whenever a vacancy was to be filled!

Moreover, the assistant postmaster was Mr. E. P. Thompson, a Republican politician who had been reinstated and who soon began to use the office for political purposes. Complaint was made to the Federal Commission, which investigated the case, Mr. Roosevelt conducting the examination of the witnesses. Two men who had been discharged some years previously had been put back into places which could only be filled from the eligible lists and had already been serving illegally nearly two months. Mr. Roosevelt exclaimed, "These men must be discharged to-day" and it was done.

Another case was that of a man who had been reinstated by Mr. Wallace although he had been discharged by a former postmaster for operating a gambling room. Thompson attempted to defend this reinstatement on the ground that the man was only engaged in "a little game of five cent ante with friends" but the proof was clear and the postmaster was directed to sever at once the connection of this man with the office.

The investigation had an admirable effect. After it the law was well observed and within the classified service appointments were made without reference to politics so that two years later, when Postmaster Wallace died, his execution of the civil service law had been a model of fairness and justice.

The conduct of the Commissioners in sustaining the law so exasperated the Republican spoilsmen that charges were preferred against them, instigated principally by Mr. Hatton of the Washington Post and an investigation was held by a Congressional Committee from which however Mr. Roosevelt and Governor Thompson came out with flying colors. In this investigation Mr. Wanamaker attempted to discredit Mr. Roosevelt by testifying that the Commissioner had sought to secure his consent to the appointment of a Mr. Shidy who had been coerced by Postmaster Paul of Milwaukee into tampering with examination papers. Shidy as secretary of the Civil Service Board had done this with the concurrence of the other members, but had afterwards turned State's evidence under

Mr. Roosevelt's promise of protection. Then he had been dismissed from the service while the other members of the board who had concealed the offense had been retained, and Roosevelt sought to get Mr. Wanamaker's consent to secure for Shidy another position. Wanamaker testified that Roosevelt had recommended him as a "worthy man" but was confronted with the fact that the public reports of the Commission which he admitted he had read, showed exactly what the circumstances were.

Mr. Roosevelt was much exasperated by this testimony. I recollect one evening when dining at his home that he dismissed an emissary of Mr. Wanamaker with the statement, "You may tell the Postmaster-General from me that I don't like him for two reasons, in the first place because he has a very sloppy mind, and in the second place because he doesn't speak the truth."

JOHN WANAMAKER

I had occasion later to make my own commentary upon this text. As chairman of a committee of the National Civil Service Reform League to investigate the condition of the civil service under President Harrison, I desired to see the record of removals and appointments of postmasters, and addressed a letter to Mr. Wanamaker asking for an inspection of the files of the Postal Bulletin containing this record—files which were in reality public property as the newspapers were furnished from day to day with a statement of their contents.

The Postmaster-General asked me to call upon him. I had already criticized him in a communication to the New York *Evening Post* for his testimony against Mr. Roosevelt, and he commenced the conversation by saying, "Mr. Foulke, I suppose I ought to feel angry at you, because you have deliberately published falsehoods about me. But I do not feel angry." I inquired immediately, "What have I said that was not true?" Then he tried to avoid the subject by saying, "We will not go over the details, because I don't suppose you meant to say what was not true." And he spoke of what he was pleased to call Mr. Roosevelt's attack upon *him*, adding, "The trouble with civil service reformers is that they do not consider that anybody can tell the truth but themselves."

I now introduced another subject of difference.

Soon after Mr. Wanamaker became Postmaster-General, Mr. Marshall Cushing, who within a short time became his private secretary, addressed a circular letter to a large number of men in public life stating that he was making inquiries on behalf of a Cabinet officer in regard to civil service reform and asking why both parties should not "abandon their insincere professions for the law and have the patriotism" to go back to the old system. It struck me as remarkable, I said, that a Cabinet officer should thus declare that the principles of the party with which he came into power were insincere and unpatriotic. Just about this time Mr. Cushing walked into the room. Mr. Wanamaker said he did not know of a letter of that kind. I produced a copy and showed it to him. He glanced it over and replied, "But this letter merely says the inquiry was made in behalf of a Cabinet officer. It doesn't say it was made in *my* behalf and Mr. Cushing was not my private secretary at that time." "He became your private secretary soon afterward," I responded, "and it was natural to infer that he meant you." Mr. Wanamaker at first seemed disposed to argue the point. I thereupon turned to Mr. Cushing and asked, "Who was the Cabinet officer for whom you wrote that letter?" but before he could utter a word the Postmaster-General interposed with, "Never mind, that has nothing to do with it." I now turned to him and said, "Mr. Wanamaker, this letter was written by a man who shortly afterwards became your private secretary and when I ask him to say who was the Cabinet officer for whom he wrote it you won't let him speak. Don't you think there is a pretty strong inference that he meant you?" "Oh, well," said the Postmaster-General, "I didn't tell him he should not answer you. I have nothing to conceal. He is at liberty to tell you what you want to know." "Then, Mr. Cushing," said I, "What Cabinet officer was it for whom you were making these inquiries?" "I was making them," he answered, "in my own way; but the officer for whom I was writing happened to be the Postmaster-General." "It seems, Mr. Wanamaker," I remarked, "that my inference was correct." "I don't know," answered the Postmaster-General, "how that letter was written. I never saw it before."

Mr. Cushing reminded me that he was a newspaper man, and said that he was trying to get at the facts and resorted to this device to accomplish his purpose. He then asked me whether I did not myself believe that the parties were insincere in their platform professions. I answered that I did not, that I thought when General Harrison was elected, he intended to carry out his pledges for this reform.

There was another rather significant incident in our conversation, Mr. Wanamaker referred to the wisdom of having reliable information to proceed upon. I told him that that was the very reason I had made my effort to inspect the authentic record of removals and appointments and remarked that I had merely asked for leave to consult the past files of the Daily Bulletin which contained lists of the post office changes and other material facts. "If you want the number of removals," he said, "we shall be glad to give them to you." "That is not what I want," I answered. "I want to look over the back files of the Bulletin. I have some of them, but they do not extend back to the beginning of this administration. I want to see the earlier ones." "Well," said he, "I can't let you see them. You have no business to see them." "But you give them to the public press," I argued. He assented. "Then" said I, "I don't understand why I cannot see them." "You cannot," was all the response he made, so I quitted the office.

After this conversation I naturally shared Mr. Roosevelt's opinion of the Postmaster-General.[1]

---

[1] On December 16th, of this year, 1889, I was invited to address the Commonwealth Club of New York City and after relating to that body the foregoing experience with Mr. Wanamaker I added, "There is one thing of which the politicians of the country may be well assured, whether or not the people favor civil service reform, they will not continue to have confidence in the party which knowingly with its eyes open, fails to perform its solemn promises. There is something more immoral in this than even in the

THE INVESTIGATING COMMITTEE

In December, 1889, a committee was appointed by the Reform League to investigate the condition of the civil service under President Harrison.[1]

I was chairman of this committee and was placed in general charge of the work. The results of our investigation were contained in six reports which we made to the League, embracing the following subjects: first, Congressional Patronage; second, the Patent Office; third, Presidential Postmasters; fourth, Removals upon Secret Charges; fifth, Political Changes in Post offices; sixth, The Census Bureau.

We were in constant communication with members of the Civil Service Commission, especially with Mr. Roosevelt and Governor Thompson and it was here that my strong personal friendship with Mr. Roosevelt began. I often dined with him and we sometimes took excursions together, walks in the country and rows upon the Potomac. Some of the pleasantest experiences of my life were connected with this investigation.

CONGRESSIONAL PATRONAGE

Our first inquiries were addressed to Republican members of the House of Representatives asking for the number of

---

spoils system. The Republican party has been successful in the past because it has been true to its great promises and plans—emancipation, the preservation of the Union, enfranchisement, payment of the National debt—these became embodied as fixed facts in the history of our country. The party was as good as its word. But if at the last convention it has in the most solemn manner made a distinct pledge to the people, and if it fails to keep that promise now, the people will know the value of every pledge hereafter made."

[1] Charles J. Bonaparte of Baltimore, Sherman S. Rogers of Buffalo, Richard H. Dana of Boston, Wayne MacVeagh of Philadelphia, and myself were the members of this committee. Four of us out of the five had voted for Mr. Harrison. On the 15th of February, 1890, we had our first meeting in Philadelphia and outlined our general plan. We determined to establish our headquarters at Washington, to examine the records of the various departments and to address communications to officials removed and those appointed in all parts of the country; to interview Congressmen and heads of departments as to the changes made and the working of the various branches of the service so far as possible.

offices in which the appointments depended upon them, the number of applications received during the last year and the amount of time and correspondence required. From the answers received it appeared that about 250 appointments depended upon each of the Congressmen and that the average number of applications to each was about 1700; that the correspondence involved in this office brokerage was enormous and that more than one third of their entire time was devoted to it. In the meanwhile their proper legislative duties, as appeared from the Congressional records, were neglected so that out of more than 17,000 measures introduced less than 3500 were finally acted upon by Congress, either one way or the other.

Our conclusions as contained in our report on Congressional Patronage published in April, 1891, were as follows.

The men selected are chosen, not on account of the knowledge of their fitness possessed by the appointing officer, but because they are recommended by certain representatives or senators. The head of the department or bureau feels little responsibility for their acts. It often happens that he is not at liberty to discharge an inefficient man, lest he may offend the Congressman whose influence secured the appointment of that man. The Congressman, on the other hand, does not feel the responsibility for these appointments, for he is not nominally nor legally the appointing officer. In many cases it is not known on whose recommendation the appointment is made. This system "invades the independence of the executive and makes him less responsible for the character of his appointments. It impairs the efficiency of the legislator by diverting him from his proper sphere of duties and involving him in the intrigues of the aspirants for office."

Sometimes, as we found in our investigation, members of Congress endeavored to avoid the responsibility of making appointments, such as that of postmaster, by holding informal elections among Republican patrons of the office. An amusing account of an election held in his district was given in an interview with one of these Representatives. He said:

I have held one election only under this administration, and that had a most disastrous result. It resulted in several men losing their characters; one or two were turned out of church, and all was turmoil and confusion.

Carriages were hired to bring voters fourteen miles distant, and citizens of another State voted. The doors of the polling places were broken in. Democrats were allowed to vote. There were no safeguards about the polls. No oaths were required, and there was no respect for the election. The judges certified the election of one man, but sent a statement with the certification that the election was carried by fraud. The consequence was, I went outside for the postmaster and chose a man who had not voted and took no part in the fight. He moved into town and took the office (worth not more than $150 per year); but they would have torn the election nominee to pieces if I had recommended him. I look upon these elections as a party disaster.

THE PATENT OFFICE

Some two months later we issued a report concerning the Patent Office. The beginning of the administration had found this Bureau in control of spoilsmen who held all the places both above and below the classified list. Mr. Montgomery, the first Commissioner who had been appointed by Mr. Cleveland entered the office without any experience in patent law and appointed his brother his confidential clerk to distribute the subordinate positions among the friends of influential Congressmen. The Bureau was honeycombed with politics and the abuses were very serious. Later in his administration President Cleveland transferred the Commissioner to a different field and appointed as his successor Benton J. Hall of Iowa, who devoted his energies mainly to preserving the remnants of good service from further inundations but who was still surrounded by many incompetents whom he failed to discharge.

President Harrison at the request of the patent bar appointed Mr. Charles H. Mitchell as Commissioner, a man of extensive experience and recognized standing and there was a decided improvement. Our Committee went into considerable detail as to the former abuses and the reforms accomplished from which it appeared that it was the competitive system applied to the examiners which had preserved the Bureau from utter demoralization during President Cleveland's administration and it was the extension of civil service reform tests and principles which had improved the service under the

Harrison administration. This investigation of the Patent Office was the only one made by our committee in which it appeared that any improvement had been made.

Our committee next took up the subject of Presidential Postmasters. The Congressional Record and certain reports of the Postmaster-General gave us the needed information. From these it appeared that nearly 64 per cent. of these offices were changed during the first year of the Harrison administration.

The statement made by the Post Office Department however indicated that only about 23 per cent. of these changes had been made by the removal of the incumbents, the remainder being by deaths, resignations, and the expirations of official terms. The number of deaths was very few, only forty-eight in all and we now proceeded to examine whether the resignations were voluntary or compulsory and whether the removals were really to secure a better service, or were made for political reasons. We therefore addressed communications both to the postmasters displaced and to the new appointees asking the causes assigned for the removals, the politics in each case, what political services had been rendered, and upon whose recommendation the change was made.

As soon as we commenced making these inquiries, First Assistant Postmaster-General Clarkson, in an interview published by the Associated Press, attempted to forestall our investigation by giving a hint to the new appointees that they were not to answer, or if they answered what the tenor of their answer was to be. He said:

It is evidently an effort to get statements from removed and disappointed officials for political use, and some of the letters show an intention to try to induce the new postmaster to make statements of defense where no defense is needed. The postmasters seem to realize that they have reports to make only to their superior officers. No political capital can be made out of these changes. The President has made no removals except for cause,—for delinquency in official duties, inefficiency of service, or violation of law. *He has refused to make any changes for partisan reasons.*

The answers to our inquiries however showed that in regard to resignations about two thirds were voluntary and one third not voluntary but were requested by the Congressman of the district or other influential parties who were believed to have the disposal of the office in their hands. In some cases inducements were offered in the shape of a postponement in the time for the change or the offer of a good price for office fixtures. Sometimes the resignation was procured by threats of immediate removal. Our committee concluded that many of these so-called resignations were not such in fact but that the changes were substantially changes for political purposes.

Some of the answers we received to our inquiries were amusing. For instance a western editor quoted from his letter of resignation, sent to the President, in which he said:

I am moved to tender you my resignation because of the anxiety of a barnyard of patriots to succeed me. I believe the tariff is a tax. They do not. Therefore they are of your own kith and kindred, and he who provides not for his own household is worse than an infidel. I am told that you are not built that way. The boys who are anxious to be my successor are very hungry; they have been feeding on icicles and shucks for four long, weary years; the official calf is fat and they yearn to taste its tender joints. They carried torches, drank with the "coons," sang *Grandpa's Hat Will Just Fit Benny* and did divers and sundry foolish things, none of which they would have been guilty of doing had they not scented an aroma of postmaster on the crisp morning air. And the pæans of praise which they sounded when it became evident that you "had got there Eli" will ever be a Sahara in my memory.

REMOVALS ON SECRET CHARGES

Our fourth report discussed the subject of removals of presidential postmasters on secret charges. On this we said:

Out of 356 answers received to our questions whether or not any cause for the removal was given to the man removed, it appeared that in only 47 cases was such cause assigned, in ten cases the matter was disputed and in 299 cases it appeared, from uncontradicted statements, that the incumbent was removed without any cause being given.

In a very large number of cases he solicited information from the Post Office Department as to the character of the charges; but this information was almost invariably refused. If he ever learned what the charges were, he learned it by private inquiry from other sources, generally from hearsay and rumor merely. In many instances the new appointee, in answer to our inquiry as to the causes of the removal, while declining to state these causes himself, refers us to written charges on file in the department. As Mr. Wanamaker tells us that "all papers in appointment cases have invariably been deemed privileged and confidential" and as the postmasters themselves are refused access to the charges upon which they are removed, but little can be done to lift the veil which conceals these secret accusations.

Case after case is given in which the man removed asked to be informed what the charges were and to be given an opportunity to answer them which he failed to secure. Clarkson writes: "It is not the custom of the Department to furnish postmasters with copies of charges." In answer to a similar request, Wanamaker writes another postmaster that the change was made "in the interest of better mail service."

Many similar cases were adduced and in conclusion we said:

This system could easily be abolished if the inspector of the department, previous to the removal, should be required to acquaint the officer accused with the nature of the charge against him and hear what he had to say. If such a vast number of removals were not made for purely political reasons this would not be by any means an impossible or even a difficult task. It is only because the energies of the department and of the inspectors are exhausted in an improper and immoral effort to turn men out without cause for political reasons that they might find it difficult to give the necessary time to an investigation of charges, where publicity would be some guarantee that they were honestly made.

It would be just as absurd to expect a judge to decide a case properly when he heard nothing but the plaintiff's statement as to expect removals to be properly made under such a system. Your committee is of the opinion that there is no evil in the spoils system as inherently wicked as this, whereby both the livelihood and reputation of innocent men are liable to be overthrown by secret and false accusations.

In connection with these removals upon secret charges, it may be well to recall the expressions made by Mr. Harrison in the Senate upon this subject in his speech of March 26, 1886, as reported in the Congressional Record, vol. 7, No. 3, page 2790 et seq. In reference to Executive nominations then pending in the Senate he said:

"In many of these cases, it leaked out in the community where the officer resided that charges had been filed against him. Some base fellows had been used for that unholy office; and, being advised that charges had been sent, the appeal was made to heads of the different departments, and, I believe, in many cases to the President himself, to be advised of the character of the charges made. . . . Here was an accusation, a hearing, a sentence, and an execution without the accused being advised of the character of the charges against him. . . .

"What is it these people ask? An honorable discharge after honorable service. That is all. . . .

"I do lift up a hearty prayer that we may never have a President who will not pursue and compel his Cabinet officers to pursue a civil service policy pure and simple upon a just basis, allowing men accused to be heard, and deciding against them only upon competent proof and fairly—either have that kind of a civil service or, for God's sake, let us have that other frank and bold, if brutal, method of turning men and women out simply for political opinion. Let us have one or the other."

It seems incredible that the administration of the man who uttered these words should perpetuate this system of removals upon secret charges. Yet such is the fact!

Your committee concurs most heartily with the expressions quoted above. They furnish the best standard of criticism possible of the system of removals which is still practised in the Post Office Department. It can never be unjust to the President to judge him by his own standard of duty, by his own conceptions of justice and fair play. The fittest condemnation of his own acts is found in his own words. Nor will it do to shift the responsibility from the Chief Executive to the heads of these departments. Mr. Harrison has told us why it cannot be so evaded. "I do lift up a hearty prayer that we may never have a President who will not either pursue and *compel his Cabinet officers* to pursue a civil service policy pure and simple or" etc. It is not the Postmaster-General and his First Assistant who, in the last analysis are responsible. It is the President, who appointed Wanamaker and Clarkson, and who permitted these things to be.

POLITICAL CHANGES IN POST OFFICES

The review of the changes of Presidential post offices was continued in the next report. In this our investigation showed that out of 437 changes, 427 removals were of Democrats and out of 513 appointments 510 were Republicans. This uniformity indicated that political motives rather than the good of the service dictated the changes. In many cases very full inquiries were made as to the political faith of the appointees before their commissions were issued, post office inspectors being often employed for this service at government expense. In most of the cases the new appointees had been active in party work as committeemen, delegates, county leaders, etc. Some of the new appointees related their services to the Republican party in great detail and with apparent pride, as well as the political influence behind them. Sometimes their petitions would be signed by all the members of the Legislature. Editors of party newspapers were chosen in considerable numbers and the appointments were almost uniformly dictated by Republican Congressmen, the Post Office Department stating that Congressional recommendations "were in accord with the long standing practice of the Department and deemed to be the best ground of action." The relatives of Congressmen were often appointed to places in these post offices and in many cases it was stated that the appointee was active in Congressional nominations in the interest of the Congressman by whom he was recommended.

"Offensive partisanship" was employed as an agency of removal in the same way as under President Cleveland. The statements of Mr. Clarkson that the President had made no removals except for cause, inefficiency, delinquency, or violation of law and had refused to make any changes for partisan reasons was thus shown to be untrue. Our committee quoted a letter of Mr. Wanamaker to Congressman Rockwell of Massachusetts in which he said, "The Postmaster-General declines to recommend to the President the appointment of a Democrat unless it is clear that there is no Republican to fill the place." It did not seem hard to determine the motive for removals and appointments under such an administration of this department.

THE CENSUS INVESTIGATION

Our final report contained the results of our investigation into the Census Bureau.

In the summer of 1889 President Harrison had refused to include any part of the Census force in the classified competitive system. This was a keen disappointment to many who had supported him. I was in Europe when the announcement was made and, on September 1st, I addressed him from Switzerland the following letter:

The papers just received announce your decision not to include the clerks of the Census Office in the civil service rules. I find it almost impossible to believe that this determination has been finally made by the Administration of a party which promised that the reform system should be extended to all grades of the service to which it was applicable. To what grades could that refer if not to such as these? If the successful experiments already made elsewhere with exactly this branch of the service do not show the applicability of the system, what could demonstrate it? If this is really your conclusion, let me, with all respect, most earnestly remonstrate. Can any party long retain popular confidence if the promises of its own platform become discredited?

And now, something over a year later when the Census had been taken, our committee observed:

If an administration has a free choice between a non-political and a political agency for taking the enumeration, and chooses the latter, composed of officials of its own political faith, the presumption is against the fairness of a census so taken. The results of such a census will be apt to reflect something of the bias of those who take it. And, even if it were fair, many would not believe it to be fair. Suspicion is cast on such a census in advance of enumeration; and if, at the close of the work, many inaccuracies are shown, resulting in the advantage of the party by whom it is taken, the work is sure to be discredited.

Our report showed that the President had been asked by the Civil Service Commission to adopt competitive examinations but had declined to do so, leaving with Mr. Porter, the Superintendent of the Census (a man who had expressed his opposition to Civil Service Reform) the power to make the selections for that service. The Superintendent recommended the supervisors and these designated the enumerators. But as the supervisors were appointed by political methods, naturally the appointment of enumerators became a matter of political patronage. Republican members of Congress nominated great numbers. Sometimes Democratic members procured the appointment of a few, but the great mass were Republicans. In many places the enumerators were instructed by the supervisors and others to do political work.[1]

[1] Thus Supervisor Douglas in New York wrote to his enumerators, "As it is of the utmost importance that a Republican member of Congress be elected in this district I shall feel personally obliged if, on the day of the election, you will work specially for Benj. H. Williams, the Republican candidate."

5

The worst effects of the patronage system of census appointments were apparent in the city of New York where C. H. Murray, a Republican politician, was made supervisor. The following circular letter from him showed the manner in which the enumerators were selected.

DEAR SIR: You will please forward to this office a list of the applicants that the Republican organization of your district desires to have named as census enumerators. This list must be sent here on or before April 1st.

Of this method of appointment President Walker, of the Massachusetts Institute of Technology, who had been Superintendent of the Ninth and Tenth Censuses, said, "If the selection of the enumerators was made upon any such basis as is implied by that, the census could not have been otherwise than bad." Such a method was a direct violation of Section 5 of the act providing for the census, which prescribed that

---

Section 8 of the Act, required that each enumerator should subscribe an oath that he would not disclose any information contained in the schedules, lists, or statements to any person except his superior officer, yet in spite of this, the enumerators in Monroe County, Indiana, who were selected upon the recommendation of the Republican County Committee were engaged in making poll lists for the Republican party. This also occurred in other counties and States.

Our committee observed that if enumerators were allowed to remain ignorant of the law imposing secrecy, the Superintendent of the Census deserved the greatest censure and if they were permitted to violate it wilfully he was an accessory to a crime.

A letter from Congressman Raines to one of the enumerators in his district was as follows:

"MY DEAR SIR: As it is quite likely that you will in a few days be appointed enumerator for your district, I write you this in the strictest confidence. I would like very much that you should take the trouble, before you make your report to the Supervisor of the Census, and after you have taken all the names in your district, to copy in a small book the name and post office address of every voter on the list. After you have done so, I wish you to send the book to me at Canandaigua. I ask you to do this as a personal favor and to make no mention of the matter to anyone. What I want is a full list of all the voters in your enumeration district. Will you please treat this matter as strictly confidential?"

Mr. Raines told me he had sent this letter in ignorance of the law which required enumerators to keep secret the results of the enumeration.

enumerators "should be selected solely with reference to fitness and without reference to party affiliations."

It is evident enough that among men thus appointed there must have been a considerable number who were utterly unfit for the work, and it is not surprising that among these men Police Inspector Byrnes should recognize well-known criminals. Mr. Byrnes said:

> I know that some of the enumerators in this city were thieves. This very morning one of these enumerators came here to call upon me. He had been three times an inmate of the State Prison. He was appointed upon the recommendation of a Republican judge. This thief's name is known to all the city detectives, and his picture occupies a prominent place in the Rogues' Gallery. He did not take the oath in his own name, and his dealings with the Census Bureau were under an alias.

The danger of employing such men as enumerators is very evident. Private houses were opened to them with the understanding that the government was satisfied with their trustworthiness.

Many facts indicated that the New York census was inaccurate and incomplete and the police authorities by order of the Mayor had a recount made and the result showed a population nearly 200,000 more than that shown by the federal authorities. The Mayor asked the Census Bureau for a recount but this was refused. The New York authorities then determined to take one of the wards as a sample and secured a copy of the federal list for the second ward, the smallest in the city. It contained 826 names while the police enumeration showed 1340 names or 41% more. The New York authorities now procured from the persons omitted in the federal enumeration affidavits showing their residence in that ward. Three hundred and twenty-eight such affidavits were furnished.

I personally inspected the lists in the police and federal enumerations respectively and ascertained by visiting the ward that a large number of residents therein were omitted in the federal census. I found that in two squares alone, twelve houses, in which thirty-eight persons resided had been wholly omitted.   John Kiernan, the enumerator, who secured his appointment through the "regular channel" as an enrolled Republican of the Third Assembly District, told me that certain schedules had been lying somewhere around the house but could not be found.   In this he was corroborated by other members of the family.   In a number of cases even the names reported by Mr. Kiernan did not appear in the federal lists.

As the enumerators in New York were Republicans and as the city had a large Democratic majority and the result was that the population was enumerated as less than it actually was, it was naturally inferred that the error was intentional and made for the purpose of reducing the representation of New York in Congress.

Our committee concluded its report by insisting that the refusal to apply competitive examinations in appointments to the clerical force of the Census Bureau was a violation by the President of a promise contained in the Republican platform in 1888 and indorsed in his letter of acceptance; that by the appointment of enumerators on political grounds in open violation of the law great numbers of incompetent men had been engaged, that in many cases the work had been carelessly and badly done and was open to the suspicion of partisan considerations and that there was a widespread distrust of the accuracy of the result which greatly impaired its value, all caused by the fact that the Census Bureau had been conducted upon the spoils system.[1]

---

[1] During our investigation, the criticisms of Mr. Porter's methods of taking the census were so widespread that he undertook a defense of his course in an article in *Frank Leslie's Illustrated Newspaper* in November, 1890.   On the 12th of that month I addressed to him an open letter which was widely published.   It contained the following:

"Realizing at last that the census taken by you through officials chosen by partisan machinery has become so generally discredited that a personal defense over your own signature was necessary, you seek to show in an article in *Frank Leslie's Illustrated Newspaper* that your work has been honestly and fairly done.   You would be more successful in this effort if the methods pursued at the outset in the taking of the census had been less tinctured by those political elements which were calculated to cast suspicion upon its results.   As you have addressed the people and thus invited public discussion of your management, permit me to make a few inquiries through the same channel of the press.

"You say that a partisan census is an impossibility. If this be so why did you recommend to the President that this census be taken by enumerators appointed upon the recommendation of Republican Congressmen and other influential party men? Why did you refuse to adopt the system by which appointments in your bureau should be non-partisan, made upon competition among those seeking appointment without regard to their political affiliations? The Civil Service Commission desired that the merit system should be applied to your office but you resisted this just and reasonable demand and insisted upon retaining the patronage of this vast bureau which you parcelled out among politicians.

"Did it not occur to you that by this act you were to discredit the results of your work? Even if the enumeration were fair and accurate, was it not certain to be clouded by suspicion if made by one party alone? Would you believe in the accuracy of a Democratic enumeration made in the same way? Do you, in fact, believe in the accuracy of the police enumeration made in New York taken under Democratic direction? If not, how can you expect others to believe in the accuracy of your own? You say that even to hint at such an infamy as a partisan census is an outrageous assault upon the integrity of every one who has taken part in the work and yet you assert that the police were appointed in New York for the sole purpose of finding more population than the federal enumerators found and that the general rule adopted was, 'When you are in doubt, add one.' Is not this an equally outrageous assault upon the integrity of those who took part in that enumeration?

"You say that your enumerators were selected with the greatest care from the best material available. How do you know this when you refused to subject your appointees to an examination in which their ability could be tested in comparison with that of others?

"You say that no one has been able to ascertain whether the discrepancies in the New York count are due to careless omissions in June or intentional additions in October. Is it not your duty to ascertain whether a discrepancy of two hundred thousand is due to the careless omissions of your agents? Do you expect the people to believe in the accuracy of your census when you admit that it is possible that two hundred thousand names have been left out by the careless omissions of your own enumerators? And why do you speak of these additions as 'intentional' and of the omissions of your own bureau as simply 'careless.'

"But I desire to address you not simply as a citizen, but as a Republican, as one who, like yourself, did all I could for the success of the party in 1888. Our party promised in its last platform that the reform of the civil service auspiciously begun under a Republican administration should be completed by the further extension of the reform system already established by law to all grades of the service to which it was applicable. So far as the Census Bureau was concerned there could be no doubt as to its applicability. The places in that bureau are subordinate, non-political, administrative offices.

"The pledge made in the Republican platform could have no possible reference to anything if it did not refer to such a bureau as yours where experience had already shown the applicability of the reform system. Yet you recommend to the President a violation of that pledge and the retention of political patronage in the appointment of the fifty thousand officers of whom you speak. Do you believe that any party can long retain power when the promises in its own platform become discredited?"

To this letter Mr. Porter replied on November 13th, that my first assumption that he sought an opportunity to defend the census in *Frank Leslie's Illustrated Newspaper* was not true, because the article was written at the very earnest solicitation of the editor of that paper. That my second assumption was equally incorrect that he recommended to the President that the Census be taken by enumerators appointed upon the recommendations of Republican Congressmen and influential party men since the law made it the duty of the supervisors to select their own enumerators. It would have been impossible to submit an army of fifty thousand enumerators to an examination since in many parts of the country it was difficult to secure persons for the work at less than $3.00 a day for employment lasting from fifteen to thirty days. Mr. Porter said he would believe in the accuracy of an enumeration conducted by a Democratic administration in the same manner and spirit as the Eleventh Census but that a list of names secured by the policemen in New York was quite different from a census of the United States. The intent of that enumeration was to find more people than were found by the federal enumerators who were bound by their oath of office and instructions to the strictest rules and regulations. He knew that his enumerators had been selected with the greatest care because in New York City they had been subjected to a quasi civil service examination by the supervisor and those who were not fairly accurate and rapid writers were refused employment while in other cities the supervisors were instructed to test personally each applicant and ascertain if he had the necessary ability.

Mr. Porter denied the charge that there was any politics in his appointments. Every important place, every expert, every man or woman in charge of work had been appointed solely on account of ability. In fact the merit system had been successfully applied and as a result he had one of the most efficient clerical forces in the public service. No pledge made by the Republican party had been violated.

On the following day I rejoined in the letter here given:

" DEAR SIR: In your open letter just received, you say my first assumption was that you sought an opportunity to defend the census in *Frank Leslie's Newspaper* and that this is not true because the article was written at the solicitation of the editor.

" I certainly was slow to assume that an article defending your own management was solicited and written in the ordinary course of the business of such a journal. That your conduct of the office should create a demand which made such an article a valuable commodity and that you should then satisfy it in this manner I certainly did not wish to believe.

" You say that my second assumption—that you recommended that the enumerators should be appointed on the recommendation of party men— is equally incorrect and that these enumerators were appointed by the supervisors.

" But were not these supervisors themselves political appointments? Was partisanship absent in their selection?

" I have known several and they are all Republican politicians. Did you not state on September 9th, before a Congressional Committee, that appointees were generally recommended by Republicans? . . .

" Was this your idea of the meaning of the Republican platform? Republican supervisors are appointed and they appoint Republican subordinates for political reasons and then you claim that all this is non-partisan. . .

" Is there not a presumption that when you thus made selection between the old plan and the new you did it for a purpose? And that this purpose was to aid in some way the Republican party, either in the manipulation of patronage or in the control of the results of the census?

" You say that you know the enumerators were selected with the greatest care because in New York they were subjected to a quasi civil service examination by the supervisors and those who were not fairly accurate and rapid writers were refused employment.

" I do not quite understand that mongrel variety of reform embodied in a quasi civil service examination by partisan supervisors. In such examination did any one who could show his proficiency and qualifications whether Republican or Democrat, have an equal chance with others?. . .

" But I am still more puzzled in comparing two other statements in your letter. On the first page you say "an attempt to subject this immense army to a civil service examination would have been a farce, if it would not have been impossible," while in a subsequent part of your letter you speak of this quasi civil service examination by the supervisors and say that the supervisors were personally instructed to test each applicant. If the other system was absurd and impossible why was not this absurd and impossible? If you can thus examine a man who has come with a recommendation why could you not competitively examine, without regard to politics, all those who desired to be appointed? . . .

" The words of the Republican platform demanded the extension of the *system already established by law.* What was that system? It was a system of appointments without regard to political consideration upon open, competitive examination, made under the direction of commissioners of both parties appointed by the President. . . .

" Was the classified system extended to any part of your bureau?

"You think it would not be practicable to extend it to census enumerators, but you have given no reason why it should not be extended to the bureau in Washington, to clerks and other employees in your office. Did not the Civil Service Commissioners desire that it should be so extended? Did you not oppose this? Has it been so extended? You did, indeed, institute a sort of pass examination so that persons entirely ignorant might be weeded out, but Democrats could not compete on equal terms and there was no competition even among Republicans, except among those whose application had come with the proper indorsement, for you say in your testimony before the committee, 'Usually the examination was confined to those whom it was intended to appoint.'

" It is not necessary to remind you that this is not Civil Service Reform and that it is not what the Republican party promised.

" Yours respectfully,

" WILLIAM D. FOULKE."

To this letter Mr. Porter made no further reply. In respect of this correspondence Mr. George William Curtis wrote me the following:

" WEST NEW BRIGHTON, STATEN ISLAND,

" MY DEAR MR. FOULKE: Your pulverization of poor Mr. Porter is complete and your service to the good cause, as so often heretofore, is very great. It is a cause which asks for itself, only what it asks for the Civil Service, a fair field and no favor. With every friend of reform I congratulate you heartily and I am always,

" Very truly yours,

" GEORGE WILLIAM CURTIS."

CHAPTER V

Now that we are dealing with the Census Bureau it may be well to consider the subsequent history of this branch of the public service in its relation to the spoils system.

Some years after the foregoing report was published I had occasion as a member of another investigating committee of the League to examine more specifically the manner in which Mr. Porter's appointments had been made. This was after Mr. Porter had retired from office when evidence was accessible which could not be secured during his incumbency.

I found that, like the Secretary of Patronage in England in former days, he kept regular books of account with Congressmen informing each, whether Senator or Representative to whom patronage was given (and these were mostly Republicans), how many positions were at his disposal. I examined two of these books of account. In one of them the appointments were classified according to States and in the other they were charged to the particular Congressman on whose recommendation they were made. The latter book was a ledger of over four hundred pages. At the head of each page appeared the name of the Congressman charged with the appointments. In the left-hand column were the numbers of the files containing the recommendations and credentials, then followed the names of the appointees and the grades and salaries. By means of this book the relative rights of members of Congress could be adjusted and it could be seen at a glance whether any particular member had overdrawn his account. A peculiar feature of this book was that after a Congressman retired the clerks appointed by him were transferred to another account where the appointees of ex-Congressmen were all thrown together, perhaps as the subjects of early decapitation.

I was informed there were other books of the same character as this ledger in the Census Office covering other periods of time. I could not help thinking of the similarity of this catalogue to a live stock register. The clerks appointed seemed to be regarded as the property of particular Congressmen. There was however no reference to their records and personal qualifications. Such a record might have been unpleasant reading, for one of the employees in the Bureau told me that there were about five thousand people in Washington who had been at one time or another in various departments and been turned out for one reason or another; that these persons had made it uncomfortable for Congressmen until they got new places and that great numbers of them were foisted upon the Census Bureau. Some of them had had relations with the Congressmen which made refusals difficult. While under the competitive system it was hardly possible that applicants could get places *because* of corruption or immorality, yet when appointed through Congressional favor this was often the very reason for the appointment and after getting their places in this way removal from the bureau even for just cause became difficult and often impossible. Persons dismissed for inefficiency or misconduct were actually reinstated even against the will of the chief of the bureau himself at the demand of some political friend too powerful to be offended.

The purpose of this distribution of patronage was not only to strengthen the party, but perhaps more important, to secure ample appropriations, and some $10,620,000 was thus secured. Indeed Mr. Porter himself once told me that his plan had greatly smoothed the way for the passage of such appropriations and other friendly legislation.

Extravagance was a necessary result and certainly any political advantage sought to be secured in this way was entirely illusory since the most severe defeat ever sustained by the party then in power occurred at the close of the very year in which these appointments were parcelled out, principally among the representatives of that party.

When Mr. Robert P. Porter retired as superintendent, Carroll D. Wright took charge of the permanent Census Bureau and spoke strongly of the inefficiency and extravagance which the patronage system had entailed. He estimated (see letter to Henry Cabot Lodge, Congressional Record, Dec. 16, 1897, page 174) that two million dollars and more than a year's time would have been saved if the Census Bureau had been placed under the civil service law,[1] and he added:

> I do not hesitate to say that one third of the amount expended under my own administration was absolutely wasted and wasted principally because of the fact that the office was not under civil service rules. . . . In October, 1893, when I took charge of the Census Office, there was an office force of 1092, there had been a constant reduction for many months and this was kept up without cessation to the close of the Census. Nevertheless while these general reductions were being made and in the absence of any necessity for an increase of the force 389 new appointments were made.

That is new appointments were made where they were not needed, the new men replacing experienced clerks and filling the office with beginners at the end of the work because these appointments were political.

It is interesting to note that at a later period Mr. Porter himself became a convert to the necessity of placing the Census Bureau in the classified service. He told me himself that if he had it to do again he would select his clerks by civil service examinations. In an article in the *North American Review* in December, 1897, he enumerated among the faults of the existing system the following: "Placing upon the shoulders of the superintendent, whose mind should be fully occupied with his experts in planning the work, the responsibility of an office force of several thousand clerks." And he asked, "Why transform the office at its busiest season into an examination department for clerks and the director of a vast scientific investigation into a dispenser of political patronage? It is simply unjust to such an official. Having passed through the

---

[1] Mr. Porter disputed the statement of Mr. Wright that it was so much as two million from this cause alone.

ordeal once, I am satisfied that the other way is more practical and in the end will be better for all concerned."

When therefore on March 16, 1897, Senator Chandler introduced a bill for the taking of the Twelfth and every subsequent census, Section 3 provided that employees should be appointed according to the provisions of the Civil Service Act. The bill was referred to the Census Committee which in spite of the disastrous experience of the preceding census, struck out Section 3 and substituted a provision renewing the system of Congressional patronage with its attendant evils.

I was again appointed by the National Civil Service Reform League as chairman of an investigating committee to report upon the effect of this new law. On January 17, 1898, before the bill passed we made and published a report showing the disastrous effects of this plan on the preceding census, the extravagance of the bureau, the demoralization of the force employed and the comparative worthlessness and lack of public confidence in a census thus taken. We set forth in our report the opinion of Mr. Wright, the changed views of Mr. Porter, the patronage books of account and the evils and unreliability of the former census as shown in our previous investigation, and we urged in the strongest language we could command the classification of the Census Bureau under civil service rules.

But all to no purpose. The bill as passed provided for the appointment of supervisors, statisticians, and other clerical employees by the director after such examinations only as he might prescribe. The President appointed as director ex-Governor W. R. Merriam, of Minnesota, a selection made for political reasons, and Mr. Merriam determined to make the appointments subject to the patronage of Congressmen. He made an allotment to each State and then a subdivision among Congressional districts and the Senators and Representatives were asked to furnish the names of such persons as they desired to be examined for places in the Bureau. No one else was considered for appointment. In this allotment of patronage Democrats were not entirely overlooked. They were allowed a smaller number of appointments than Republicans and the members of the House of Representatives did not get so many as Senators but nobody got less than six and regular books of account were kept as in the preceding census, in which the appointments were charged to the Congressmen recommending them.

Governor Merriam however secured a rather better set of employees than Mr. Porter had done ten years before. The examination was severe and in a limited way it was competitive because each Congressman nominated about twice as many as the number of a pointments he was entitled to and those who passed best were chosen unless (as often happened) the candidates could not pass at all in which case new persons had to be nominated.

The appointments, however, still went by favor through personal and political influence and were tainted with the same essential vice as those made under Mr. Porter. It was inevitable that the appointees should use the power given to them for the benefit of their party and of the particular Congressman who gave them the appointment. This led to abuses of which the following case is an excellent illustration.

THE MARYLAND SCANDAL

The Hon. S. E. Mudd, a Republican Congressman from Maryland, secured the appointment of one Rollins, as supervisor for his district. The constitution of Maryland provides that any county of less than 18,000 inhabitants shall have two members in the House of Delegates; if it contains a population of between 18,000 and 28,000, three members; if between 28,000 and 40,000, four members; if between 40,000 and 55,000, five members and the apportionment is to be made on the basis of the federal census, if no State census is taken.

It was thus to the interest of Republicans and of Mr. Mudd personally as the leader of the party in his district to have the representation of the Republican counties as large as possible.

There were three counties where he hoped to gain delegates; St. Mary's, Charles, and Anne Arundel. But the population of the first two as shown by preceding censuses was somewhat short of 18,000 each and in Anne Arundel by the census of 1890 it was about 6000 short of 40,000. But after the census was taken and the population of these three counties was announced in December, 1900, it was found that each was just a little over the limit required and that there would be a gain of one Representative in each county. Suspicion was aroused, since elsewhere there was little growth in population, and in February the governor of Maryland called an extra session of the legislature to amend the ballot law and provide for a State census on account of the belief that there were frauds in the federal enumeration.

Mr. Merriam, the Director of the Census, determined to investigate and to begin in St. Mary's County. Congressman Mudd now requested of the Census Bureau that the man in charge of the inquiry should be instructed to confer with one Joseph H. Ching, at Leonardtown the county seat, and this was done. In the schedules returned by the enumerator, the first eighteen, which contained 1713 names, were found correct but 528 names on the last six schedules could not be accounted for. Ching claimed they were genuine inhabitants but gave no information where they could be seen. A house to house canvass of the county followed and the results were developed in a trial of an indictment against Ching, who with one Abell and other enumerators was charged with conspiracy in making fictitious returns.

It appeared that in the preceding July the enumerators had completed their schedules and their returns showed the population to be 16,998 or 1002 less than the 18,000 limit. Ching went to Washington and complained to Rollins, that the enumerators had omitted a considerable number of inhabitants and Congressman Mudd asked the chief statistician whether the supervisor could not send out additional schedules where he believed that people had been overlooked. The answer was that it was his duty to do so. So the supplementary schedules were sent out and four enumerators, Abell,

Bowles, Guyther, and Graves returned them with 1138 additional names, sufficient to raise the population to over 18,000.

When these men were tried, Guyther pleaded guilty and turned State's evidence. He testified that Ching told him he ought to get from 150 to 200 additional names. Guyther answered that he did not know where to get them. Ching replied he could go to the summer hotels and enumerate the guests, adding, "Are there no graveyards in the district?" Guyther made up 198 additional names, partly from people who had moved away, partly from summer boarders and nurse girls at hotels and partly from imagination, filling up the ages and occupations at will.

Ennumerator Graves sent in 100 additional names partly duplicates of the names already submitted.

Of 528 additional names returned by Abell on his supplementary list 73 were in Ching's handwriting, 29 had been dead from a few months to twenty years or more, 127 had never lived in the district; other names were entirely fictitious. In one case Ching not only enumerated a dead woman but also the Washington undertaker who had come down to bury her.

Bowles returned 312 additional names, 55 were those of dead people and the balance were non-residents or fictitious. Some of the statements in his schedules were amusing. Eccleston S. Graves appeared as a school-teacher, six years old. Thomas J. Graves, age two years, was described as a farm laborer employed during the entire year who could read, write, and speak English. Joshua Niles, two years old, was said to be a carpenter.

The enumeration in Charles County also contained many names which ought not to have been there and in Anne Arundel County between three and four thousand berry pickers who were in the county temporarily for a few weeks were included.

The federal grand jury which brought in the indictment said in their report: "So long as such appointments are treated as part of the spoils of politics the recurrence of such frauds and scandals as have been revealed by our investigation may be expected."

The foregoing facts were embodied in a report published by our Investigating Committee on June 24, 1901. Ching, the ringleader in this conspiracy, was convicted and punished.

ROOSEVELT AND THE TRANSFERS OF CENSUS CLERKS

In 1901 I was appointed on the United States Civil Service Commission and had not been long upon that body before we began to see trouble ahead in respect to the employees of the Census Bureau.

The work of taking the census of 1900 was now nearly over and the time was soon coming when a force of several thousand clerks and other employees would be discharged. Although they knew perfectly well when they took these places that the appointments were temporary yet they were none the less reluctant to go and we foresaw that each one would naturally betake himself to his "influence," that is, to the Congressman who had secured his place, to keep him in office or get him another job. The Congressmen were already at work insisting that the clerks recommended by them should be appointed to permanent positions and urging their superior qualifications. According to civil service rules they could not be admitted to the classified service, for no one who enters without passing a competitive examination can be transferred to a competitive place. But there were very few places left in the unclassified service and the only way Congress could provide for these census clerks was to enact a law authorizing their transfer to the classified service whenever there was a vacancy. If that were accomplished we felt the Commission might as well go out of business for the next year or two as far as department clerkships were concerned. Whenever favoritism and competitive examinations come into conflict before a Cabinet officer favoritism is pretty sure to win because each department depends so much upon Congress for appropriations and friendly legislation that the wishes of Congressmen prevail over the merits of the applicants. In this case then the great bulk of appointments would be made, not through examinations but by transfers. It was not long before such a bill was introduced and we determined to oppose it.

Mr. Proctor, the president of the Commission, and I appeared before a committee of the House of Representatives for this purpose. I made a statement to the Committee that we did not object to incorporating into the classified service all who were to be retained in the permanent census office but we objected strongly to that service being flooded by these temporary appointees, who were now about to be discharged. I spoke of the injury to those who had already passed our competitive examinations on the implied promise of the government that if they were highest on the list they would be considered for the first appointments. To fill their places with persons appointed on the nomination of Congressmen would be unjust. This measure would discredit the competitive system and lead to patronage seeking and favoritism in place of honest competition. If the census clerks were a peculiarly capable body of employees as was claimed, they might attend our spring examinations and if they were more capable than others they could show this in fair competition.

The committee, however, was violently hostile and nothing would prevent the House of Representatives from providing places for these protégés, so the bill soon passed that body and came up for consideration in the Senate. Mr. Proctor and I now appeared before the Senate Committee. The members were more reticent but were evidently opposed to us. They were afterwards confronted however by a legal proposition which puzzled them. The Supreme Court had decided that the chief officer of a bureau like that of the census was not the head of a department within the meaning of the Constitution so as to authorize Congress to vest in him the power of appointment. These employees therefore, it was feared, had not been legally appointed in such manner as to justify their transfer to the classified service. The bill was therefore changed so as to provide that all employees of the Census Office might be appointed by the director with the approval of the head of the department and when so appointed were to be placed without further examination under the provisions of the Civil Service Act. Now we knew that the spoilsmen were defeated, for according to the law it was optional with the

6

director and the head of the department whether they should appoint these employees or not and we knew that President Roosevelt would never permit the head of any executive department to flood the classified service with these parasites. I brought the matter to his attention. Elihu Root, then Secretary of War, who happened to be present, argued on the other side, speaking of the very small number of those who were interested in the competitive system and opposed to the desires of the representatives of the people. But the President was inflexible and the appointments were not made.

THE CENSUS OF 1910

When preparations began for the following decennial census, Representative Crumpacker of Indiana, introduced a bill providing that the force should again be selected by non-competitive examinations and therefore subject to Congressional patronage. The fact that they were to be nominated by Senators and Representatives was not stated in the bill, but it was well known that the director would find his task of taking the census burdensome and unpalatable, if not impossible, if he did not take the men who were foisted upon him by the members of Congress. It was further understood among these members (in order to secure Democratic support for the measure) that there was to be no discrimination between Republicans and Democrats as to the number of appointees each was to have. Every member was to be entitled to so many, whatever his politics. In other words, these places, instead of being the spoils of victory were to be divided even more basely between the two contending parties as sheer loot for which a struggle was unnecessary. This too, was not "nominated in the bond." It was merely the Congressmen's private understanding, the "agreement between gentlemen."

On January 6, 1908, President Roosevelt sent a special message to Congress urging that the census employees be selected by civil service rules stating that the Commission was able through its regular channels to supply all needed eligibles. He declared that non-competitive examinations served only as a cloak to hide the nakedness of the spoils system and were useless as checks upon patronage appointments and that the employees of the two last censuses had been far below the average of persons appointed by competitive examinations. The additional employees would seek to be retained in the permanent service at the close of the work and the very men who most strongly objected to having them put under the civil service law would then endeavor to have their transfer protected by that law.

But the President's message had no effect on Congress. The bill passed the House by a large majority and came up for consideration in the Senate where it was pitiable to listen to the ridiculous arguments in its behalf.

Its advocates still prated of their unwillingness to curtail the "discretion" of the director in making these appointments, as if he had any such discretion, and of the "aid" which he might receive from members of Congress in learning the "qualifications" of those whom he had to appoint. The bill with this spoils feature in it passed the Senate by a vote of about two to one.

It is extremely fortunate for the country that the concurrence of the Executive is essential before a bill passed by Congress can become a law. In regard to the Civil Service, as well as other important questions, the Executive, representing the whole body of the people, and not any special district or interest, is the one branch of the government upon which the people at large have to rely for the protection of their interests in opposition to special privileges and favors.

A committee had been appointed by the League to resist the spoils feature of the bill. President Roosevelt was urged to veto the measure and he did so.

The spoilsmen in Congress now determined to await the advent of the new President, in the hope that he might be more amenable to their designs. President Roosevelt had, however, conferred with his successor at the time the bill was vetoed.

I was again made chairman of the League's special committee on the census and on January 7, 1909, we issued a circular letter detailing the abuses and demoralizing effect of patronage appointments. The director of the census himself asked to be relieved from making these appointments and President Taft told Congressmen and others that if the bill came to him in this shape he would veto it.

Then the patronage mongers determined to take a new tack. They would not pass a census bill at all and the decennial enumeration would have to be taken under the old law by which, as they thought, they could retain the patronage. But here too they were disappointed for they ascertained that if this were done, the President by executive order would require competitive examinations. Beaten at every point Congress finally yielded and passed a bill allowing such examinations as to a considerable portion of the employees.

The act, passed July 2, 1909, provided that the additional clerical force required should be subject to an examination by the Commission open to all applicants, selection to be made in the order of rating, the act going even further than the general civil service law in that the director could not choose any one of the three highest candidates but must appoint the highest.

The census appointments were of four principal classes: the clerical force; the supervisors, some 330 in number; the enumerators temporarily employed from fifteen to thirty days, amounting to some 65,000, and some 1800 special agents to collect statistics of manufactories, mines, and quarries. The supervisors were to be confirmed by the Senate and therefore could not be made subject to examination.[1]

An examination was provided for the enumerators but it was not made strictly competitive on account of the temporary service and low compensation. The law did not provide for an examination of the special agents but the census director, Mr. E. Dana Durand, who was a friend to the merit system, prescribed a competitive examination to be conducted by the Civil Service Commission.

It was felt that all had been done which the conditions then

[1] President Taft did the utmost possible to eliminate abuses by prescribing that supervisors and enumerators must abstain absolutely from participation in all political movements under pain of dismissal.

existing permitted, to secure a non-partisan census.   In
regard to the appointment of the supervisors, however, the
"courtesy" of the Senate still foisted some improper persons
upon the service and this in its turn worked injury in the
appointment of the enumerators.   The friends of the competitive system believe that some better system of choosing
supervisors and enumerators must yet be found and applied
in the censuses which are still to come.

CHAPTER VI

WE must now go back in our narrative to the administration of President Harrison which we left in order to bring to its conclusion the account in regard to the census. The appointment of Wanamaker to the Cabinet and of many discredited politicians to other places; the continuation of Cleveland's removals upon secret charges; the partisan changes in the post offices and the perversion of the Census Bureau to political purposes had given great dissatisfaction to those who were interested in civil service reform. Moreover we were grievously disappointed that the President had made no extension of the competitive service. Those of us who had supported him, relying upon the promises of the platform and the candidate, were particularly exasperated. His administration was generally unpopular and when the Congressional elections came on in 1890 in the middle of his term there was a sweeping Democratic victory all over the country. In Indiana which had supported him in 1888 the Democrats carried the election by a large majority.

Whether it was on account of the wholesome discipline administered by this election or whether it was the result of a previous resolution long deferred, President Harrison now began to do something for the reform and on April 13, 1891, he extended the competitive system to about seven hundred places in the Indian service. But considering that there were still in the whole service about one hundred thousand positions still unclassified, this was a rather pitiful concession.

Later in the year the Secretary of the Navy, General B. F. Tracy, established rules of his own for the registration of laborers and for admission to other positions in the Navy yards, removing them from political manipulation.

The main body of the postal and customs service, however, still remained under the spoils system. We were therefore far from satisfied with the concessions made.[1]

Later I determined to make a personal appeal to the President, calling his attention to the promises of the platform which were still unfulfilled, and on December 26th, I sent him the following letter:

In the last Republican platform it was declared that the classified system "should be extended to all grades of the service to which it was applicable." This declaration was made a pledge which the party promised not to violate. In accepting the nomination you made this promise your own, expressing your concurrence in your letter of acceptance. In common with many others I labored earnestly for your election, with confidence that this promise would be observed. The Civil Service Reform Act designated post offices and custom-houses having less than fifty employees as offices to which the system is applicable by providing for its extension to these places whenever so ordered by you. The declaration of the platform could have no meaning if it did not refer to such offices. The able Civil Service Commissioners appointed by you have repeatedly urged that this system be extended to post offices having twenty-five employees or more, yet during nearly three years of your term you have not made this extension. May I ask, with all respect, while this promise remains unfulfilled, how shall we know hereafter upon what pledge of the Republican party or its candidates we can rely?

To this letter the President five days later replied as follows:

I have your letter of December 26th. I have not time this morning to discuss at any length the question which you present or to attempt any restatement of what I have attempted to do in the promotion of Civil Service Reform movements since I have been here. My thought was that

---

[1] During this year I did what I could to disseminate the merits of the competitive system at every opportunity which offered. On September 3d, in an address at the Social Service Congress at Saratoga, I spoke on the philosophy of the spoils system as well as of the competitive system by which we were endeavoring to supplant it. (This address will be found in Appendix III.)

On September 20th, at the annual meeting of the League in Buffalo, I spoke on the subject of the secret sessions of the Senate. (This address will be found in the Appendix IV.)

the first thing to do was to satisfy the country that the law was being faithfully and impartially administered as to those offices already classified. I think a good deal has been accomplished in that direction, and there has been an important extension of the classified service. The subject presented by you, as well as some other suggested movements, has been having and will have my consideration, but I am not now prepared to announce my program.

This letter, as may be imagined, was far from satisfactory. Moreover, Mr. Harrison was now especially discredited in his own State. He had disappointed the independents because he had used the offices as spoils and he had disappointed the politicians because he had given them to the wrong men. As the campaign for the Presidency again drew near it was also found that the civil service law itself was being flagrantly violated in permitting political assessments to be levied upon officeholders and campaign contributions to be collected even in federal buildings.

The Minneapolis Convention, at which Harrison was renominated, was filled and controlled largely by placeholders. John C. New, an intimate friend of the President who had been appointed by him Consul-General at London, a place then yielding $30,000 to $40,000 a year, returned from England to manage his campaign in the convention. More than 140 officeholders had votes in this body and some 3000 others gathered around and bore down opposition.

Mr. Blaine, at the very last moment, declared himself a candidate, and some of the leading bosses of the Republican party, Platt for instance in New York and Quay in Pennsylvania, to whom Harrison had yielded much but not enough to satisfy them, now came out as the supporters of the Maine statesman. Platt said, "It is a much-to-be-regretted fact that the President has placed his campaign in the hands of those who hold office under him. It will be a serious matter in case of his nomination should this fact give rise to the charge that he was forced to give his campaign to these men *because he could get no others to assume the task.*" But "these men" were so well organized that the convention was carried for Mr. Harrison, "a victory," said Carl Schurz, "for officeholders against disappointed officeseekers." Moreover the sweeping declarations and promises in favor of reform made by Republicans four years previously had now dwindled to the doubtful declaration of the platform, "We commend the spirit and evidence of reform in the civil service and the wise and consistent enforcement by the Republican party of the law regulating the same."

It was now the Democratic party which was enthusiastic for better things, reaffirming its radical declarations of 1876, denouncing Harrison's nomination by officeholders and pledging itself to a reform of all such abuses!

Many of us determined that we could not support a nominee chosen as Harrison was under these conditions; that Cleveland was preferable to this and we resolved to make our opposition as emphatic as possible.

I had been invited by the members of the Massachusetts Reform Club to address them upon the subject, "Harrison's Record as a Civil Service Reformer," and on September 10th, at the outset of the campaign I presented an elaborate résumé of his shortcomings,[1] which was printed in full in the New York *Times* and was quite generally noticed throughout the country.

I now took an active part in the campaign, speaking at many places in New York and New Jersey and then returned to Massachusetts where I spent a week upon the stump at a number of towns in the neighborhood of Boston.

It was during this week's canvass that I got some knowledge of the way in which speeches were reported in the daily papers in Massachusetts. The Boston *Herald* sent each morning a stenographer to my room with the request that I dictate to him what I was going to say that evening. He transcribed his notes and the proof was sent to me for revision in the afternoon. I found the work accurately done with the exception that at the end of every few sentences there appeared the words "Applause—laughter; prolonged applause," etc., this applause having been given wholly in anticipation. The applause was not always administered at the designated places.

[1] See Appendix V.

When the November elections came on, Harrison was overwhelmingly defeated and his own State gave a large majority against him. His course toward the reform of the civil service was by no means an unimportant factor in the result.

After this defeat, however, he did something quite substantial to advance the competitive system. He included in the classified service all the clerks and carriers of the free delivery post offices, a most important addition, which if made earlier would have taken away much of the basis for our criticisms, but now it looked like an effort to keep in place his own Republican appointees. But whatever the motive, these legacies from departing administrations, little by little extended the system and in every compromise made with spoils politics, something was always gained.

GEORGE WILLIAM CURTIS

It was in September, 1892, in the midst of this campaign, that George William Curtis died after an illness of several months and at the next meeting of the League, Carl Schurz was made president in his place.

The gracious personality of the first distinguished leader of the civil service reform movement in America cannot be forgotten by those who were familiar with him and participated in the great work of his life. His presence would be remarked among a thousand; his smile, his gentleness, and his charming voice, his faultless English, and his wonderful diction could not fail to leave an ineffaceable trace upon the memory.

Mr. Curtis while he lived was the unquestioned head of the League, presiding at all its meetings as well as those of the Executive Committee and directing its counsels. He was followed by all the members with singular unanimity. We loved him dearly. He was always so fair, so eminently reasonable that it was impossible to resist his winning arguments or to refuse to acquiesce in a leadership which secured the best possible results with no greater antagonisms than unflinching loyalty to principle demanded. The name of Mr. Curtis gave strength and dignity to our organization and the wonderful eloquence of his annual addresses gave distinction to our meetings. These addresses were usually written out in full and he read them to audiences which could not fail to regard with admiration their literary quality, their faultless reasoning and their impressive delivery.

But he was greatest of all at the dinners which followed, where he spoke extemporaneously. On these occasions the grace, the brilliant allusions, the spontaneous wit which adorned his remarks gave them a beauty which cannot be described. His last after-dinner speech was delivered at Baltimore. It was not taken down in shorthand and no record of it is preserved. It was an extemporaneous poem, the most beautiful of its kind I ever heard. He began by likening Baltimore to the city of Viterbo in whose coat-of-arms was found, not the wolf of Rome nor the winged lion of Venice but "La bella dama." He continued in the same strain, every sentence touched with delicate imagery, sometimes with raillery, sometimes with deep emotion. He carried us away with him on the wings of his fancy and entirely captive to his wonderful oratory. We little knew at this time that these were the last words we should hear from his lips. Sometimes his addresses contained the inspiration of prophecy. At the very first conference on August 11, 1881, that led to the foundation of the League, he uttered this memorable sentence: "We have laid our hands on the barbaric palace of patronage and have begun to write upon its walls, '*Mene, Mene*,' nor do I believe the work will end till they are laid in the dust."

During his presidency the annual dinners of the League were graced with a succession of wonderful speeches not only by him but by Mr. Herbert Welsh whose fervid appeals were marvelously impressive, by Charles J. Bonaparte whose delicate sarcasm had an inimitable literary grace, and by a number of invited guests distinguished for their eloquence. I have never heard at the banquets of any other organization any speeches that were at all comparable to those I have heard at the dinners of the League.

After Mr. Curtis's death this feature of our annual meetings was by no means so brilliant. Mr. Schurz was even more powerful than Mr. Curtis in elaborate argument and wealth of illustration but he lacked the light touch, the delicate wit, the literary flavor so necessary for the after-dinner speaker. We still had many fine addresses but the average was nothing like that of the earlier days. Sometimes however there was amusing repartee. I remember one of these occasions at the Hotel Savoy, in New York, at which Bishop Potter presided and which Mr. Roosevelt, then Governor of New York and soon to become Vice-President, attended. Mr. Roosevelt spoke entertainingly on the subject of civil service examinations insisting that they should be practical, that scholastic qualifications were often unimportant and he recommended that the Collector of Customs at such a place as El Paso, who had to be "handy with his gun" on the Rio Grande border, ought to pass an examination in marksmanship. Mr. Wayne MacVeagh rallied the Governor as a champion of civil service reform constantly exempt from examinations himself and one who uniformly hung on to every place he had until he was sure of a better one. Mr. Bonaparte, who sat next to me, suggested as a modification of the El Paso examination that the candidates should shoot at each other, the survivor receiving the position, a suggestion which I afterwards related to the guests attributing its sanguinary character to the Bonaparte blood and expatiating upon its manifest advantages in saving the Civil Service Commission from the necessity of rating the papers, the appointment being made by the direct process of the survival of the fittest.

While Mr. Curtis was living he always made it a point to encourage the efforts made by the younger members of the League to spread the gospel of the reform. On one occasion, I think it was in 1890, I had been asked by a literary organization of the Society of Friends of New York to deliver an address upon the subject in the lecture room of Friends' Seminary on Rutherford Place adjoining the meeting house. I had been in my youth a pupil in Friends' Seminary and there were a good many of my friends in the audience, but what was my surprise to see Mr. Curtis there among them as well as Mr. E. L. Godkin, the distinguished editor of the New York

Evening Post, whose services on behalf of the reform system have also been incalculable. After the address those who were present were invited to take part in the discussion and Mr. Curtis delivered extemporaneously a very admirable speech on behalf of the reform system. Mr. Godkin also was called upon and in illustrating the methods of appointment under the patronage system he told a story which I shall not forget.

I was present [he said], on one occasion in the office of a member of the Cabinet when a Senator came with a delegation to present the claims for office of one of his constituents. The proposed appointee was a rather beefy or beery looking individual but the Senator in urging his claims invested him with every possible virtue. Not only was he adequately equipped for the filling of the responsible position which he asked but the voice of the entire district demanded the appointment as necessary to harmonize the party and to fulfil just expectations. Indeed any other course than the appointment of this particular man would be disastrous not only to the service but to the State and to the country at large.

After the delegation had departed I said to the Secretary, "That man was very earnest and seemed to make a very strong case." Whereupon he opened a drawer and took out a letter addressed to him by this Senator.

"DEAR MR. SECRETARY," it read, "I will be with you tomorrow to urge the appointment of ——— to the office of ———. Don't believe a word of what I am going to say to you and don't appoint the man."

Nor was this an isolated instance. Indeed the general run of applications, letters, endorsements, etc., on behalf of applicants for office is apt to be of just this character. In my own town I know of a petition circulated in favor of a man for the position of consul-general at Berlin. It was filled with fulsome adulation, while in fact the man was the common laughing stock of the community, not fit by qualifications or attainments for any public office whatever and yet that petition was signed by the president of every bank in town, by the judges of the courts, by all the members of the bar, by the clergy of the most important churches and by the heads of our leading industrial and commercial institutions. The appointing officer who depends upon testimonials from "prominent citizens" relies upon a broken reed.

CHAPTER VII

CLEVELAND'S SECOND TERM

It will be remembered that after the election of President Harrison I had discussed the meaning of the Republican platform and considered what civil service reformers had a right to expect from the incoming administration. Harrison had disappointed us, and now on the accession of Mr. Cleveland I took up at the annual meeting of the League in April, 1893, in New York, the general question of platforms and promises from the beginning of the reform movement and especially the platform upon which Mr. Cleveland himself had now come into power, what he had promised, what the promise meant, and what we had a right to expect. (See Appendix VI.)

Mr. Cleveland's failures during his first term forbade any extravagant anticipations. Still we did not question that he was friendly to the reform movement and would aid it so far as he could withstand the pressure of his own political partisans.[1]

---

[1] Right at the beginning of his term, President Cleveland announced that he would look with disfavor on the application of persons who had held places under his former administration for reappointment to their old positions and that such reappointments would be made only where the applicants had proved to be exceptionally competent officers, where no other available Democrats applied, etc., etc.

Mr. Francis E. Leupp, the able editor of *Good Government* the organ of the National League, wrote to a number of the members for their opinion in regard to this announcement and I sent him the following which was published in the issue of April 15, 1893:

"As a matter of principle it is hard to justify the new rule. A man who has performed his work well, even though there be nothing exceptional about it, would seem better qualified than one without experience. To

The appointment of Mr. Bissell as Postmaster-General, of Secretary Herbert in the Navy Department, Secretary Lamont in the Department of War, Secretary Morton in the Department of Agriculture, and Secretary Gresham in the State Department all argued well, but John G. Carlisle, a thorough-going politician was made Secretary of the Treasury, Hoke Smith, Secretary of the Interior, and Josiah Quincy, First

---

take the chances on a new man in every case must lead to some unfortunate results. Yet there is no doubt that this plan is generally popular, and, when I heard it, I did not feel as much disapproval as it seemed to me I ought to have felt.

"Civil Service Reformers, as well as the rest of the world, have a certain sympathy with a rule excluding any class which is clamorously demanding spoils. No doubt many of the old officeholders constitute such a class and I think we share a certain diabolic joy in seeing their hopes thus nipped in the bud. The men appointed by Mr. Cleveland four years ago to the subordinate offices—to postmasterships, small collectorships, etc.—were very largely local bosses, and these men want the plums again. They used their offices to maintain their political influence, and now they expect to use that influence to get the offices. If we have a new set of men, we are very likely to have fewer of these local politicians. Under the present rule I do not think we shall have so many editors of country organs as we had before.

"I can hardly blame the President for shutting off by a single rule any considerable tributary to the great stream of office seekers now surging round him at Washington. This test of exclusion, however, is by no means the best. It shuts out the good as well as the bad—the men who stay quietly at home, as well as those who throng into the Departments and make life a burden to the President and his Cabinet. There was a principle enacted into a law, several hundred years ago, which would, if it were renewed today, accomplish this result much more effectively—a statute of Richard II., under which the great appointing officers of the crown were obliged to take an oath to observe the following rule: 'That none that pursueth by himself or by others, privately or openly, to be in any manner of office, shall be put in the same office or any other.' If such a rule as that could be adopted, there would be some relief from the interminable hauling and pulling that now goes on, and the chances are that we should have a much better class of public servants.

"So far as Civil Service Reform is concerned, I do not think the rule adopted by the President will have much effect one way or another. It does not apply to places in the classified service, but only to the positions which still remain political spoils. The final way out of this business is to extend the classified system as rapidly as circumstances will permit."

Assistant Secretary of State.   These were unfortunate selections and Mr. Quincy, who had the consular appointments in
charge, soon made an almost clean sweep in that branch of the
service, removing Republicans and putting Democrats in with
"unprecedented vivacity."

Notwithstanding the determination of the Postmaster-
General to enforce the civil service law some curious things
occurred in his department.   It will be remembered that just
after Harrison became president the Republicans improved
their time up to May 1st when Cleveland's classification of
the railway mail service took effect, in turning out Democrats
and getting in their own men.   The same thing was now done
by the Democrats.   The Attorney-General on May 5th gave
an opinion that the classification of free delivery offices by
Harrison took effect only after an examination had been
provided for the particular office to which it was to be applied
and the politicians now began to get very busy in ousting
Republicans and putting in their own men before these
examinations were provided.   Indiana furnished a typical
illustration.   An examination was to be held at Terre
Haute, a free delivery office, on May 6th and something had to
be done instantly if a clean sweep was to be made.   So Daniel
W. Voorhees one of the Senators from Indiana despatched a
letter to the Civil Service Commission, stating that the local
board at Terre Haute was composed of three intensely partisan
political workers, and that no Democrat contemplated going
before it for examination, feeling that justice could not be
obtained.   Upon this the Commission postponed the examination until the 13th of May so that they might enquire into
the matter.

Now the statements made in Senator Voorhees' letter were
entirely without foundation.   The majority of applications for
examination were from Democrats.   The purpose of asking
the postponement was to enable the new Democratic postmaster, Mr. Donham, to make a clean sweep of the employees
and put Democrats in their places.   Accordingly on Friday,
May 12th, one day before the examination, Mr. Donham,
accompanied by three political friends who had been selected

for the three principal places, came to the office of the post-master, Mr. Greiner, and demanded immediate possession. Greiner answered that this was impossible as the inventory was not completed and he asked for delay until the following Monday morning. Donham refused. Greiner telegraphed to the Postmaster-General asking instructions and was directed to transfer the office Saturday night. Greiner then asked Donham to vacate the office so that the business might go on. Donham refused, remained in the postmaster's room, and about nine in the evening made forcible entry into the principal room of the post office and stayed there all night. In the meantime he had sent to the residences of the letter carriers and other employees notices that they were dismissed. On the morning of Saturday, the day of the examination, Donham with his friends attempted to take possession of the whole post office building and excluded the letter carriers and other employees therefrom, in some instances using force, and he again notified these employees that they were discharged and that their places would be taken by various successors, whom he had appointed and had caused to be sworn in on Friday afternoon. Greiner again wired the Postmaster-General who telegraphed to Donham that he had instructed Greiner to deliver posses-sion on Saturday night and that postmasters could not employ, re-instate, promote, or remove carriers. The civil service examination was held on Saturday and completed about four o'clock in the afternoon and the papers were forwarded to Washington. That night Greiner gave the keys to Donham.

All the above facts were ascertained by a committee of our Indiana Civil Service Reform Association consisting of Mr. Lucius B. Swift and myself, who went to Terre Haute and personally investigated the case. I asked Donham if the men removed had been guilty of any misconduct. He answered that he had made the charge of general insubordination. I asked in what that consisted. He answered that when he came in to take possession he met with resistance. I asked if the Post-master-General was not equally guilty of insubordination. He answered he did not know about that. I inquired why he was in such a hurry and he said on account of the civil

7

service law. Mr. Swift asked if he had worked with these new men politically and he said he had.

Upon these facts we made a report (copies of which we sent to the President and the Postmaster-General) that Mr. Donham had attempted to take violent possession of the office and had unlawfully removed the letter carriers and other subordinates without cause for the purpose of effecting a complete partisan reorganization of the office and giving places to his friends before the civil service law should take effect. The Civil Service Commission ordered an inquiry, Theodore Roosevelt, one of the Commissioners, went to Terre Haute and personally investigated the case and on May 25th, he made a report detailing Donham's illegal acts and stating that in other places, Galesburg, Bloomington, and Quincy, Illinois, Plattsburg, New York, and Columbus, Georgia, wholesale removals of Republicans and appointments of Democrats had been made in a similar manner. On this report all the employees whom the new postmasters had attempted to introduce into the service were removed and the old employees were reinstated.

In this Terre Haute case the effort was to make the clean sweep just before the civil service law was applied. But these efforts did not cease even after that, though the methods were different. The plan then was to prevent Republicans, as far as possible, from taking examinations and thus to get a Democratic eligible list and then to turn out the Republicans in office and put in the Democrats who passed. Our Association heard that this method was being pursued at Fort Wayne so Mr. Swift and I, as an investigating committee, betook ourselves thither and interviewed the postmaster and some twenty odd employees and other witnesses. The examination had been held on May 7, 1893, but Mr. Rockhill, the new Democratic postmaster who was the editor of the Fort Wayne *Journal* did not take possession of the office until July 20th. It had been previously announced in his paper, however, that "bright young Democrats should appear at the examination." It was believed that Democrats only would be appointed so there were very few Republicans applied. In the unclassified service all the Republicans were dismissed except one (the nephew of the Postmaster) and their places (also with one exception) filled with Democrats.   Then the dismissals began of the men in the classified service.   In no instance was any statement made to the men dismissed of any complaint against them until after they were notified of their discharge.   Some of them asked the cause and were given no answer, in other cases it was "for the benefit of the service."   Sometimes charges were trumped up after the dismissal, charges, for instance, of the non-delivery of certain letters for which the carriers were in no wise responsible, while the new carriers misdelivered the entire mail of certain buildings with impunity. The postmaster excused the changes by the pressure for place and the statement "Everybody has his friends."

Our committee reported these matters in detail and by the order of the Association we sent our report to the President, the Postmaster-General, and the Civil Service Commission. The Commission some time afterward reported that of thirty-six employees twenty-seven had been separated from the service and that the presumption was that the postmaster was controlled by political considerations, yet no action was taken upon its report.

The system of removals upon secret charges still prevailed though Postmaster-General Bissell, at a later period, put an end to it so far as carriers in free delivery offices were concerned by an order (dated June 28,1894) that no such carrier should be removed except upon written charges of which he should have notice and an opportunity to make defense.

THE VAN ALEN CASE

There was another event during the early days of Mr. Cleveland's second administration which greatly weakened the confidence of many who had been his friends and supporters.

Almost immediately after Mr. Cleveland's inauguration, some of his friends learned that a Mr. Van Alen, a wealthy man, prominent in Newport society but without diplomatic experience, had contributed some fifty thousand dollars to the

Democratic campaign fund of the previous year through Mr. Whitney, and now applied for the office of minister to Italy. The President was warned of the scandal which would follow such an appointment.

Mr. Horace White, editor of the *Nation*, wrote him on April 7th, that if the bargain was ratified the administration might as well be dead and buried; likewise the individuals composing it; likewise the Republic if it followed so pernicious a precedent and that the money must be paid back. Mr. White stood ready to contribute more than his share to that end.

But this was said to be Mr. Whitney's "one request" of the administration. Mr. Whitney was not only the close friend of the President but the political manager to whom more than to anyone else Mr. Cleveland was believed to owe his election. On June 20th, Mr. Whitney wrote to Mr. Cleveland, saying: "This, as you know, is the first time you have been approached by me on the subject of appointments." After some delay the nomination was sent to the Senate.[1]

---

[1] On September 28th, I wrote to Walter Q. Gresham, Secretary of State the following letter:

" DEAR SIR:

" The recent publication of Mr. Whitney's letter in regard to the appointment of J. J. Van Alen to the Italian mission makes it clear that Mr. Van Alen, a gentleman who has not been generally known in American political life, contributed a very large sum to the late Democratic campaign fund. His appointment to the Italian mission would appear to be largely the result of what Mr. Whitney calls 'his patriotic, generous and cordial support of the party in the late campaign, when friends were few and calls were great.' The circumstances were so similar to those in regard to the appointment of Mr. Wanamaker that those of us who did what we could to make the country ring with that scandal can, if these things are true, hardly afford to be silent now. Such an appointment is sure to give rise to the popular belief that the distribution of many of these high offices is too much according to the methods of the auction mart, in which cabinet offices have commanded their hundreds of thousands under Republican rule and foreign missions their tens of thousands under Democratic administration. The question whether or not there was any agreement when Van Alen gave this money is not by any means a conclusive one. The precedent set when such important appointments follow such important contributions is most disastrous to the political morality of the people. Every

The Senate confirmed the nomination. The appointment was criticized in the newspapers and elsewhere, and at a meeting of the executive committee of the League on November 16th, I introduced the following resolution:

Resolved, That the National Civil Service Reform League through its Executive Committee expresses its earnest remonstrance against the bestowal by the President of high offices of State in return for the contribution of large campaign funds. It must regard any appointment made on account of such contribution as implying a forgetfulness of the trust conferred upon the Chief Executive, as a violation of the professions upon which the present Administration came into power and as an example which, if followed, must lead to the destruction of free institutions.

I remember the occasion very distinctly. The meeting was held at Clark's on West Twenty-third Street. The attendance was large. Carl Schurz presided and those most prominent in the reform were present. Theodore Roosevelt was also there but when this question arose, involving a direct attack upon the administration under which he was serving, he withdrew.

I called attention to the indignation which had been felt throughout the country at the appointment and insisted that there was no civic organization whose duty it was to speak unless it was the National Civil Service Reform League. Mr. Schurz in supporting the resolution said that if Mr. Cleveland were a candidate now, it would not be possible to urge the moral principles on which the last campaign for him was conducted without awakening a smile and I remember that after the meeting he said to me, "A great many people supported Mr. Cleveland because they believed he would be incapable of just that thing."

Edward Cary of the New York *Times* offered the following

---

man of large means sees this way to political preferment clearly pointed out. If there is any reason why these conclusions are not justified, I should, as a supporter of Mr. Cleveland, be very glad to know it."

Secretary Gresham answered on October 10th that he saw the force of what I said but that the President had not made the appointment as a consideration for the contribution made by Van Alen and that he himself had nothing to do with the patronage of the State Department.

resolution which was incorporated with mine and both were unanimously adopted:

Resolved, that the League through this committee declares its opinion that appointments should not be given to such contributors and profoundly regrets that the President has departed from this rule.

Mr. Page, editor of the *Forum*, asked that I write an article for that periodical under the title "Are Presidential Appointments for Sale?" It was published about the middle of November, 1893,[1] and was widely reviewed in the newspapers under such titles as "Offices at Auction," "A Lasting Scandal," "No More Van Alens," etc.

The New York *Evening Post* which had supported Mr. Cleveland said:

There is a terrible indictment of President Cleveland in the last number of the *Forum* apropos of the Van Alen affair, by Mr. W. D. Foulke of Indiana. The worst of it is that it is every word true. . . .

President Cleveland was about the last man in America to expose himself to this rebuke. Nor did he incur it hastily or ignorantly. He appointed Mr. Van Alen with a full knowledge of all the facts and after months of reflection. In one short hour he made all his own homilies against the use of money in politics ridiculous and more than this, he let loose the Republican tongues, which the sale to Wanamaker had tied up. The solitary defense for him which has been attempted, so far as we know, is that he could not refuse anything to Mr. Whitney, who had done so much for him. But he owed his election largely to the popular belief that he was one of the few men that could be relied on to refuse what was wrong, not to Mr. Whitney only, but to everybody.

The English have just filled a similar vacancy at the same post. We published yesterday the official career of their appointee. Contrasted with Mr. Van Alen's it is enough to make an American hang his head for shame.

But Mr. Van Alen did not go to Italy. On the 20th of November he wrote to Secretary Gresham, declining his appointment. He admitted having made a large contribution to the Democratic campaign fund but added that it was from disinterested and patriotic motives, and not with the idea that it entitled him to special consideration. He went on to say:

[1] See Appendix VII.

A large number of my fellow-citizens have been led, either by coincidence of circumstances or by false report, to look upon my appointment as in some way inconsistent with the professions of the Democratic party, and the President's high ideals of public service . . . I do not think that I could now remove this impression from the minds of many right-minded and thoughtful people whose judgment, I frankly admit, may possibly be correct.

It is clear that at all events I find myself in a false position with reference to this office and appointment. Acceptance of the office would make me appear willing, for the sake of personal gratification, to discredit, in the eyes of many, the political party to which I am attached, and to bring undeserved rebuke upon the administration which has honored me and whose success I earnestly desire.

It therefore seems to me sufficient to add that self-respect compels me to adopt the only other alternative and to decline the high office to which I have been appointed.

The President, to whom this letter was referred, answered it on the 22d, requesting Mr. Van Alen to reconsider his resolve and saying:

I did not select you for nomination to the Italian mission without satisfying myself of your entire fitness for the place. I am now better convinced of your fitness than ever. You know and I know that all the malignant criticism that has been indulged in regarding this appointment has no justification and that the decent people who have doubted its propriety have been misled or have missed the actual considerations upon which it rests. We should not yield to the noise and clamor which have arisen from those conditions.

Mr. Van Alen replied on the 24th, refusing to be moved from his purpose, and adding:

My only regret in this decision, which I must beg you to consider as final, is that it is contrary to the personal preference which you so kindly express. But I cannot think it would be advisable for me to invite further misrepresentation by taking advantage of your generosity.

This correspondence did not however wipe out the unfortunate impression which the appointment made upon the public mind.[1]

[1] Thus on December 6th, Mr. Lucius B. Swift wrote me: "I think Cleveland's letter came from the heart, and that he felt ugly at being baffled. Van Alen for some reasons determined to get out of the scrape

CLEVELAND'S SERVICES TO REFORM

In matters where Mr. Cleveland was at greater liberty to act upon his own convictions he rendered most substantial service to the competitive system. In the first place he kept upon the Civil Service Commission, Mr. Theodore Roosevelt, the most efficient and aggressive Commissioner the country ever had and he removed from that body Commissioner Johnston, who had seriously obstructed the work of reform and put in his place, upon Mr. Roosevelt's recommendation, John R. Proctor of Kentucky, one of the most admirable men who ever filled that office and who continued in place through the subsequent administrations of Mr. McKinley and of Mr. Roosevelt himself.

Mr. Cleveland also gave to the Commissioners much fuller coöperation than President Harrison had done, and, while their recommendations were not always followed, they felt that they had behind them a man who was in full sympathy with the general purposes of the law.

The political changes outside the consular service were not so rapid as under Mr. Harrison. Mr. Cleveland generally adhered to the principle that officeholders should be removed only at the end of four years' service. Moreover, beginning in May, 1894, after he had been in the office about fourteen months, he made a series of most important extensions of the classified lists[1] culminating in his so-called "blanket order" of May 6, 1896. These formed the most valuable and splendid services yet rendered to the merit system by any president.

---

and wrote an adroit letter. It does not in any manner alter the facts. I think your *Forum* article brought the thing to a head."

[1] On May 11, 1894, assistant teachers in the Indian Service, on May 28th, meat inspectors in the Bureau of Animal Industry, and on November 2, messengers and watchmen in the Departments were included, and the classification was extended to custom-houses having as many as twenty employees so as to bring within it all employees except mere laborers; then a large number in the postal service was added to the competitive class. On November 17, steamboat clerks and transfer clerks in the railway mail service were brought under the rules; on December 12, the internal

By this order of May 6, 1896, Mr. Cleveland extended the classification to some 31,372 places, practically the entire executive service throughout the United States with the exception of places subject to confirmation by the Senate, fourth class postmasters, laborers, and minor positions specifically excluded. It was estimated by Mr. McAneny, secretary of the League, in his report to the executive committee, October 3, 1896, that the number of excepted places was 865. All chiefs of division, chief clerks, and disbursing officers were included. This was the most valuable addition ever made at one stroke to the competitive service.

---

revenue service; on January 3, 1895, the superintendents of post office stations at which carriers were employed; on March 4, the census division of the Interior Department; on May 24, all places in the Department of Agriculture not previously classified; on June 13, every employee in the Government Printing Office; on July 15, the clerical force in the various pension agencies and on March 20, 1896, the employees of Indian agencies and school employees not previously included.

CHAPTER VIII

SUPERANNUATION

At the meeting of the National Civil Service Reform League held in Washington, December 12 and 13, 1895, I brought formally to the attention of that body the question of super-annuation in the civil service. It seemed to me that since the indefinite tenure of office established by the competitive system might tend to increase the number of the super-annuated, it was the duty of the League to consider the matter and to take measures to prevent the evils of superannuation before these should become formidable. I had indeed sub-mitted this question four years previously to George Wm. Curtis with a scheme of competitive examinations for pro-motions and demotions within the service. He presented this to the executive committee several of whom approved the project but no action was taken in regard to it. And now at the Washington meeting in 1895, I delivered a short address urging that some plan should be adopted by which the "barn-acles" might be removed.

I found, however, that there was strong opposition. We were making such satisfactory progress that many protested against throwing such an apple of discord into our midst. Nothing was then done, but I persisted year after year until on October 4, 1899, a special committee to investigate the matter was appointed consisting of Richard Henry Dana, Silas W. Burt (former surveyor of the Port of New York), and myself. We went into the subject elaborately but it was not until the annual meeting of December, 1900, that our report was finally presented to the League.[1]

[1] We showed in this report that in the departments in Washington in

We unanimously recommended a system requiring life insurance on the deferred annuity plan by all employees during probation as a prerequisite to final appointment, the policies to be non-assignable and in government control and secured by deposits from the insurance companies also in government control. The exact age at which the annuities should be payable might vary for different kinds of service and the details should be arranged by a commission composed of Civil Service Commissioners and experienced officials of the departments.

It was not long after this that I became one of the Civil Service Commissioners. The Commission made a careful examination of the subject and collected the data for determining the deductions which would be required from salaries for the purpose of paying annuities to the superannuated and disabled. The results were tabulated and submitted to actuaries and their conclusions were set forth in an appendix to the annual report of the Commission for 1902. In this report I also incorporated some observations leading to the same conclusions as that reached by the League.

On February 23, 1904, I was called as a witness before the Committee on Civil Service Reform of the House of Representatives, detailed the arguments and facts set forth by the Commission and offered as a suggestion for legislation a draft of a bill to require annuity policies.

The various members of the Committee examined me at some length. It was suggested that the government could provide an annuity more cheaply than any insurance company. I answered that I believed this was not the case, since

---

1893, only two per cent. of the employees were over seventy years of age, in 1900 very little more than two per cent. Still, as the evil might grow, we considered the following remedies:

1. A civil pension list. 2. A retirement fund to be made up by deductions from salaries. 3. Endowment or deferred annuity insurance from all seeking admission. 4. The forced retirement of a certain percentage of employees each year. 5. Recurring examinations for promotion, reduction, and dismissals. 6. A daily record of efficiency for the same purpose. 7. Fixed terms of office. 8. Forced retirement at a certain age. Also certain combinations of the foregoing.

the government must confine itself to certain kinds of securities for investment and an insurance company could get a higher rate of interest. Moreover the premiums could be made lower for government employees than for others since the commissions paid to agents constituted a large part of the cost to insurance companies and a considerable part of that cost might be eliminated. The companies had assured us that they could insure government employees much cheaper than others for this reason.[1]

[1] In 1901, after I had become a member of the Civil Service Commission and had ceased to take an active part in the work of the League, another committee on superannuation was appointed. In 1906, that committee presented an exhaustive report coming substantially to the same conclusion as the first committee.

"We recommend," says the report, "that, if any enforced provision for superannuation be deemed advisable, it take the Australian form of a deferred annuity policy, which candidates for office shall be required to take out in some company before final appointment. As this would not apply to those who are at present in the service, we recommend that a record be kept of the amount of work done by employees over sixty-five years of age and that their salaries be reduced in proportion to the amount by which their work falls short of that of a thoroughly efficient employee. This would be at once fair to the government, and humane to the office-holders."

In 1907, the committee of the League again recommended the Australian system to be supplemented however by a gift of annuities from the government to the superannuated persons already in the service. The policies were to provide that the sums paid should be returned with interest if the employee was separated by *death* or *illness*, but if he voluntarily resigned or was removed for misconduct or neglect he should be entitled only to a paid up policy based on premiums already paid and good at the retiring age only. The plan would discourage resignations during the years of efficiency, an evil which had already become serious, nearly eight per cent. resigning annually.

The proposition of the League for deferred annuity policies to be issued by insurance companies (which has always seemed to me the best) was not, however, popular in Congress and a variety of bills were introduced, mostly impracticable, proposing deductions from salaries which would in the end be found inadequate. The committee on superannuation therefore, seeing the trend of probable legislation, considered it wiser to suggest what this legislation should be in case Congress should decide (as seemed probable) that provisions for old age should be made directly by the government instead of by insurance companies.

In 1912 an agitation on behalf of a direct pension system was set on foot by the employees of the government, and Congress, instead of granting this, proposed as an antidote in a rider to one of the appropriation bills to eliminate superannuation by fixing a seven years' term of office for employees! The bill was actually passed in this shape. The League appealed to the President to veto it, which he did. This incident showed the danger of permitting the question of superannuation to go on indefinitely without some solution.

In March, 1917, the superannuation committee of the League reported to the Council endorsing the Pomerene Retirement bill then pending in the Senate. This bill provided for deductions which would be sufficient with 4% compounded annually to purchase an annuity from the United States equal to one half of the employee's annual salary after twenty years of service and proportionately for smaller periods, the annuity to be payable when he became seventy years of age. The deductions were to be invested in federal, State, or municipal bonds under charge of a board of investment. A separate account was to be kept with each individual and upon his separation from the service he might withdraw his deductions with the accumulations thereon.

The report endorsing this bill said it should be amended so as to make clear that whether the employee's separation were voluntary or enforced his deductions with accumulations should be returned to him or in case of his death to his estate. It is evident that the committee had now changed its position. Instead of requiring deferred annuity policies the government itself was to become the insurer and, by recommending the return to the employee of all the deductions made from his salary with compound interest thereon, the committee seems to have disregarded its previous argument that this would encourage resignations among the most efficient in the civil service. The Council, while approving the general principle of retirement allowances, recommitted the report to the committee for further consideration, and the question is still pending before the League.

No act providing for superannuation allowances has yet been passed.

CHAPTER IX

THE FIRST BRYAN CAMPAIGN—McKINLEY'S ADMINISTRATION

UP to this time the presidential candidates of both parties, whatever their official derelictions, had been personally friendly to civil service reform and the platforms of the two principal parties had in some shape or other given it at least their nominal adherence. But now a campaign was approaching in which the Democratic party and its candidate were to be openly hostile.

It was those who were out of power who saw most clearly at this time the excellence of the merit system and resolved that "the civil service law was placed upon the statue book by the Republican party which has always sustained it and we renew our repeated declarations that it shall be thoroughly and honestly enforced and extended wherever practicable."

In addition to this, the Republicans nominated as their candidate Wm. McKinley, who had, six years before, successfully resisted an attempt made in the House of Representatives to defeat the appropriation for the Civil Service Commission saying, "If the Republican party of this country is pledged to any one thing more than to another it is to the maintenance of the civil service law and to its execution and not only that but to its enlargement and its further application to the public service."

Moreover, Mr. McKinley in his letter of acceptance on August 27th, had promised that the party would take no backward step and would seek to improve and never degrade the public service.

Wm. Jennings Bryan, on a free silver platform, was the candidate of the Democracy. One plank in that platform opposed "life tenure in the public service" and favored "fixed terms of office and such an administration of the civil service laws as would afford equal opportunities to all citizens of ascertained fitness." Mr. Bryan, in his convention speech, thus explained the declaration: "What we oppose in that plank, is the life tenure which is being built up at Washington, which excludes from participation in the benefits, the humbler members of our society." In his letter of acceptance he added: "A permanent office-holding class is not in harmony with our institutions. A fixed term in appointive offices, except where the Federal Constitution now provides otherwise, would open the public service to a larger number of citizens without impairing its efficiency."

The National League as an organization had never hitherto taken any official action either advocating or opposing any candidate for the Presidency. But this non-partisan attitude now had to be abandoned and our executive committee in October, 1896, published an address to the voters reciting the declaration of the Democratic party and its candidate and adding:

The statement that life tenure is being built up at Washington is wholly false. All persons in the classified service are subject at all times to dismissal, the only limitation of law being that they cannot be removed for refusal to render political service or to contribute to campaign funds.

The policy of fixed terms of office demanded by both platform and candidate would result in a "clean sweep" of all public officers and employees— competent and inefficient, faithful and unfaithful alike. It involves the periodical displacement of trained servants, the substitution of those who are inexperienced, and the complete destruction of business methods in the conduct of the government . . . It is one of the chief advantages of the merit system that the humbler members of society have equal opportunities with the most influential in entering the public service . . .

That system has been slowly and laboriously evolved out of the necessities of our public service and the conditions of our political life. It has added greatly to the economy and efficiency of administration. It has given a new incentive to praiseworthy ambition and effort. It has opened a new career to industry and capability and, more than all, it has removed from our politics much of the temptation to corrupt and mercenary conduct. The subordinate places in the government have become, for the first time, positions of public trust instead of rewards for partisan service.

The merit system—the product of a generation of progress—will, if the principles of the Chicago platform be enforced, be destroyed at a single blow, the business of the government will be thrown back into chaos; the cost of its maintenance will be increased by many millions, and the spoils system, one of the gravest perils that have menaced our government since the Civil War, will again threaten the integrity and permanency of our institutions.

I took a very active part in this campaign, speaking in all sections of the country. The principal issue was of course, free silver, but the attitude of the Democratic party and its candidate on civil service reform was also considered.

At Chicago on October 17th, I addressed an audience in Central Music Hall exclusively upon this latter subject.[1]

---

[1] In this address I observed among other things: "What Mr. Bryan desires is to build up an office-seeking class, which he would lure to his own support by the hope of the places to be distributed. Terms of office are to be fixed so that more office-seekers can enjoy the patronage. The civil service is not a public trust, but a personal and party perquisite and as many of his followers as possible are to have their chance at it. Under Mr. Bryan's system of administration they are to be led in rotation to the trough.

"My friends, the people of our country have more sense than politicians think. They are tired of a system of patronage which regards the public service as a largess to be scattered among the multitude rather than a charge where duties are to be performed. They are tired of the demagogues who appeal not to their patriotism but to their supposed appetite for place. The promise of a general distribution either of the offices of the State or of the wealth of the individual will never be ratified by their suffrages."

Still more discreditable is Mr. Bryan's statement in his speech at Ada on August 10th, "that he was not yet engaged in distributing post offices, but that he hoped soon to be." God grant that that hope and every iniquitous longing for the partisan plunder of a great public trust may be blighted forever!

There was reserved for the present candidate of the Chicago convention the unique distinction and bad eminence of being the first nominee for presidential office willing to defy the moral sentiment of his time and to ally himself openly with one of the great crimes of the century. It was reserved for the convention assembled at Chicago to make the first open attack upon the competitive system.

It must, indeed, be confessed that this attack is in perfect harmony with the conduct of the candidate and his followers upon other issues. It was to be expected that a candidate who publicly appeals to selfishness and class prejudice as the controlling motives of political conduct, who sneers at the patriotism of those who demand the honest fulfillment of obligations, should also hold out to his hearers the hope of the distribution of post offices

Washington Hesing the postmaster of that city who had been a sturdy adherent of the merit system which he had consistently enforced in his office spoke on the same theme at the same time.

McKINLEY PRESIDENT

Mr. Bryan was overwhelmingly defeated and now the question arose, Would President McKinley be as good as his word? In his inaugural he had renewed his assurances, but right at the outset of his administration there came murmurs of dissatisfaction from all around him. Various members of his Cabinet, chiefs of bureaus, and others high in authority insisted that Mr. Cleveland, by including practically all places in the competitive service after so large a proportion of them had been filled by Democrats, had been unfair and that many of the more important places ought now to be excepted. There was this much legitimate foundation for the complaint. When the Civil Service Commission drew up the order of May 6, 1896, for presentation to President Cleveland and some doubts arose as to whether the classification could be properly applied to certain positions, it was determined that the wisest course was to include everything and then ascertain from future experience whether there might be some cases (which were thought to be extremely few) where this would be found impracticable. If so, exceptions could afterward be made. But naturally when the new administration came into power the disposition was to multiply these exceptions and to magnify the need of them. The clamor against the civil service law was loud and vehement.

The League saw the danger, and at a meeting of its executive

---

as part of the general plunder to follow his election. It was to be expected that a convention which denounced a President for enforcing the laws he was sworn to execute, which proposed to reconstruct our highest court to carry out the bidding of the multitude, and which openly offers as the price of a vote the confiscation of just debts, would also appeal to the rapacity of the unscrupulous by promise of the lawless pillage of the public service. The creed which inculcates national dishonor ought logically to encourage official debauchery.

committee on February 1, 1897, Mr. Dorman B. Eaton moved that a committee be appointed, of which I should be chairman, to represent the League at Washington and that we be empowered to present communications and issue public statements with the concurrence of the president, Carl Schurz. The motion was adopted and the committee appointed and I spent considerable time at the capital upon this work. I interviewed the members of the Cabinet, the chiefs of bureaus, etc., who were most dissatisfied.

Mr. Cornelius Bliss, the Secretary of the Interior, was one of these and when I reminded him of the promises of the platform and of Mr. McKinley's letter of acceptance and inaugural he showed considerable feeling, declared civil service reform had gone too far and that he would not have taken the office had he supposed he would have been so crippled in the choice of his subordinates. He complained that men with whom he had the most confidential relations, for whose acts he was responsible and whose judgment on important matters he had to take, were appointed through the Civil Service Commission and that he had no opportunity to select those he could trust.

It so happened that during this conversation there was an employee in the room who was listening with considerable interest. I afterwards learned that this person was one of the "confidential" men whom Mr. Bliss had recently appointed but that in fact he had known nothing about him. He had simply given him the place at the request of the President himself and it turned out that he was a man who had been removed during the previous administration for improper relations with his female subordinates, this fact being of course unknown either to the President or to Secretary Bliss. This seemed an impressive commentary upon the supposed need of personal choice in these "confidential" places.

The next day I visited Mr. Benjamin Butterworth, Commissioner of Patents, who with Mr. McKinley had been a warm friend of civil service reform on the floor of the House of Representatives. He told me that he considered it all wrong that chiefs of divisions, chief clerks, private secretaries, and financial secretaries should be included within the rules, and he read me a report he had prepared for the Secretary of the Interior, and for the use of a Senate Committee which was now investigating the question. This report was quite rhetorical, it spoke of the classification of these high offices as tending to create an "office-holding aristocracy"; it said that the Cleveland administration had brought the reform up to its high water mark after it had filled these responsible offices with its own friends; spoke of the confidential relations which must exist between the Commissioner and these officers, who, he said, were selected by a Commission which knew nothing about the duties of the place and cared little about them, insisted that the head of a bureau like the Patent Office ought to have some privileges, and that if the necessary changes in the rules could not be made it would be better to repeal the whole law than to continue the present system of civil service gone mad.

I reminded him that his communication was quite different from the position he had taken in Congress; I assured him that under the rules he was allowed to select his chief clerks and chiefs of divisions out of the whole civil service and was not confined to those who were certified. I made a good deal of fun of his report, especially the peroration, and told him he had taken his stand with the ward heelers. I think he finally saw he had gone too far, for he said he would leave out all about the office-holding aristocracy and the repeal of the law, and would add that he considered the law itself needed no amendment, but only the rules, and that it was highly beneficial, etc. He told me, however, that he had not found a single Senator, Congressman, or public officer who favored such a monstrous thing as the inclusion of these high places. I asked him why it was that his report was all on one side. He said he thought it necessary to talk strongly, since otherwise the President might not do anything.

I next learned that in the Pension Office, lists were being prepared stating the politics of the employees, a sinister augury of the early decapitation of the Democrats.

A few days later I visited Mr. John Sherman, Secretary of State. He claimed he had always been friendly to the reform but said he was now having so much difficulty that he did not know but it might be necessary to abolish the whole system! I asked him if he thought he could carry on the business of the Department if that were done and he admitted it would be difficult. I asked what particular trouble he had found and he referred to the appointment of a chief clerk. It seems he had discharged an efficient chief clerk of large experience and had asked for the appointment of one Major Michael, an old politician who had filled many places in a shifty manner and had been closely associated with Mr. Sherman. The Civil Service Commission thought Michael could not be lawfully transferred to the office of chief clerk in the Department of State. All of Mr. Sherman's objections seemed to resolve themselves into this one complaint and at last he said the Commission had growled but had finally assented to the appointment and that now it was all right. When I asked whether we might not expect his coöperation against any interference with the present rules he assented and the conversation ended quite differently from its beginning. When, however, a day or two later Mr. Sherman learned that the Civil Service Commission had referred to the Attorney-General the question whether Michael should be transferred, he made what Commissioner Proctor called "a diplomatic remark." He said "he wished the Civil Service Commissioners were in hell."

I also learned that Mr. Wilson, Secretary of Agriculture, was much dissatisfied and I felt sure that a great deal of pressure would be exerted on Mr. McKinley by his own Cabinet. The Public Printer also appeared before the Senate Investigating Committee and insisted that his office should be excluded from classification.

I communicated my various interviews to Mr. Schurz, the president of the League, who wrote me as follows:

NEW YORK, 4 May, 1897.

MY DEAR MR. FOULKE:

I think you should see the President and talk to him frankly. In my opinion we ought to let them all know that an order withdrawing the chiefs of division from the classified list will be regarded by us as a cause for *war.*

Bliss has sent his report to the Senate Committee substantially as he gave you to understand. I have a copy of it. I think we shall now let the press open on him. He seems to be much under the influence of Boss Platt for the sake of "harmony." Harmony is Bliss's weak point.

Let us watch whether he has not some party heelers dumped upon him for almost every one of those "confidential places." He is in an irritated state of mind, judging from the tone of the letters he writes.

They ought all to be made to understand that if their backsliding goes any farther, we shall open on them along the whole line. The reactionary movement is indeed strong in official circles, but I do not think it has touched the people.

I am glad you will stay at Washington a while longer.

Sincerely yours,

C. SCHURZ.

To this I answered on May 7th:

I note your remark that "we ought to let them all know that an order withdrawing the chiefs of divisions from the classified list will be regarded by us as a cause for *war*." I lay awake one night thinking over this. I would enjoy a fight upon this subject immensely, but before we go into a conflict of this sort we ought to see pretty clearly where we are coming out. Hitherto we could afford to attack an administration if it failed to do its duty in respect to civil service reform, without much regard to consequences. If we crippled the administration the country would not greatly suffer. The choice was between Harrison and Cleveland, and the changes from one to the other were, in the end, quite sure to be favorable to civil service reform, so we could go on whacking away according to our power without much care where the blows fell. But a new condition confronts us now. As the only alternative of a Republican administration, the black spectre of repudiation and national dishonor rises before us. Nothing will justify us in adding the weight of a feather to the balance on that side of the scale, especially since the Democratic party announces the annihilation of civil service reform as one of its tenets. Now we cannot declare war without weakening the administration and the Republican party, which is at present the ark of our safety (I fear my metaphors are getting mixed). If we fight at all we must fight to win. The conflict will be long, uncompromising, and bitter. In the end we shall either fail or succeed. If we fail, then it will appear that the fight has been useless. If we succeed we shall have weakened the only political party which can reasonably hope to be elected which displays any interest at all in our reform. It looks to me a little like the Turko-Greek war, where the invader cannot hope to gain anything even if he wins. I should say, therefore, that while it is our duty to remonstrate very earnestly, both with the heads of departments and with the President, yet to attack McKinley himself or the administration generally can lead to nothing but disaster. . . .

I have also just seen Mr. Brosius,[1] who tells me that he has had a conversation with Mr. McKinley, and feels satisfied that the President would not allow any change in the law, but only some changes in the rules and the administration of the law, which he thinks will not be very extensive.   I told him that the main fight was for the chief clerks and for the chiefs of divisions, and that I had received a communication from you that they ought to understand that such a change as this would be regarded as a cause for war.   He seemed to deprecate this strongly, and believed that some few concessions might be necessary for the purpose of keeping what we have got, and said that these offices were not numerous, and it seemed to him that they were quasi-political in character.   He said he would regret the change, but did not think that we ought to consider that enough to constitute a cause for war.

To this Mr. Schurz answered on May 8, 1916:

Nobody can be more anxious than I am to keep the government from falling into the hands of the silver Democrats.   But I am profoundly convinced that we shall only increase that danger if we fail to hold up the Republican party strongly to its responsibilities.   If we let the Republicans understand that we shall feel bound to stand by their organization whatever they may do, they will do no end of mischief.   To be sure when the emergency comes I shall do whatever the best interests of the country may demand under the existing circumstances.   But in the meantime I shall consider it not only my duty but also good policy,—good "political policy" as the politicians say—to criticize every serious delinquency on the part of those in power as straightforwardly and severely as possible.   It seems to me that the Republican party is now on the high road to defeat.   The best friend to-day is the "disagreeable" friend who tells it the truth without mercy.

When I spoke of "war" I meant that such an act as the withdrawal of the chiefs of divisions from the classified service must be followed on our part by an attack along the whole line on the Republican party for its treachery.   And, personally, I shall make that attack on all the responsible parties as vigorous as possible.   Please come by way of New York when going home.

To this I answered:

I cannot go to New York just now.   I see fully the force of all you say in your letter.   I never thought that we ought not to criticize wrong-doing everywhere as severely as it deserves but as Curtis said of Sumner our criticism of the administration should be that of a friend and not a relentless enemy.

I also agree with you that we must not let the Republicans understand that we shall stand by them whatever they do.   We never gave that

---

[1] A member of the House, friendly to our reform.

assurance even when we were members of the party. But we ought not to threaten war unless we mean to make war to the death. Probably I exaggerated the meaning of this word in your letter. It seems to me that at present our duty should be limited to influencing the administration by every legitimate argument and to criticism of shortcomings which need not be any the less candid and complete because its tone is entirely friendly.

Our committee had several interviews with the President in which he declared his intention of supporting the existing system without material change and of extending it to other places. Indeed for a considerable time he resisted the onslaught made upon him to restore these places to the spoils system. In one respect he greatly strengthened the competitive service for, on July 27, 1897, he made an order providing that no removal should be made from any position subject to examination except for just cause and upon written charges filed with the appointing officer and of which the accused should have full notice and an opportunity to make defense. This order was designed to abolish the iniquitous practice of removals upon secret charges, and it was greeted with general public approval. But in a number of cases it was not observed and the President did nothing to punish the officials who violated it.

It was true that in his annual message, December, 1897, he declared: "The system has the approval of the people, and it will be my endeavor to uphold and extend it." It was also true that in this session of Congress he opposed all efforts to repeal or change the law. But in the administration of it the executive department showed great weakness. The President gave out that he proposed to issue an order excepting certain important classes of offices, and the heads of departments and bureaus at once proceeded to act as if the places had already been excepted. Internal revenue collectors removed their deputies and appointed others in violation of the rules under the pretense that they were only anticipating this order, and the Treasury Department, although mildly remonstrating, did not punish them for so doing. In the Department of Justice the same thing occurred and the remonstrances of the Civil Service Commission were ignored. In the Interior Department many appointments in the Land Office were made in disregard of the rules. Many persons were employed without examination as laborers and then assigned to classified work.

The Pension Commissioner circumvented the law regarding the appointment of examining surgeons by creating new examining boards and sending all applicants to these. As such boards became classified only when the amount of fees received was three hundred dollars annually, they were treated as unclassified and the old classified boards were thus driven out of business.

In the Post Office Department political applicants were sent to post offices where free delivery service was about to be introduced and appointed to clerkships without examination, and then as soon as these offices were classified and these persons were thus admitted to the competitive service, they were transferred to other post offices which had been previously classified, thus crowding out the men upon the eligible lists who were entitled to appointment. Cases of this description accumulated until there were more than a hundred of them and a considerable number of these appointees were then given the important place of Post Office Inspector. In other offices like the San Francisco Custom House, persons were appointed to positions in the excepted list and then assigned to other duties while the duties of the excepted places were performed by classified employees.

Other tricks were resorted to in order to get rid of classified employees. They were laid off for "lack of work" or given an indefinite furlough without pay and their positions immediately filled by others.

When the Spanish War broke out and the emergency appropriation bill was up in Congress it was provided that the additional force should be appointed without regard to civil service rules although the Commission had eligible lists from which this force might have been taken.[1]

In the consular service the places were changed even more

---

[1] On August 1, 1889, Elihu Root succeeded Mr. Alger and the political loot of the War Department was arrested.

rapidly than by Quincy under the Cleveland administration, more than ninety per cent of these places being refilled during the first year. The pass examinations which Secretary Olney had established after Quincy had looted the service now became a farce, so much so that at first the State Department refused all information as to such examinations, declaring that they were "strictly confidential." But when John Hay became Secretary of State he let in the light and it was found that the questions were so put as to require no capacity whatever to answer them. For instance, there was a requirement that an applicant for a consulship should know the language of the country to which he wished to be sent, but the questions were so framed that the candidate for a French consulship was not asked to write or say anything in French, but might state in English his knowledge of the French language, that is he might say how much he thought he knew of it. The questions on the different examination papers were all the same and inevitably leaked out so that the "coaching schools" had complete assortments of the answers. Out of 112 candidates during McKinley's first year only one failed to pass!

Abuses crept into other branches of the service. Temporary appointments were made without being authorized by the Commission. Appointing officers failed to assist the Commission in preparing examinations by stating the qualifications required. In some cases they refused to appoint those on the Commission's eligible lists and chose others instead. Worst of all when violations of the law were investigated by the Commission and reported, *not a single man guilty of such violations was dismissed.*

The government kept paying the salaries of those illegally appointed as if the civil service law did not exist. The Controller of the Treasury, Mr. Tracewell, in April, 1899, wrote an opinion that even though the Civil Service Act declared that no person should be appointed to a classified position except under certain conditions, yet if a man were so appointed the appointment was not illegal; that the civil service rules had no force except such as the Executive or head of the Department chose to give them and that all persons on the pay-roll would be assumed to be regularly appointed! Mr. Tracewell even became sarcastic at the expense of the law which he was bound to enforce.

> If this ruling has a tendency to muddy the stream of civil service reform which should always flow pure and clean from the fountain throughout its course, I can only answer that it would be as futile for me to attempt with my limited jurisdiction to purify this stream as it would be to bail the ocean of its waters with a pint cup.

MCKINLEY'S ORDER, MAY 29, 1899

One would suppose that when the law could thus be violated it was hardly worth while for the President to make an order exempting places from competition, but this was considered desirable in order to give legality to the political appointments already made. The President had delayed issuing this order for more than two years. It had been the subject of elaborate discussion and correspondence between George McAneny, the Secretary of the League and Lyman J. Gage, Secretary of the Treasury, who, having been previously an advocate of civil service reform was now put forward as the defender of the administration in this backward movement.[1]

But remonstrances were in vain. On May 29, 1899, the President's order was promulgated. It removed from competition, as then supposed by the League, about ten thousand places, although it was later ascertained that less than half this number were actually withdrawn. It made valid many appointments previously made in violation of the law. It weakened the rules by facilitating transfers and reinstatements without examination, allowing reinstatements without regard to any limit of time, and making temporary appointments per-

---

[1] It was about this time that I addressed to the President a letter containing the following in reference to the administration of the Philippines recently acquired:

"How can we hope to administer the government of our colonies successfully if, at the very beginning of such administration we take a distinct step backward in our home government; if our chief executive at this critical time shall remove from the operation of the competitive system a large number of important offices and turn them over to the scramble of place-hunters and political adventurers?"

manent. It thus permitted new and serious abuses. It marked the first considerable reduction in the area of the merit system since the civil service law was enacted in 1883.

When the new order appeared, the spoilsmen hailed it with a shout of triumph but the press of the country was almost unanimous in disapproval. It was considered the first important step backward in the reform, a step which the President had promised not to take.

It was not long, however, until the President made some atonement for this and rendered a very important service to the merit system in extending it to the Philippine Islands by his instructions to the Philippine Commission in April, 1900. In the following September that Commission passed a civil service law applying to the great bulk of the executive positions in the islands, and a system of rules was adopted more comprehensive and satisfactory than those in the Federal civil service.[1]

The Federal Commission loaned to the Philippine Civil Service Commission Mr. F. M. Kiggins, one of its ablest officials, and subsequently Mr. Leon Pepperman and Dr. Wm. S. Washburn, to aid in organizing the service and administering the new law. As a result the competitive system was soon established in the islands under peculiarly favorable conditions.

---

[1] (1) The scope of the Philippine Act was broader, applying to laborers as well as to higher administrative officers.

(2) Competitive examinations were required for promotion.

(3) Examinations were also given to test the qualifications of those in the service to retain the places they held.

(4) A thorough physical examination was required.

(5) Power was given to the Civil Service Board to administer oaths, summon witnesses and require the production of official books and records.

(6) Whenever the Civil Service Board found that a person held office in violation of law and certified the fact to the auditor and disbursing officer all subsequent payments of salaries were illegal.

(7) The Philippine Act prohibited the solicitation of political contributions from officers or employees by any person whomsoever.

(8) The laws regulating preferences to veterans and natives prevented any from being certified out of the order of their relative standing.

(9) A supplementary act passed by the Philippine Commission directed a re-classification of the service.

DORMAN B. EATON

It was on December 24, 1899, that the League sustained its second greatest loss in the death of Dorman B. Eaton, the historian of the reform movement in Great Britain and one of the most eminent of the pioneers in the reform movement in America. No one who was favored with the opportunity of association with him can fail to remember his noble presence, his benevolent face and his deep interest in all that concerned good government. He was single hearted in his devotion to the merit system. Though he was interested in the betterment of municipal government and wrote an elaborate work upon the subject, though he was an advocate of minority representation and other devices to secure better political conditions yet civil service reform always stood paramount in his affections. Many of us had been converted to it by the facts and arguments of his convincing history. He had been the principal draughtsman of the admirable Pendleton Law and under that law he had been the first President of the Commission, having been appointed by President Arthur in 1883, and also holding office under Arthur's successor President Cleveland with whom his relations were most cordial.

His work in the establishment and organization of the competitive system had been of the highest order; in the administration of the law he was not quite so successful. Impressed as he was with Mr. Cleveland's earnest desire to advance the reform and knowing his efforts to resist the tremendous pressure upon him for spoils, Mr. Eaton had too much of the milk of human kindness in his nature to criticize the President and call him to account for his inconsistencies or to act vigorously in resisting his serious infractions of the law and when some of the rest of us investigated and exposed the abuses in the public service, he seemed to us far too ready to explain and to excuse. He was very elaborate, often prolix in argument in the meetings of our League and its Executive Committee and I have sometimes felt that we did not always treat him with the tolerance which his most distinguished services undoubtedly merited. He prided himself on being above all things "a practical man." It did not seem to some of us that he was altogether this, but rather that he was a high-minded idealist who brought into the struggle against the spoils system the most unselfish devotion and untiring energy. His magnanimity toward those of us who sometimes criticized and opposed him was very great and there were none who after his death did not hold his memory in most affectionate regard.[1]

CAMPAIGN OF 1900—SCHURZ RESIGNS

As the campaign of 1900 drew near the opinions of civil service reformers were divided. McKinley was the Republican candidate and Bryan was again the Democratic candidate upon a platform which re-affirmed the hostile declarations of 1896 against the competitive system. Anti-imperialism however was declared to be the paramount issue. Some of our number who were opposed to the acquisition of the Philippines supported Mr. Bryan in spite of the fact that he and his party had declared their opposition to reform. They felt a deep resentment at the backslidings of McKinley and could see nothing in his extension of the competitive system to the Philippines which could atone for breaking his promises regarding that system in the United States. Others believed that there was far less to fear from the Republican party led by McKinley and Roosevelt than from the Democratic party with Bryan and Stevenson.

I was one of the latter and took part in the campaign in favor of McKinley. Carl Schurz, the president of the League, was

---

[1] The New York Civil Service Reform Association appropriately said of him: "He was a maker of laws without ever being a member of a legislative body. Important acts of legislation originally drawn by him stand on the statute books of the United States as well as of the State of New York. He may well be said to have been the legislative architect of civil service reform in this republic, for every law now in force that embodies the true principle of civil service reform was either originally framed by him, or at least shaped in its principal features upon the lines which he had originally laid down. To the cause of civil service reform he gave its most instructive literature; to it he devoted the last efforts of his life, and with it his name will forever be most honorably identified."

such a pronounced anti-imperialist that he supported Bryan, and since Bryan and his party were opposed to the merit system, he believed that this action might embarrass the League and therefore on September 22, 1900, announced his purpose of resigning from the presidency. The general and executive committees, however, declaring that it was the uniform practice of that body to hold that the independent political action of any member should not affect his standing, requested Mr. Schurz to withdraw his resignation. But he answered that he continued to believe that his position with regard to other policies of the national administration would create practical inconveniences and he persisted in his determination, so at the December meeting of the League, Mr. Daniel C. Gilman, president of Johns Hopkins University was elected in his stead.[1] At this time many of the members regarded the outlook for our reform as a very gloomy one. I did not share this feeling but, while I concurred in their criticisms of the President's shortcomings, it seemed to me that many were disposed to look only on the dark side of the picture and did not give sufficient credit to the administration for the good things it had done. It was the President who helped to resist

[1] In 1907, Joseph H. Choate former ambassador to England succeeded Mr. Gilman, in 1908 Charles W. Eliot former president of Harvard University succeeded Mr. Choate, and in 1913 Dr. Eliot having declined a re-election, Richard Henry Dana became president of the League. In making this choice the League again selected a man to whom the reform of the civil service was the leading interest of his public career. This had been true of George William Curtis and was measurably true of Carl Schurz in spite of his manifold activities. With Presidents Gilman, Choate, and even President Eliot who were men of varied and illustrious careers, civil service reform had been only one of many important public questions to which their lives had been devoted and they were not so closely associated with the detailed work of the League. But with Dana, civil service reform had perhaps the first place in his heart. He had inherited his devotion to its principles from his distinguished father, he had been a member of the League ever since its organization, had been chairman of its Council and had taken part in all its more important investigations and measures giving it many years of devoted service. He was not so eloquent as Curtis or Schurz but there never was a man of higher ideals, of purer personal character nor one whose knowledge of the spoils system and of the details of reform methods was more thorough and complete.

the adverse legislation of Congress, it was the President who had abolished the system of secret removals, and it was the President's commission that had already begun the work of extending the competitive system in the Philippines.

I had an interview with President McKinley in which I urged him to extend the civil service system to Porto Rico also. The difficulty was that the rules provided that none but citizens of the United States should be admitted to examination. The inhabitants of Porto Rico had been declared to be citizens of that island but had not been created citizens of the United States. I considered that they were such in the international sense which required allegiance on their part and protection on ours but since there was a difference of opinion on that subject the President submitted the matter to the Attorney-General and gave me the assurance that if it were held they were not citizens of this country an amendment of the rules would be made extending the right of examination to them. Shortly afterwards the system was extended to the Customs service both there and in Hawaii.

MCKINLEY'S CHARACTERISTICS

In this interview I was struck with Mr. McKinley's extraordinary skill in conversation, his diplomatic temperament, and his very accurate knowledge of human nature. He contrived to say what he desired without offending and much more adroitly than the presidents who had preceded him. There was a saying current in Washington attributed to a Congressman who had failed to get what he wanted, that Harrison used to freeze applicants out of the White House, Cleveland would kick them out, while McKinley kissed them out.

Indeed I had much the same impression of these three presidents. General Harrison, a man of personal rectitude and high character was reserved and cold to all except his close personal friends and even with these, and when he most desired to be agreeable he was not always genial.

Cleveland on the other hand in the single interview I had with him gave me the impression of a man of rugged frankness,

He seemed coarse-grained and almost brutal in his treatment of those who displeased him.   I remember that the man upon the line ahead of me was a federal territorial judge who was endeavoring to explain to the President some matters for which he had been criticized.   But the scoring he got for his conduct in the presence of a large number of persons would be enough to discourage anyone else from attempting explanations.   Cleveland simply trampled upon him.

Mr. McKinley on the other hand had a most insinuating and winning way, indulging occasionally in delicate courtesies involving a rather innocent kind of subtle flattery.   For instance in the above interview he asked me in the most confidential manner (although I was almost a stranger to him) if I could advise him of a suitable person to appoint as Attorney-General of Porto Rico saying, "If this were in our own country I would have no difficulty, there are many men who would do, but we must take a great deal better care of the people of Porto Rico than of ourselves."

Mr. McKinley was personally on good terms even with those who criticized him most severely.   Mr. Bliss, Secretary of the Interior, once said to me, "I have been in his cabinet now a long time and I never heard him speak an unkind word of any human being."   No doubt there was a great deal of policy in this.   He was a consummate manager of men but beneath all that there could be no doubt there was a genuine kindness of heart.

CHAPTER X

HOWEVER divergent were the views of the members of our League in regard to Mr. McKinley we were all united upon one thing and that was upon the necessity of keeping a close watch upon all that was done and of criticizing with impartiality any proved shortcomings of the administration. Another investigating committee was appointed. I was made chairman and, in April, 1901, I went to Washington and began work upon a series of investigations which resulted in nine reports to the Council of the League, which were extensively published by the press of the country.

INDIAN AGENTS

The first of these, issued on May 5, 1901, was on the subject of Indian Agents. Few political appointments had given rise to greater scandals. The agents were generally selected by the Senators from the States in which the agencies were respectively situated and for the personal or political advantage of these Senators.

During Cleveland's first administration in sixty agencies all the agents were changed but two. Under Harrison there were seventy-six changes and only eight agents were allowed to serve out their terms; in Cleveland's second administration there were eighty-one changes and only four served out their terms; under McKinley among fifty-eight agencies there were seventy-nine changes, only nine were permitted to serve out their terms and only one was reappointed.

We believed that nothing could be more unfortunate for the

9   129

Indians since no plans for tribal improvement could be effective when they were stopped almost at the beginning by changing the agents. The men appointed were mostly improper selections. The Indians were despoiled by fraudulent contracts and their morals corrupted by drunken, brutal, licentious, and dishonest caretakers. We gave many instances supported by affidavits showing all kinds of corruption and debauchery. We insisted that whatever temporary improvement might be made by changes in the personnel, no lasting reform could be inaugurated without a change in the system and we recommended that all appointments should be made by promotion from superintendents of Indian schools, from higher grades of the classified Indian service, and by details from the army.

I communicated this to the President on April 26th, in a letter containing the exhibits and evidence upon which our report was founded. He made some improvement in the personnel of the service but the system remained unaltered. This reform had to await the advent of Theodore Roosevelt.

THE HICKS CASE

Our second report was upon the violations of the civil service law by Postmaster Thomas L. Hicks of the Philadelphia post office. As early as January, 1898, a committee of the League had sent to the President a report showing a number of such violations but no action was taken and Mr. Hicks, emboldened by the impunity he enjoyed, continued to ignore the law until near the close of 1900 when other irregularities came to our knowledge.

On the 22d of January, 1901, Mr. Dana and myself representing the investigating committee, went to Philadelphia and in conjunction with Mr. Francis R. Wood, of the Philadelphia Association, we visited the post office and interviewed the postmaster. Mr. Hicks made statements to us and showed us documents indicating many clear violations of the law.

The rules forbade laborers to be employed on duties of classified employees but the Philadelphia post office had a large number of such laborers appointed without examination and doing service as bookkeepers and clerks.

Postmasters were required to abstain from partisan activity but Mr. Hicks admitted to us that he always took an active part in politics and preferred to appoint those nearest to him politically. He called meetings of carriers for political purposes and in his addresses at these meetings and elsewhere he spoke in favor of the repeal of the civil service law and declared that none but Republicans ought to be appointed.

The law forbade coercing employees in political matters yet we had written statements from men who had been directly asked by the postmaster to take part in a political contest for State Senator and one of these had been discharged for refusing to do so.

By the rules no classified employees could be discharged except for cause on written charges nor could they be removed for political reasons yet thirteen Democrats, superintendents of stations, were displaced and given lower positions without any charges against them and twelve Republicans and one Democrat put in their places. Some of the superintendents thus reduced were then put at work which they could not perform and were thus crowded out of the service.

It was forbidden by law to require that a surety bond should be made by any particular company, yet Mr. Hicks told us that he would take no bonds from his appointees but those of the National Surety Company with which he admitted he had a special arrangement, the nature of which he declined to state.

The law and rules governed dismissals and transfers yet men appointed to take charge of sub-stations by Mr. Hicks had to sign a written agreement that their appointments were temporary and that he could transfer or dismiss them at his pleasure.

The law authorized the Civil Service Commission to make an investigation of his office, yet when its secretary, Mr. Doyle, who was lawfully detailed by that body, came to the Philadelphia post office for this purpose, Mr. Hicks refused to permit inquiries and instructed his subordinates to give Mr. Doyle no information.

The law forbade admissions to the classified service without examination, yet Hicks in conjunction with Perry Heath, First Assistant Postmaster-General, fraudulently nullified this prohibition by sending persons whose appointments they desired to small post offices which were about to become classified. As soon as these offices were brought within the competitive system, the appointees, who had now become classified, were transferred back to the Philadelphia office. A sister of the postmaster was thus admitted to the service.

In April, 1901, our committee had an interview with the President and called his attention to the fact that there were many violations of the Civil Service Act which had not been punished and we urged upon him the necessity of making an example of the delinquents. He asked us to bring to his notice some clear cases. Accordingly I wrote to him calling his attention to this variegated assortment of breaches of the law, giving the names and the circumstances attending each and concluding as follows:

Will you permit me to suggest that if such things are permitted to go unpunished, it will be construed as notice to the world that there is to be no enforcement of the Civil Service Act. It has been suggested that Mr. Hicks should be permitted to remain in office until the close of his term (which is soon to expire) and then be succeeded by someone else, but such a course would manifestly fail in producing the wholesome effect of making an example of a flagrant violator of the law and would seem itself to be a violation of the rule which requires that such a man should be dismissed from office. . . . May we not hope that an example will be made of a man who has been guilty of a greater variety of violations of the law than any other case which has come to my knowledge.

On the same day I sent a copy of the letter to the Postmaster-General. No action having been taken, our Investigating Committee on May 13th, made and published its report to the League.[1]

The conclusion of this case was what might have been expected from a President of the temperament of Mr. McKinley.

[1] The Postmaster-General, Mr. Charles Emory Smith of Philadelphia a political friend of Mr. Hicks, published on June 17th an attempted exoneration of the Postmaster but it was far from convincing. I answered with a letter giving a detailed analysis of the evidence and the law.

In spite of our convincing array of facts, Postmaster Hicks was not dismissed until Roosevelt became President.

LLEGAL EMPLOYMENT OF LABORERS

Our third report, published on May 20, 1901, dealt generally with the question of the employment of laborers for the purpose of assigning them illegally to clerical duties. We showed that in three years, from June, 1896 to June, 1899, the labor force of the departments had increased more than 50 per cent owing not merely to the natural growth of the service but also to the fact that laborers were employed to perform the duties of classified employees.

These cases had become so numerous that there was danger that the competitive system would be seriously undermined by them.

We recommended for the correction of this evil the establishment of a labor registration system such as had already been created in the Navy Department. This would eliminate politics and personal favor. Indeed it was only a short time after our report was published that such a registration system was adopted in the War Department and a substantial improvement made.

THE SAPP CASE

The fourth report of our committee issued on May 27, 1901, related to the violations of the civil service law in the Internal Revenue service in Kentucky under C. E. Sapp. This was one of the most picturesque cases of the management of a government office under the spoils system which ever came to my knowledge. In 1899 Mr. Sapp issued to one Joseph Potoning a written authority to collect campaign assessments as follows:

Knowing your zeal in such matters and the campaign funds being low and being very desirous of nominating Attorney-General Taylor for governor, I respectfully appoint you a collector and hope you will push the matter and do everything you can for us.

Respectfully,

CHARLES E. SAPP.

Potoning accordingly levied an assessment of five per cent on the salary of each of the employees, payable monthly and he demanded payment both by letter and in person and often in the building occupied for official duties, which the law prohibited. He made monthly reports to Sapp as to the employees who had or had not paid, and upon these reports the assignments to duty of these employees as store-keepers, gaugers, etc. were made and their pay was regulated accordingly. Those who contributed were given good appointments and those who failed, poor assignments, and some were laid off and dismissed.

The collector compelled his employees to stay away from the meeting of the "Hambrick" faction, to which he was opposed, by standing at the entrance of the building where they assembled and warning them not to go in. He required them to attend the meetings of the Davis faction to which he belonged.

By means of his official authority he controlled the Republican primaries of Louisville held June 10, 1899, to elect delegates to the State Convention.

In the fifth ward he caused J. J. Bryan, one of his gaugers, to be made chairman and directed him to call the meeting to order by solar time, eighteen minutes faster than standard time by which all business in Louisville was transacted. The Internal Revenue men went into the hall, locked the doors, appointed the delegates to the State Convention and filed out five minutes before 1 o'clock, the hour set for the meeting standard time. Then the opposition numbering over 200 gained admission but the District Convention held that the delegates appointed by the earlier convention were elected.

In other wards similar transactions occurred. Two depositions, that of William Holbourn, attorney, and that of John Gimbel, cigarmaker, threw interesting side lights upon the statesmanship of the collector. One presented an inside and the other an outside view of the situation.

Mr. Holbourn stated that he went to the meeting in the 12th ward at half-past 12 o'clock. When he got there he found sixteen men congregated together. There were seven others who came in afterwards making twenty-three in all when the doors were closed and locked. The men inside were principally officeholders.

The convention was called to order at a quarter of one, city time, and was over before 1 o'clock. They went through a kind of "service" that they had, of nominating delegates to serve in the coming convention. . . . After it was all over we came out and went into the other room and found about 200 of the 12th ward people massed there waiting for the convention to be called to order. . . .

Mr. Gimbel testifies concerning a ward meeting at 307 East Market Street. The time appointed was 1 o'clock. He arrived about 12.30 and waited near the building till fifteen minutes before one, when the doors were closed. After this three employees of the Internal Revenue Service, with about ten other men went around the corner of the block and through the yard of a person residing on Shelby Street and jumped the fence back of said yard. In less than five minutes they came out again and announced the names of the delegates to a reporter.

By such simple methods a majority of the ward conventions were "carried" by government employees, acting under collector Sapp. And when the Republican Convention met at Lexington, on July 12th, over sixty of these employees (including the collector, the chief deputy, the assignment clerk, etc.) composed about one third of the entire delegation from the county, and Attorney-General Taylor (the candidate mentioned in Sapp's letter to Potoning) was "enthusiastically" nominated for the Governorship.

The Civil Service Commission investigated these facts and sent an account of them to the Secretary of the Treasury, to the President, and to the Department of Justice. A year elapsed. The papers had been forwarded to the District Attorney at Louisville and were now submitted to the Federal Grand Jury but the jury ignored the charges. In April, 1901, I called the facts to the attention of the Secretary of the Treasury, the Commissioner of Internal Revenue, and later of the President himself. Nearly a month elapsed and nothing was done. Then our committee gave its report to the public concluding with the following remarks:

It is interesting to observe the political results of the lawless policy adopted by the collector in levying assessments and packing primaries for the purpose of securing a "Taylor" delegation in the State Convention. Taylor, who was nominated to the governorship by such means, is now a fugitive from justice, indicted for complicity in murder, while the Republican majority in the Fifth Congressional District (in which these transactions occurred) was reduced from 12,500 in 1896 to 3700 in 1900. Your committee is personally assured by men of standing and responsibility in that community that this difference of over 8000 votes is largely due to general indignation at the political methods of collector Sapp.

Still Sapp remained in office. In October, 1901, the Commission made a further investigation and on November 7th, transmitted to the President a report showing that the collector still continued to violate the law. By this time Mr. Roosevelt was President and results were soon apparent. Collector Sapp, on November 11th, resigned his office.

THE EL PASO CASE

On June 3, 1901, our Investigating Committee published a report on the flagrant violations of the law at the El Paso Custom House. In July, 1908, a competitive examination was held for places in this office and Moses Dillon, the collector, told W. S. Holmes, a member of the local civil service examining board, that there were four applicants, Fink, Bloom, Mc-Dougal, and the collector's son, whom the collector desired should pass this examination. Holmes was ordered to communicate this to Race, the secretary of the board, and tell him it would not be wise for him to refuse. Race accordingly gave Holmes copies of the questions, Holmes brought them to Bloom and Fink, two of the candidates, who studied them and were examined and appointed.

The collector also received contributions for political purposes in his office at the federal building from inspectors and other federal employees. This case, with the testimony of the witnesses, was laid before the Department of Justice but by this time the witness Holmes was dead and others refused to testify because the evidence would incriminate themselves so no indictment was found.

On the morning of April 18, 1901, I submitted the foregoing facts to Mr. Gage, Secretary of the Treasury, who told me that as the office of collector was a presidential office, complaint should be made to the President. Two days later I communicated these matters in writing to the President but when six weeks elapsed and nothing was done our committee gave its report to the public.

Still no action was taken until after Mr. Roosevelt became President. Then on November 4, 1901, the Civil Service Commission submitted to him papers showing the charges and the facts and the collector was removed from office.

CENSUS FRAUDS IN MARYLAND

Our next report of the frauds in the taking of the Federal Census in Maryland has been already referred to in a preceding chapter.

EMPLOYEES OF THE HOUSE OF REPRESENTATIVES

In July we issued a report on the abuses in the appointments of subordinate officers and employees of the House of Representatives, which was a review of an investigation made by a special committee of the House, known as the Moody Committee on the 28th of February.

The civil service law did not apply to these positions, hence we had an opportunity to set forth the charms of the spoils system in a place where it was permitted to bloom and bear fruit unrestrained by inconvenient rules requiring competitive examinations. While subordinates in the House of Representatives were nominally appointed by the clerk, doorkeeper, etc., the places were really apportioned as patronage among various members of Congress, mostly those belonging to the party in power. Persons appointed to perform certain work were assigned to occupations entirely different. Thus the House telegrapher worked in the stationery room, while the man who actually performed the work of telegrapher was paid from an appropriation of $900 for the "hire of horses and wagons and cartage for use of clerk's office." Meanwhile the man who received $1200 as telegrapher spent his time in the library compiling biographies of the members of Congress, a "leisurely place" where "you didn't have to perspire a great deal," though $400 additional appropriation was recommended by the clerk in evident appreciation of the statesmanship recorded in these biographies. One of the pages "who could not read and write" was put to driving a team and the man employed as driver cleaned the floors and scrubbed the spittoons. The locksmith served as a messenger and though he was absent from April until after the Christmas holidays, he received $1440 a year.

The librarian and his subordinates were also absent for long periods and the library, consisting of some 300,000 volumes was scattered from dome to basement with piles of books in unused rooms until the librarian himself testified that it would be all right for a barnyard but for books it was terrible.

One Smith, who was pretty fond of "old barleycorn" got an appropriation of $600 for "loafing about." He had a good run of the books which were in the rubbish pile and knew to what part of the pile to go to for certain volumes. The business of keeping this rubbish pile was farmed out by other employees to this man.

The folders were absent a great deal and others were employed and paid to do their work.

The door-keeper testified, "I do not like to criticize members, but that is the situation. They go and say, 'I have got to have my man home' and he must go home."

The door-keeper was further asked: "Have there been any other cases of absenteeism except among the folders?" To which he replied, "No, except those who naturally go." Of this our committee observed: "It would appear that these two classes, those who naturally go and those who go through the artificial assistance of Congressmen form a pretty large aggregate."

There were dozens who were paid when they were not there at all. One of the employees in the cloakroom was there on and off for only three or four months during a period of three years and he was spared from going to Washington even to receive his salary. The vouchers were sent to him and he filed receipts in the disbursing clerk's office "just as all the other gentlemen who go home do."

The disbursing officer testified: "It is no question for me to find out whether they are there or not."

The office which kept such admirable check upon expenditures itself cost about $14,000 a year.

This system had existed for many years and it was evident that places in the service of the House were considered not as positions where there were duties to be performed, but as sinecures for which money was appropriated or as plunder to be divided, and in the minds of our committee the sinister question arose whether honest legislation could be expected from Congressmen thus guilty in withdrawing from the Treasury these numerous small sums for the objects of their patronage. Was public virtue in larger matters possible in a body where such peculation was an established institution?

More places had been promised than the officers of the House were able to discover. So those who were appointed contributed to pay people not on the roll.

The barbers in the Republican cloakroom were each assessed $10.00 a month to pay one in the Democratic cloakroom who had no place and had to be carried. "A gentleman on the Democratic side suggested taking care of him in that way."

Two colored men employed as laborers in the House bathrooms at $720 a year had each to give two months' pay to a white man who did nothing. Afterwards they had to give $10.00 a month to a colored man and sent it to him by registered letters for eight months. They said this was done by order of the Clerk of the House, which, however, he denied.

The reading clerk was carried on the rolls at a salary of $3600. He turned over this salary to the disbursing clerk who returned him $2000 for himself, gave $1200 to one man and $400 to another. This $400 was actually paid to one of the Congressmen who sent it to his protégé. Not only was there no record of these transactions but the employee was often deprived of his memory concerning them. The clerk of the House thus described how things of this sort were done:

Salaries have been divided for years, and it is generally caused by the Members; you understand that. For instance, two men draw two positions. One is $1200 and the other $800. They both want the $1200 position; and they compromise by one taking the $800 position and the other the $1200 and they figure 8 and 12 is 20, one half of 20 is 10. This is a matter which they figure among themselves.

Enormous salaries were paid for trifling work—$2000 a year for a newspaper clerk who had charge of the subscription lists and files, and $1314 for the man who brought up the newspapers and put them on the files.

The House carpenter designated his own work, and made out his own bills, which were paid without auditing or supervising. There was one bill of $3218 for packing boxes alone.

The report of the Congressional Committee which investigated these abuses *did not give the names of the members who caused them.*

Our Committee after describing all these things remarked: "The entire force consisted of 357 persons. If such abuses could exist in a force of that size what would be the effect of restoring the patronage system in the eighty-five thousand places now subject to competitive examination?"

EVASIONS THROUGH SPECIAL LEGISLATION

On July 29th our Committee published a report on the evasions of the civil service law through constructions placed on special legislation. We showed that although the rules applied to all new positions as soon as these were created except where Congress expressly provided otherwise, yet in a great number of cases some ambiguity in the language of the bills had been improperly construed by appointing officers so as to exclude these positions from the competitive service. Thus the number of exceptions kept constantly growing and the civil service law was circumvented.

For instance appointments to the Rural Free Delivery service were made without examination for the ridiculous reason that that service was spoken of as "experimental" and this was continued long after it ceased to be experimental at all.

The act appropriating money for the Forest Reserve Bureau provided that the employees should be appointed "wholly with reference to their fitness and without regard to their political affiliations." This language did not interfere with appointments under the civil service law but rather the reverse. Yet the Secretary of the Interior claimed the rules did not apply, a letter from the Civil Service Commission contesting this view remained unanswered, and the Bureau was treated as unclassified.

Certain temporary clerks in the office of the First Assistant Postmaster-General were also appointed without reference to the civil service rules, though these rules made special provision for temporary appointments. Copyists in the General Land Office were similarly appointed because the work was said to be of an "emergency" character; temporary stenographers and typewriters in the Department of State on the ground that the word used was "select" and not "appoint," etc. We insisted that if the practice of securing exceptions by such methods should not be checked the Civil Service Act would be gradually nullified and we called upon the President to classify these places and put a stop to these practices. But no action as taken until Mr. Roosevelt became President.

JERSEY CITY POST OFFICE

On August 12, 1901, we issued a report concerning the violations of the law in the Jersey City post office. E. W. Woolley, Assistant Postmaster, was president of the Hudson County Republican Committee and the Jersey City Republican Committee which sent to the carriers letters requesting contributions to meet campaign expenses both for local and national campaigns.

In addition to this it was shown that Mr. Woolley together with Superintendent of Carriers Bertsch had coerced employees of the office and had illegally discriminated against those who refused to contribute by changing their routes and giving them undesirable vacations in the winter time while those who contributed avoided trouble.

In making these assessments a curious method was adopted to avoid direct personal solicitation. There was a box placed on a little table in front of the time-keeper's desk in such a position that when the carriers came up to report they could not fail to see it. This box contained a rabbit's foot and had an official envelope with the corner of a $10.00 bill sticking out. Other envelopes had on them the names of the carriers from whom contributions were desired. When asked the meaning of this one of them testified, "The rabbit's foot meant good luck, that those who paid $10.00 would be in good luck."

The claim was also made that the vacations had been drawn by lot although the *carriers were not permitted to be present when this was done.* In view of the fact that these undesirable vacations uniformly fell to the lot of the non-contributors I observed to the Postmaster-General that in this case we had a remarkable illustration of the direct interposition of Providence in favor of campaign contributors for Hudson County elections.

I called the attention of the Postmaster-General and the President to these facts. The case was submitted by the Civil Service Commission to the Attorney-General, who declined to prosecute, and accordingly in August our committee published these matters, calling attention to the fact that the offenders still remained in office and had actually repeated their political assessments in open defiance of law.

A curious thing occurred while we were publishing this series of reports. President McKinley, in spite of the fact that we were criticizing his administration so severely, told me in one of my interviews with him that he was not satisfied with all the members of the Civil Service Commission and that he desired to appoint me as one of the Commissioners. I was at first inclined to wonder whether this was not merely one of his compliments till I heard he had also spoken to others of appointing me. There had been so many things however which he had expressed his intention of doing in regard to the civil service which had not been done that I did not give the matter serious consideration. I am inclined to think that his idea was that in appointing one of the most active of his critics to an administrative position he would disarm much of the criticism and perhaps satisfy those who were making it how difficult it was to enforce the law against strong political pressure.

Our investigating committee had prepared the drafts of two more reports, one of the Internal Revenue service and one on the appointments under the War Emergency Acts. These were to be submitted to the President on his return to Washington in the fall.

We had also collected a mass of information relative to the results of his unfortunate order of May, 1899, as to the work of the Census and other matters when suddenly the tragedy at Buffalo and the accession of Mr. Roosevelt to the presidency completely changed the aspect of affairs.[1]

[1] The preparation of these reports and the collection of this information were mainly the work of Mr. George McAneny who had been secretary of the League since 1894 and had conducted its affairs with signal ability up to 1902 when he was called to other duties, becoming executive officer of the New York Municipal Civil Service Commission under Mayor Low, then president of the Borough of Manhattan, afterwards president of the Board of Aldermen, and at one time acting Mayor of New York. He was ably seconded in his work for the League by his assistant Elliot H. Goodwin who succeeded him as secretary upon his retirement in 1902 and continued as the executive officer of the League until 1912 when he became general secretary of the United States Chamber of Commerce. A great part of the material in our work of investigation was prepared and arranged by the assiduous labors of these two men and the whole was greatly improved by their revision. There were no men connected with the reform movement whose judgment was more unerring. The League has been specially fortunate not only in the leadership of George Wm. Curtis, Carl Schurz, and Dorman B. Eaton but in having at its command perhaps the most efficient men in the country in conducting its propaganda, in marshaling the facts regarding the spoils system, and in devising suitable remedies for abuses. No history of the Civil Service movement will be complete which cannot present more fully than I am able to do in these pages the invaluable services of these men to the reform.

CHAPTER XI

ROOSEVELT was the antithesis of McKinley. While Mc-
Kinley administered the government by soft, flexible, diplomatic measures, moving along the path of least resistance
and seeking to be friends with everyone, yielding to pressure
and floating on the currents of popular opinion rather than
directing them, Roosevelt attained his objects by the directest
road, bearing down obstacles by the force of his will. He had
a far more definite knowledge of the needs of the civil service
than had McKinley. His six years' experience as Commissioner had shown him clearly that little could be done by
compromising with spoilsmen; that the law needed to be
strictly enforced.

Early in October I had an interview with him regarding
such enforcement and the extension of the classified lists.[1]

It was not long after this that I received a telegram from

[1] In this interview he assured me that he intended to:

(1) Remove all officers charged with violations of the law who were
unable to present an adequate defense and whose cases had not already
been adjudicated.

(2) To restore the old rule limiting reinstatements to one year except
in the case of veterans.

(3) To amend the rule governing temporary appointments so as to
require that when there were less than three on the eligible list one of these
should be given the temporary appointment until the examination for
permanent appointment should be held.

(4) To amend the rules so that Porto Ricans and other inhabitants of
insular dependencies could be examined.

(5) To require all civil employees to furnish testimony when asked by
the Civil Service Commission under penalty of dismissal.

(6) To provide that when any person was appointed without com-

him asking me to take a place on the Civil Service Commission. He had indeed, as I learned afterwards, spoken of this matter to some of his friends immediately after taking the oath of office at Buffalo, and later he had assured himself of the approval of Senators Fairbanks and Beveridge from my own State. The offer when I received it was extremely attractive to me. I was a warm friend of Mr. Roosevelt and I believed in him absolutely. I knew well his interest in the reform and felt sure a great deal of effective work could be done under his administration. The offer was also attractive because I would be associated with so able a defender of the reform system and so charming a man as John R. Proctor, the president of the Commission.

But there was one consideration which restrained me from an immediate acceptance. I was to be appointed in place of a man who had been for a number of years a conscientious Commissioner and who would be thrown out of office without support in his old age if I were to take the place. I talked with Mr. Proctor about this and he told me that that contingency had already been provided for, that he had seen the President and had asked him to make some other provision for this man, since he doubted whether I would accept the place if this were not done. Mr. Roosevelt answered him characteristically: "Old man, do you know the thing you are proposing is distinctly a spoils proposition! I would be making a place, not for the benefit of the service but to provide for some particular man. But in this case," he added, "I am with you, and I am going to do it." A place of some consideration was accordingly provided where the ex-commissioner was still

pliance with the civil service rules auditing and disbursing officers should refuse payment of the salary of such appointee. He said that at a later period after the law had been better enforced, he would consider the classification of the Internal Revenue service, the registration of laborers, and if possible the classification of the consular service, but that his plans might be changed to meet the suggestions of his Cabinet or in case any legal difficulties should intervene.

I reported the successful result of my interview to the Executive Committee of the National Civil Service Reform League which on the motion of Mr. Schurz accepted the report with special and cordial satisfaction.

able to do effective work. And I, who was equally regardless of consistency, as soon as I learned of this decided to accept the Commissionership.

ON THE COMMISSION

I secured a very tiny but attractive house on New Hampshire Avenue where I lived while I remained in Washington. On the 15th of November I was sworn in. The Commission was then housed in a rather shabby rented building opposite the Post Office Department and here it was that I began to learn the details of the work and coöperate with the other Commissioners, Messrs. Proctor and Rodenberg, in the work of strengthening and extending the classified system.

Within three days we procured from the President an order repealing the exemption from examination of a large number of employees in various departments at large of the United States army, ten days subsequently the President promulgated a rule providing that superintendents of Indian schools acting as agents might be classified, also a rule restricting transfers, and on the following day, November 27th, the classification of the free delivery, a very important branch of the service, was authorized.

It was not long after I began my duties that I learned some extraordinary things. I found for instance, that much of the opposition to civil service reform roared loudly and thundered in the index, but yet was very gentle and mild at heart. We heard, for example, a cry coming up from the departments with singular unanimity to the Commission: "Save us from the office seekers; include in the classified service anything and everything you can; we don't want our lives worn out by these interminable applications; but for heaven's sake don't tell the Congressmen we asked you to do this!" I found that the Commission played to the remaining departments and bureaus of the government very much the same part that Jorkins played in the firm of Spenlow & Jorkins. Spenlow was always accommodating, but it was Jorkins, who sat in an unknown room upstairs, whom nobody saw—it was Jorkins who always fiercely resisted the demands for every concession. So it was with us. Every department official would be only too glad to oblige, but for that infernal Commission which blocked the way to every primrose path of patronage. It perhaps was fortunate that there were those on the Commission who were quite willing to be Jorkins, or even something worse, if they could thus prevent the demoralization of the service. Sometimes even the legislators who denounced the competitive system and the Commission upon the floor of Congress would privately tell us they did not mean half they said, that they really were glad to be relieved of distributing patronage, but that they had to make a showing to the office seekers among their constituents.

But this was not true of all, and where a Congressman really wanted to secure the appointment of some useful dependent or retainer, or the relative of some influential constituent who *had* to be placated, many were the evasions and tricks by which he sought to squeeze his protégé into the service in spite of the law. How many "temporary appointments" he used to solicit which threatened to last a lifetime! How often would he try to have his friends appointed as "mere laborers" and then to have them assigned to clerical work until the Commissioners threatened to issue a new edict, "Scrub or get out"! How many places like those of census clerks were made political patronage because they were merely temporary, and then when the work was over it was attempted to transfer them bodily into the classified service in order that so large a multitude should not be cast forth into a cold and unfeeling world!

There were other discoveries made by the new Commissioner. I found a curious impression prevailing, that we were ourselves the general distributors of patronage.

Even before I went to Washington I began to receive letters from various persons, known and unknown to me, asking for positions. It seemed to be considered that I was to be a general employment agent of the government. This fact gave rise to a practical joke upon me in my own household. Among my letters was the following, mailed to me at Richmond:

DEAR SIR: I dislike to bother you, but it would give me great service by seeing if there would be any place in Washington where I could give my services. I can manicure nails and can take care of babies.

I thought I would preserve the letter and lay it before the other members of the Commission for their amusement when we should meet. I related the incident to my family that day at dinner and told them of my purpose, whereupon my youngest daughter, a little girl of seven, archly asked me if I could not guess who was the author of the letter, which was signed by a name I did not know. I answered that I had not the slightest idea. She could contain herself no longer, but burst out laughing, and confessed she had risen early that morning, had written the letter, and had gone before breakfast to the post office to mail it.

One day a gentleman called at my office and informed me that he was the historian of the Army of the Potomac and that he wanted me to get him a good place in the government service which would support him while he was at leisure to prosecute his great work! I assured him that while I was personally much interested in history and in literature, his aspirations lay quite beyond my official jurisdiction. Yet this used to be the way in which many places in the government services were filled.

Even in the routine work of the office I was sometimes startled by the peculiar character of our duties. For instance, there was a place of "disciplinarian" in the Indian School service, somewhat different from that of either principal or teacher, and I understood, confidentially, that one of the chief functions of the disciplinarian was to do the spanking. We received one day a requisition for a disciplinarian "with a good knowledge of music." This filled the Commission with food for earnest thought.

Before I went to Washington I determined that I would never make any recommendations to the President for any civil position whatever, and when I came on the Commission I found that this rule had already been adopted by the other Commissioners and we none of us gave the President any advice as to any person proposed for an office unless he requested it.

But notwithstanding the fact that we made no recommendations I soon found that I had the reputation of having great influence at the White House and the correspondence soliciting my interposition became quite extensive. One of the newspapers had an editorial with the headline, "Dudley's at the Bat," referring to the consternation of old-time Indiana politicians who began to fear that there was not a job to be given out or a pie to be cut, but that "Teddy would pass it to Dudley." The article pictured them as weeping at the doors of the White House as I passed in at pleasure and held the ear of the President while others were compelled to wait for a smile of recognition and the smile was all they got.

Other papers began to talk about a "kitchen cabinet" composed of a group of Mr. Roosevelt's personal friends. Indeed our relations with the President were quite intimate. Proctor and I had many of our interviews with him while he was in the hands of his barber, just after lunch. A President has to economize his time and naturally it is with his closer friends that he must improve such opportunities. We used to call such an interview *le petit lever* and many of the measures for improving the civil service were discussed and often adopted on these occasions.

Everyone who lived during the early part of Roosevelt's administration will remember what an excitement was aroused in the South when he entertained Booker T. Washington the negro at the White House table. We had something which occurred in the Commission which seemed like the Booker Washington case *in petto*. The circumstances were these:

Since 1894 Congress had refused appropriations for any increase in the clerical force of the Commission, although the classified service had grown enormously. We were unable to conduct even our ordinary business with the force at our disposal. We brought this matter to the President's attention. He directed the members of his Cabinet to detail to us from their departments a force sufficient to carry on our work, and we began to confer with the representatives of these departments as to the persons they were to send us. One day there came into my office a representative of the Treasury Depart-

ment. He gave me a list of those they proposed to send. He
read the names and finally came to that of a clerk whom we
will call Margaret Brown. He described her qualifications—
she was accurate, neat, faithful, deserving in every way—and
"black as the ace of spades." Two of the heads of our
divisions were present and they both exclaimed," That will
never do, we have some Southern women in our divisions
and they will at once resign." I observed that there was no
law requiring them to remain in the service against their will
and asked the representative of the Treasury Department
how this clerk had entered the service. "She entered by
passing your examination," he replied, "and she passed it well."
I answered that I would begin by making her my own clerk
in my own office and I did, and found her extremely well-
behaved and efficient. I was much struck with the attitude
of Commissioner Proctor, who at the time was absent from the
city. When he returned I reported what had occurred. He
was a Southerner and had been a Confederate soldier. I
thought he might look at the matter in a different light, but he
answered, "You did perfectly right. The law makes no discrimination and we can make none. She would have been as
welcome to a place in my room as she was in yours."

One afternoon, shortly before the holidays, while I was
going home from the Commission I saw a letter carrier engaged
in angry altercation with the driver of a private carriage. The
carrier was standing at the edge of the sidewalk and the coachman, a negro, was on the box in the middle of the street. The
carrier was swearing furiously at the coachman and calling
him vile names. It seems that he had almost run into the
horses on his bicycle and had frightened them and the colored
driver had protested. The carrier, who was a Southerner,
resented this as "a piece of impudence which he would never
brook from a nigger." The carrier now drew a revolver. The
coachman asked someone to hold the horses, jumped from his
seat, and rushed toward the sidewalk. It seemed as if a fight
were imminent and I sprang between the combatants. The
carrier's hand was unsteady and he seemed to me intoxicated
but he was taking as deliberate aim as he could at the coach-

man and I was just between them, and I thought that by putting on a bold front something might be done, so I cried out at the top of my voice, "Drop that pistol," and advanced straight toward him. The plan worked and he dropped his arm. The lady who owned the carriage now came down the steps of the house before which the quarrel had occurred. The coachman returned to his box and the carrier walked away. I at once went to the post office and made a complaint against him. There I was told that he was in the habit of taking drugs and it seemed to me that a man who did this and carried at the same time a concealed weapon ought not to be in the service. An investigation followed and the carrier was suspended for thirty days without pay, which seemed to me an inadequate penalty, but of course that was a matter for the Department. This was only one of many instances which have convinced me that large numbers of employees are retained in the civil service who ought not to be there; that this is done principally on account of the kindness of the superior officer and his unwillingness to inflict the severe punishment of dismissal, and I have come to believe that a concurrent jurisdiction on the part of the Civil Service Commission giving that body the power to inflict such punishment after proper investigation would be a valuable aid to discipline.

CONSULAR SERVICE

One of the important matters which received the attention of Congress in the early part of 1902 was the question of the consular service. At this time it was not quite in as deplorable a condition as it had been during the worst days of the spoils system, but it was still pretty bad. The service had attained an importance far beyond that of earlier times. We had become the foremost productive nation of the world, seeking markets everywhere. There was need of the highest kind of ability in the consular service to make the most of our opportunities. The system of political appointments however seemed to proceed upon the idea that anybody was fit to be consul without any training for the place. In many

places we had politicians, broken down professional and
business men, invalids, men who desired to go abroad for the
purpose of educating their children, and sometimes men who
were not good for anything else and were made consuls on
that account.   The terms were so short and the pay generally
so meager that first-class men would not offer themselves.
The most ludicrous stories were told of the ignorance, boorish-
ness, and incapacity of many of our consuls.   Their speeches
at public reunions have many a time caused Americans to
blush for their country.   Some of them were habitual drunk-
ards.   One entered in his expense account " 15 yards of 'roap,'"
so much "hamb," so much "bleeched" "musslin."   Another
refused to certify to a collection of dried insects as museum
specimens, believing that they were medicinal substances!

On the other hand, many of the ablest reports on the foreign
markets were made by American consuls who appeared to
have won their places, however, quite by accident.   A few
feeble efforts had been made to remedy this system.   "Pass
examinations" were repeatedly instituted but had fallen into
disuse, and now once more the matter was up for consideration
in Congress and the proposition was made that some sort of
examination should be established.   This, however, was
vigorously opposed by many, among them by Champ Clark,
the Democratic leader of the House, who declared that he
was not opposed to a merit system, and repeated it with
emphasis "so that no idiot could go away and misconstrue
it"; but his idea of a merit system was that when the Republicans carried the election they had a right to the offices
and when the Democrats carried it they had a right to them.
"But here is the objection," he added, "in this consular
business.   In the civil service reform examinations as now
conducted, they do not ascertain a man's fitness to be a
consul, because the examinations are not about things which
a consul ought to know in order to render the best service."
As there were no civil service examinations at all for the
position of consul I wrote to Mr. Clark, "Might I ask to
what examinations you refer?" and I added, "If there are any
examinations of the Commission for any offices in any branch

of the services which are defective or are not practical I should like to know it, to the end that such defects may be speedily corrected." I received no answer and when Mr. Clark was asked by a newspaper man if he intended to reply he said, "I received a letter from Mr. Foulke and threw it into the waste basket where it belongs. I do not consider my remarks any of Mr. Foulke's business and if he will attend to his business I will attend to mine."

This action upon the part of one who afterwards became Speaker and a candidate for the nomination for the presidency, thus criticizing examinations which never had any existence, is a startling commentary on the character of much of our Congressional representation.

Congress, however, took no action and in December, 1902, I suggested to the President that since that body would not enact a competitive system into law he might still provide rules for the purpose of aiding his executive discretion in making nominations to the Senate. He told me he would much like to do this, but that he felt it would not be wise; that in view of the refusal by Congress to act he doubted whether persons nominated by him under such a system, if established by the Executive alone, would be confirmed by the Senate at all. The Senate could reject any of his appointments and if they considered that the adoption of this system was an invasion of their prerogative, they would be very likely to refuse confirmation. He thought it would be unfortunate to attempt to establish such a system and fail and he believed that at the present time he would not succeed.[1]

[1] Sometime after I left the Commission, however, important steps were taken to improve the consular service. On April 5, 1906, an act reorganizing it was approved by the President and on June 27th he promulgated an executive order providing that all positions where the salary exceeded $2500 should be filled by promotion based upon ability and efficiency in service, while the consulships of a lower grade should be filled either by promotion from consular clerks, vice-consuls, deputy-consuls, and others, or after a pass examination. Among the obligatory subjects of examination there was to be at least one modern language other than English, political economy, international, commercial, and maritime law, and an account of

CONTROVERSIES WITH CRITICS

A good part of my duties as member of the Civil Service Commission consisted in the work of propaganda, in speeches and articles in support of the competitive system, and also in answering attacks upon the reform in Congress and elsewhere. I always felt that it was as much a part of my duty to defend the action of the administration in support of the reform as it would have been the duty of a Cabinet officer to defend the general policies of the President.

There were a few of his appointments that were criticized by his old friends of the National Civil Service Reform League, for instance, that of John S. Clarkson, "a pronounced enemy of the system with a record as a spoilsman," as Surveyor of the Port of New York. Many of us were astonished at this appointment by the President.

I said to him that Clarkson had the appointment and management of a large number of subordinates in the civil service; that it might well be doubted whether a man who was opposed to the competitive system, as he had been, would enforce that system in his own office as well as one who was friendly to it; and I suggested that it would be a good thing to caution Mr. Clarkson in regard to his observance of the civil service law.

---

the resources and commerce of the United States especially with reference to extending trade.

The examinations were limited to citizens specially designated by the President and if the positions to be filled were in a country where the United States exercised extra-territorial jurisdiction a supplementary examination was held in common law, evidence, and the trial of civil and criminal cases.

The President might appoint any person who had passed without regard to his relative standing.

Of course this scheme was only a halfway measure, patronage not being excluded and those designated for examination still receiving the endorsement of Senators or other political authorities in their respective States, and the nominations were subject to confirmation by the Senate. Yet it was as far as the President felt he could then go and under it an immense improvement was made in the personnel of the consular service.

Later (as we shall hereafter see) similar provisions were enacted by Congress.

The President said, "I will write to him at once," and dictated a letter beginning, "You know I am a crank in regard to the civil service law,"[1] and then proceeded to ask Mr. Clarkson to see that the law was thoroughly observed, adding, "If any question arises, come on to Washington and talk with Mr. Foulke and Mr. Garfield. They are just as good Republicans as you are." And then turning to me he added, "If I were to tell him to talk to Proctor he would think I was turning him over to be a victim of some Democratic scheme."

The President knew Clarkson better than his critics and so completely did Mr. Clarkson's views upon the subject change with his new experience that when he retired from his position in 1900 he wrote, "The Customs service will never attain its rightful and possible efficiency until it is completely separated from political influence."

Another appointment for which the President incurred much criticism was that of Henry C. Payne of Wisconsin as Post-master-General in place of Charles Emory Smith, who had resigned. Mr. Payne had been a political leader and manager in Wisconsin and the selection of such a man to be the head of the department controlling more appointments than any other awakened much animadversion. The President told me why he had made it. He said:

When President McKinley died I accepted his Cabinet in its entirety. There was not a single politician in it. He did not need any. He was such a skillful politician himself that he did not require the advice of any other, but with me it is different. I do not see as clearly as he did how my action will affect public opinion or influence political affairs and I want someone who can advise me and tell what its effect will be. That is the reason I have asked Mr. Payne to become Postmaster-General.

Whatever were Mr. Payne's aptitudes or shortcomings, he did nothing during his term of office to cripple the competitive system. On the contrary he advanced it, for he announced that it was the policy of the administration that fourth-class postmasters were not to be generally changed at the end of any

[1] On another occasion, while Proctor and I were present, he said, "I don't think I am going to have much trouble with Congress in regard to the civil service law. They realize that I am a maniac upon the subject."

particular term but were to hold office indefinitely if their service was satisfactory.

An amusing correspondence was that with the editor of the
Newport *Herald* who, in an article on May 2, 1902, entitled
"Evading Civil Service Rules," had said, first: that President
Roosevelt had ordered more places taken out of the classified
service during the past few months than McKinley during five
years; second: that the records of the Commission showed a
surprisingly large number of exceptions ordered within the
past six months; third: that some of the positions thus filled
had been restored to the Civil Service immediately after the
appointment of the individual for whom the exception was
made; fourth: that there had been three times as many
appointments under Roosevelt as under McKinley in cases
where extraordinary, special, or technical qualifications were
required; fifth: that there had been a large and unknown
number of places filled without examination for temporary job
work; sixth: that there was little to boast of in the way of
additions.

I took this article to the President.   I was rather indignant
at it, and I handed it to him without comment.   He looked it
over, put on a quizzical expression, and said, "Well, am I guilty?
I am like the man that was arraigned and asked to plead, but
said he couldn't tell whether he was guilty or not till he had
heard the evidence.   I thought I had been doing pretty well
for civil service reform.   Maybe I haven't; tell me how it is."

On May 8th, I published an answer to the article.   I compared its assertions to the celebrated definition of the crab,
"a small red fish that walks backwards," which was perfect
except that the crab was not red, was not a fish, and did not
walk backwards.

In the present case, not one of the *Herald's* statements was
correct.   The President had not ordered a single place out of the
classified service.   He had specifically excepted ten persons
from examinations.   In none of these cases did the position
revert to the classified service for it had never been taken out.
It was not true that three times as many appointments were
made under Roosevelt as under McKinley by the rule except-

ing places requiring peculiar, special, or technical qualifications. Under McKinley twenty-one were thus excepted and under Roosevelt only five. A door-keeper at the White House was so appointed, because where the life of a President was at stake unusual qualifications were required. "We had no person on any eligible list who seemed competent for this duty, and I for one was only too glad to except a man whom I believed could properly perform it."

The rule for the employment of temporary appointees for a temporary job was passed at the recommendation of the Commission, since it seemed absurd to go through the delay of certifying from eligible registers, perhaps from remote sections of the country, persons who would be employed only for a few days and then discharged.

It was not true that the Commissioners did not know how many appointments were thus made. On the contrary, it was known that the total number was 193. As to the statement that "there was little to boast of in the way of additions tending to strengthen the civil service rules" I answered that there had been no administration in which the competitive system had advanced with greater rapidity and certainty during an equal period of time.[1]

[1] The Washington *Post* in an editorial entitled "A Knock by Homer Foulke" caught me in a grammatical mistake in the above letter. The editorial said:

"In a visitors' book in one of the show places in England someone wrote an inscription in eulogy of 'The great man who it had once served for a home' and underneath this another traveler scribbled the stanza:

'I note 'twas written in a hurry,
        To criticize I won't presume,
    And yet methinks that Lindley Murray
        Instead of "who" had written "whom."'

"It is the reverse comment which we should make against a sentence in Commissioner Foulke's recent letter to the editor of the Newport *Herald:* 'We had no person on any eligible list known to be competent for this duty and I for one would only be too glad to except from examination a man whom I believed could properly perform it.'

"Far be it from the *Post* to administer so much as the gentlest rebuke to Mr. Foulke for his slip of the pen. His official position entitles him to be

In April, 1902, Commissioner Rodenberg declared his purpose of resigning from the Commission in order to make the race for Congress in his district and James R. Garfield, son of the former President, was appointed in his place. At a later period we divided our duties, Mr. Proctor taking principal charge of the examinations, Mr. Garfield superintending the internal administration of the Commission and harmonizing our work with the various departments, while the general outside business of the Commission, particularly in regard to investigations, propaganda, and resisting attacks devolved mainly upon me. This was an extremely congenial occupation. I loved a "scrap" on behalf of what I considered a good cause and I had many of them.

We Commissioners were close personal friends. We visited each other often, we made New Year calls together, both at the White House and elsewhere. We took numerous horseback rides, sometimes together, sometimes with the President. I remember one of these occasions when Proctor and I were riding in Rock Creek Park. We had reached the summit of a headland overlooking the Creek with a precipitous incline and below us we saw two horsemen struggling up the sides of this steep acclivity among the bushes. Proctor looked over and exclaimed, "Who are these damned fools who have left the road and are trying to climb this cliff?" and a moment later he cried, "Good Lord! it's the President." It was indeed Mr Roosevelt, who was followed by General Young, then the ranking officer of the army, and by an orderly some distance behind. They soon reached the top of the cliff, but here there

---

independent of all rules except those laid down by the Civil Service Commission, and as to these he is not amenable to the grammatical standards prescribed by his subordinates, the members of the examining board. To parody the lines in the visitors' book:

> "Commissioners excite no wonder
>   By writing 'whom' instead of ' who,'
> Though candidates by such a blunder
>   Might lose their chance of pulling through."

was a high fence and no means of getting over it, so the President started down again. I rode ahead and found an opening and shouted to him that he could get through. He came up again and passed into the road, crying out to Proctor and me, "Come and join us." We did so and in a few moments we all dashed down through the bushes again into the ravine in another place and galloped on without any reference to road, creek, rocks, or anything else whatever. Pretty soon we came to a field and then to a fence with an open gate. The President leaped the fence. General Young rode through the gate and Proctor and I followed his more modest example. It was a wild ride until we reached again the streets of Washington.

Unfortunately about half of the working hours of an official in Washington are taken up with interviews and conversations with various persons which cannot be avoided, and which consume time to little purpose. One person after another will bring to us, with great detail, some supposed grievance which ought to be handled by a subordinate, or some Congressman will come with a story of very pressing reasons why the civil service laws ought to be suspended in favor of some particular protégé of his own. It would not do to refuse to see any of these persons. The Commission was unpopular enough as it was and to decline to listen to grievances or explanations connected with the service would be inexcusable. The result was that the days would go by and little be done and it was only the "odds and ends and fringes of time" which were left for our most important work. If such an evil is great in respect to a body like the Civil Service Commission, how unendurable must it be to the heads of the principal departments and to the President, continually beset at all hours with the most harassing importunities!

The relations of the Commission with the various departments were excellent. We were friends with them all. Under previous administrations there had been much conflict and considerable exasperation attending the dealings of the Commission with members of the Cabinet, but in the administration of a President who was so strong a supporter of the merit system all this disappeared. We were also on very cordial terms with many of the bureaus and independent offices. I remember particularly that we were very friendly with Mr. Ware, the Commissioner of Pensions, who, quite in contrast with his predecessors, was a great believer in the competitive system and did what he could to advance it in a bureau in which politics had been deeply ingrained. In addition to being a Pension Commissioner he was a versifier and would write rhymes on every occasion. Once when he took a short vacation on account of illness he communicated the fact to the President in the following limerick:

> I take up this piece of plumbago
> To tell you I've got the lumbago,
>   So I'm off and away for a week and a day
> For I feel like a very bum Dago.

It was generally from Congressmen that the most violent opposition came not only to the merit system but to those who administered it, yet we had some notable defenders in both Houses who held up our antagonists to ridicule. On one occasion an attack was made upon the system by some enthusiastic advocates of "the good old plan" who had packed the galleries with a crowd of supporters that applauded their sentiments vociferously. Mr. Allen, of Mississippi, one of our friends, told of an unsatisfied dog who had howled on a Mississippi plantation the livelong night and kept everybody awake. The planter and one of his field hands were in consultation as to the reason for this. "Massa," said the negro, "you know what makes him howl." But the planter protested he did not. "What!" exclaimed the negro, "you live more'n forty years on dis plantation and doan' know what makes a dog howl? Why, Massa, a dog howls when he smells somethin' and can't locate it." "Now," continued Mr. Allen, pointing to the galleries, "these gentlemen smell pie, but they are unable as yet to locate it, hence the uproar."

The Commissioners were fortunate in another particular. They had an excellent corps of subordinates, able, reliable, and coöperative, willing to turn in and work overtime if necessary when something important was pending, and all warm advocates of the competitive system.

Mr. John T. Doyle, secretary of the Commission, who had been with that body since its organization, was peculiarly efficient. He had, however, strong convictions of his own as to how the law ought to be administered. He had an inscrutable face. Proctor used to say it was the best poker face he had ever known though I do not believe Doyle availed himself of its advantages. But we always noticed that whenever we tried to do anything that Doyle did not think was best, while he never opposed us, it always seemed as if Providence interposed more obstacles to what we wanted done than would seem humanly possible, and in spite of our secretary's respectful and compliant course he often had his own way. And this was probably right, for as the permanent secretary of the Commission he had a more complete knowledge of the details of the system than we, the Commissioners, who were the ephemeral creatures of successive Presidents, passing in and out as political and other considerations might dictate. We were certainly greatly attached to Mr. Doyle. The competitive system has never had a more faithful or competent administrator.

11

CHAPTER XII

THE REFORMS ACCOMPLISHED

I HAVE spoken incidentally of a number of the measures adopted to advance the competitive system. It is now time to consider more in detail the precise character of the reforms accomplished. These may conveniently be divided into three general classes: first, extensions of the competitive system; second, changes in the rules; and third, improved efficiency in the execution of the law.

The extensions embraced: the Rural Free Delivery service; a considerable portion of the field service of the War Department; the employees rendered necessary because of increased work incidental to the war with Spain; places in the Insular service; employees of the permanent Census office; Indian agents, and Cuban employees. Besides these a system of registration for laborers was inaugurated and greater permanency was given in fourth-class postmasterships.

RURAL FREE DELIVERY

The Rural Free Delivery service had been instituted as an experiment but it had become so useful and popular that its permanency was assured and it had given promise of being perhaps the most extensive branch of the entire service, superseding to a large extent the fourth-class post offices. The service had not been classified by the Commission when it was established because it was "experimental." But on November 27, 1901, twelve days after I entered that body, a rule for the purpose was promulgated by the President.

There was no choice here as elsewhere between the three

graded highest. That person was selected whose name was at the head of the list.[1]

FIELD BRANCHES, WAR DEPARTMENT

The next extensions were those of various field branches of the War Department. Prior to May 29, 1899, there was in that service a considerable number of places in the quarter-master's, medical, ordnance, and engineer's departments at large, admission to which was secured by competitive but non-educational tests prescribed by the Commission. On that day President McKinley by executive order took many of these positions out of the competitive class and provided that appointments should be made upon tests to be prescribed by the Secretary of War and approved by the President.

There were other similar places which were not embraced in the President's order and had apparently been overlooked. Moreover, no regulations or tests were ever prescribed by the Secretary of War. But Mr. Alger who was then Secretary had been succeeded by Mr. Root, and under him, in April, 1901, the Assistant Secretary recommended that the order be rescinded. This was done by President Roosevelt on November 18, 1901. The total number of positions thus restored was 1888.

SPANISH WAR EMPLOYEES

The next extension made was that of employees appointed because of increased work incident to the war with Spain. It had been provided by law that these should be employed without complying with the Civil Service Act and on April 28, 1902, 850 persons had been thus appointed without examination. On that date an act was passed providing that these employees should be transferred to the classified service and this was done.

[1] Some years later President Taft changed the rule and gave the appointing officer the choice between the three highest. This was an unfortunate change for after Mr. Wilson became President, Mr. Burleson, his Postmaster-General, permitted these lists to be used in such a way as to secure in many cases the selection of political appointees through the recommendation of Congressmen. (See *infra*, Chapter XVII.)

PERMANENT CENSUS BUREAU

Another addition to the service consisted of 837 employees in the permanent Census Bureau. The proceedings by which this was done have been already described in the chapter relating to the Census.

INSULAR SERVICE

In Porto Rico the federal positions governed by the Civil Service Act embraced 301 places of which 233 were subject to competitive examinations. By our direction, Dr. Leadley, chief of one of our divisions, visited Porto Rico in March and April, 1902, organized a board of examiners, and examined some 227 applicants, most of whom were native Porto Ricans. The Insular and Municipal service of Porto Rico did not however come under the competitive system.[1]

Our Commission also aided in the establishment of the competitive service in the Philippine Islands, sending some two hundred appointees to the islands during the year ending June 30, 1902. During the following year 153 appointments were made.

Considerable difficulty was at first experienced in securing applicants owing to inadequate salaries and unfavorable reports from the islands, but this disappeared in time when it was found that men were advanced to places of high administrative importance when they showed themselves fit.[2]

[1] In 1907, the Porto Rican legislature passed a civil service law. The act, however, was very inadequate.

The police force and teachers are now subject to a modified civil service examination by special laws. In 1916, of 5387 employees only 1101 were in the classified service.

[2] In later years the policy of the Philippine government has been to fill vacancies by the appointment of native Filipinos. The proportion of natives in the service has increased from 48 per cent in 1902 to more than 90 per cent.

Many of the Filipinos are politicians who take naturally to spoils mongering and patronage. These men are opposed to the civil service law and bills injurious to the merit system have been passed in the Philippine Assembly but have not been approved by the Philippine Commission and consequently have not been enacted into law.

THE LABOR SERVICE

An extremely important advance was made when politics was eliminated from the labor service of the government by the adoption of a registration system. On July 3, 1902, we secured from President Roosevelt an order that the appointments of all unclassified laborers should be made in accordance with regulations to be promulgated by the heads of departments and the Civil Service Commission, and on March 26, 1903, another order directed the Commission to aid the heads of the departments in establishing open competitive tests. We were directed to prepare the regulations and to apply them in Washington and in such other large cities as might be agreed upon between the Departments and the Commission.[1]

The success of the Navy Yard system devised by Secretary Tracy in 1891 showed that a similar plan could be applied to unclassified laborers elsewhere.

Boards of labor employment were shortly afterwards established by the Post Office, Treasury, Agricultural, and Interior Departments, in the Government Printing Office and the Smithsonian Institution.

There were about 2225 laborer positions in Washington and 30,000 outside. According to the new plan a physical examination was first made by a physician and a suitable deduction made for any defects. The regulations dealt chiefly with tests of fitness for appointment, consisting principally of written statements by the applicant and by three reputable citizens

---

Vigorous complaints were made in 1914, during Mr. Wilson's administration, that more than five hundred war veterans employed had either been ruthlessly dismissed or had had their salaries reduced and that honorably discharged soldiers and sailors were separated from the service without cause.

The answer of Mr. Garrison, Secretary of War, was that these changes were but little more than the average diminution of American employees for many years and were due to desirable retrenchment and reduction in the service.

[1] The Civil Service Act itself did not contemplate the classification of laborers and the President's authority to prescribe registration was conferred by Section 1753 of the Revised Statutes and by his general constitutional power as head of the executive branch of the government.

who had knowledge of his character and qualifications, and the applications were rated upon the elements of age, physical qualifications, industry, and adaptability.

THE INDIAN SERVICE

Something that amounted to an extension of the classified system was adopted in the Indian service. In recent years it had been the policy of the Indian Commissioner to abandon the Reservation System wherever practicable and give the Indians industrial training, and a number of Indian agents had been dropped. The law provided that in such cases the Indian Commissioner, with the approval of the Secretary of the Interior, might devolve the duties of agent upon the superintendent of the Indian school.

On November 26, 1901, the rules were amended so as to provide that when this was done, the agent might, in the discretion of the Secretary, be given a position in the classified service so that efficient men could receive a more permanent status than the agents used to have who were changed for political reasons with each new administration. So successful was this plan that on January 4, 1905, the Commission announced that the number of superintendents in charge of agencies had increased to eighty-six, most of whom had been continuously in the service from ten to twenty-five years, and that under this policy the Indian service had been practically taken out of politic

CUBAN EMPLOYEES

Another extension was made by the incorporation of certain Cuban employees in the classified service. These men had been appointed as the result of the occupation of Cuba which

---

[1] Later on, in November, 1904, the President created a Central Board of Labor Employment composed of representatives from the different departments and offices in the District of Columbia, and directed the Civil Service Commission to supervise its work. On January 12, 1905, similar boards were established in New York, Boston, Philadelphia and St. Louis, and later this was extended to a large number of other cities.

followed the war with Spain and as they had been chosen by the military authorities they were not political appointees. Many of them had rendered valuable service under conditions of personal danger from yellow fever and other tropical diseases. The War Department furnished us with a list of those who it was believed ought to be permanently employed. On two afternoons General Leonard Wood came to the Commission and we went over with him a list of 127 names of those whom he had found to be most deserving of retention. I was astonished at the memory and knowledge of details shown by the General upon this occasion. He gave the official biographies of each of these persons, reciting in full their acts of merit and self-sacrifice, and we recommended as to nearly all of them that they should be made eligible to appointment in the classified service. This was done by an order of the President on July 3, 1902. Some of them were afterwards sent to the Philippines and to Porto Rico, others were retained in the War Department to complete the work necessary to close out the affairs of Cuba, and a few were employed elsewhere.

FOURTH-CLASS POSTMASTERS

In addition to these extensions, there was a marked change in the policy of the Post Office Department regarding the tenure of fourth-class postmasters, of which there were upwards of seventy thousand in the country. Heretofore these officers had been subject to change every four years, although their tenure was indefinite and the law itself seemed to contemplate that they should hold their places during good behavior. While the administration did not promulgate a definite rule on this subject, the policy was inaugurated of considering all fourth-class postmasters as subject to removal for cause only. The effect of this policy was to reduce to a minimum the changes in such offices. Strange to say, the new system met with the coöperation of members of Congress as it relieved them of the pressure of making changes. It was the first step leading to the classification of the fourth-class postmasters, a measure which was begun later by President Roosevelt near the close of his administration and which was completed under his successor, President Taft.

The sum total of these extensions of the competitive system fairly startled me by its size. During the year ending June 30, 1902, there were 12,894 appointments to competitive places. This was then the high water mark of the merit system, but during the year ending June 30, 1903, 39,646 competitive appointments were made—more than three times as many as the year before. I felt during that year that we were making progress but I had never dreamed that we were doing so well as this.

CHANGES IN THE RULES

But even more important than the extension of the classified lists were the changes made in the rules for the purpose of stopping leaks and irregular appointments and securing the stricter operation of the law. These changes enabled the Commission better to enforce the provisions of the act requiring the apportionment of appointments among the different States on the basis of population; gave it power to procure testimony from employees in its investigations; to require the withholding of salaries from persons holding office in violation of the law; to stop temporary appointments of persons outside the eligible lists when eligibles were available; to require examinations as well as six months' active service for transfers to new positions from those who had entered the service by mere classification of the offices they were holding; to prevent reinstatements for the purpose of immediate transfer to other places; to limit transfers to cases when the duties of the two positions were similar; to guard against reinstatements after dismissal for cause, and against the assignment of laborers to classified work. They prevented promotions through political influence; restricted partisan activity as well as lobbying in Congress by employees, and in other ways strengthened the competitive system.[1]

[1] The apportionment of appointments among the different States had been considerably affected by a rule requiring the Commission in all cases of transfer to waive such apportionment upon the certificate by the ap-

REMOVALS

Besides the foregoing amendments an order was issued giving the proper construction to the rule concerning removals. President McKinley on July 27, 1897, had promulgated as we have seen a special order providing that no removal should be

---

pointing officer that the transfer was required in the interests of good administration. These certificates had become mere formalities. Most transfers were made for the convenience of the persons who sought them and were requested by Congressmen and others for political and personal reasons rather than the good of the service. By these transfers the purpose of securing a just apportionment was defeated. Accordingly an amendment to the rules was made on November 26, 1901, requiring that the reasons for waiving the apportionment should be set forth in detail and that the certificate should be subject to the approval of the Commission.

The Civil Service Law did not give to the Commission the power to subpœna and examine witnesses or compel the production of written evidence. In regard to persons outside the civil service this defect could not be remedied but in most of our investigations the result depended largely upon the testimony of employees of the government and in these cases the President had the right to require them to appear and furnish evidence. Accordingly on December 11, 1901, the President, at our request, promulgated an amendment to the rules making it the duty of every officer and employee to give the Commission or its authorized representatives proper and competent information and testimony in regard to all matters inquired of and to subscribe such testimony and make oath or affirmation to the same before some officer authorized to administer oaths. After one employee had been removed for refusing to testify under this rule there was little difficulty in securing evidence.

The Commission was frequently without a remedy for appointments made in violation of law since it could only investigate and report the illegality to the head of the proper department and unless he took action the man illegally appointed remained in the service. To prevent this the Commission recommended a rule providing that it should certify such illegal appointment to the head of the department and then if the person unlawfully holding office was not dismissed within thirty days the proper disbursing and auditing officers should not thereafter pay or permit to be paid any salary or wages accruing after such certificate had been received by them. This rule was adopted December 11, 1901, and after its adoption these illegal appointments ceased.

The rules required that three eligibles must be furnished to an appointing officer before he could be required to make a selection, otherwise he had the right to make a temporary appointment until such eligibles were furnished. Under this system an unnecessary number of temporary appoint-

made from the competitive service except for just cause and for reasons given in writing, and the persons sought to be removed were to have notice and be furnished with a copy of such reasons and allowed a reasonable time for personally answering the same in writing.   This rule was adopted for the purpose of putting an end to removals upon secret charges and

---

ments was made of persons outside of eligible lists, for personal or political reasons, and many were discouraged from entering the examinations.   We therefore recommended an amendment which was made by the President on December 11, 1901, providing that when there were one or two eligibles on the list the appointing officer might make a permanent appointment therefrom, but if he elected not to do so, he must select one of them for temporary appointment unless special reasons were given and approved by the Commission why such selection should not be made.

But while in these cases temporary appointments from the outside had been unnecessarily made, in other cases where they were necessary or desirable they were not permitted by the rules.   This was true in the case of job employments, temporary in character.   It was ofttimes undesirable and even impossible to select men for such employment from the eligible lists, bringing them perhaps from distant places and sometimes causing them to lose the opportunity for permanent employment.   Therefore on January 24, 1902, a rule was adopted on our recommendation, authorizing such temporary appointments for three months if approved by the Commission, which, if the work was not completed, might be extended three months longer, but must then cease.   We recognized that this amendment was liable to abuse if not carefully watched and we did not permit it to apply to employments of a clerical nature even though they were temporary, if eligibles could be secured.

Other important amendments were made relating to transfers.   Before December 11 1901, an employee might be transferred no matter how short a time he had been in the service.   Men were appointed without examination to places in the small post offices just before the classification of these offices and then immediately after classification transferred to other parts of the competitive service, thus evading examination.   But on that day an amendment was adopted that no person should be transferred who had not actually served for six months in some competitive position in the office in which he became classified.

Amendments were adopted restricting transfers in other cases.   Later, on March 13, 1902, it was provided that none should be made until the person to be transferred had passed the examination prescribed for original entrance to the position to which the transfer was proposed.

Persons who had formerly been in the service sought reinstatement not

the beneficent effect of the order was generally recognized. At the same time misunderstandings arose in regard to its proper construction. It was claimed by some that "just cause" meant that some willful act of misconduct must have been committed. But it was evident that persons ought sometimes to be removed when they were not willfully at fault—in

---

for the purpose of going back to the position they had formerly held but in order to be transferred to some other place.

The Commission believed that unless the officer under whom a person was formerly employed was willing to accept his services again he should not be reinstated. Therefore on March 13, 1902, a rule was adopted forbidding all transfers of reinstated persons until they had served six months in the department or office in which they were reinstated.

The rules had been so relaxed that they permitted transfers from one position to another without regard to the similarity of duties in the two places and many were thus given positions for which there was nothing to show that they were qualified. These transfers seriously interfered with promotion regulations and were contrary to the wholesome principle that persons should rise in the service according to their demonstrated training and fitness. Accordingly an amendment was made on January 23, 1902, that no transfer should be made to any position if there was not required therein the performance of the same class of work as in the position from which transfer was proposed.

Prior to this a person dismissed on charges of delinquency or misconduct might be reinstated at any time provided the appointing officer certified that he had thoroughly investigated the case and had found that the charges were not true. The purpose of this rule was to remedy personal wrongs, but its practical operation was injurious. Most of those reinstated had been out of the service from five to fifteen years. They had been separated when it was customary to make removals for political reasons and when records of the charges were seldom kept; hence only *ex-parte* evidence could be obtained and the reinstatements were often due to political influences. Where an appointing officer had dismissed men, ostensibly upon charges but really for political reasons, and his successor dismissed the men appointed in their places and reinstated those discharged, it was evident that at some future time a new appointing officer might do the same thing and thus a rotation in office would be established. Upon the recommendation of the Commission this provision was stricken out on January 23, 1902.

The rule that no laborer should be assigned to work of the same grade as that performed by classified employees had been ineffective because appointing officers decided for themselves that the work of a particular position was not of this grade and they accordingly filled the position as though it were unclassified and then either failed to report the appointment or else

cases for instance where they had become disqualified through physical or mental disability or in cases where their services were no longer required.

It was further believed by many that the rule provided substantially for a trial, for the taking of testimony, and for proceedings similar to those in a court of law. To do this would not only involve enormous labor but would give a permanency of tenure quite inconsistent with the efficiency of the service. Yet so widespread was this misapprehension that appointing officers often hesitated to remove subordinates who had become useless or who had lost the confidence of their superiors because specific acts of misconduct could not be established by sufficient evidence to authorize dismissal. The President, therefore, upon the recommendation of the Commission, issued on May

---

reported it as an appointment to an unclassified position. To remedy this it was provided that every appointing officer should furnish to the Commission a list of all employees and positions which had been treated as below classification with the duties of each position stated in detail. The Commission then treated as classified all grades where the duties required either special qualifications or a knowledge of reading and writing.

We found that about eight hundred persons appointed without examination as mere laborers had been assigned to classified duties. We did not seek at once either to classify or remove these employees but took measures to prevent appointments of this sort in the future. To classify them would have been to confirm the illegality of their employment and to make them eligible for promotion, which, backed as they were in almost every instance by political patrons, might injure those who were in the classified service in a legitimate way. At the same time it was recognized that the sudden dismissal of a large number of laborers doing classified work would be disastrous and would raise an antagonism in Congress, in the Departments, and with the public, which would be quite disproportionate to the good results obtained. We believed that after a while many of these employees, finding promotion impossible, would give up their places or else secure entrance into the classified service through regular examinations and that possibly the remnant might be classified without serious injury.

This was afterwards done by President Roosevelt in an order dated January 12, 1905, after the labor registration system had been further developed and registries established. This order included some 640 persons. He directed, however, March 11, 1905, that laborers classified as clerks should not receive further increase of compensation without competitive examination.

29, 1902, an order declaring that the term "just cause" was intended to mean any cause (other than one merely political or religious) which would promote the efficiency of the service and that nothing contained in the rules should be so construed as to require the examination of witnesses or any trial or hearing except in the discretion of the officer making the removal. The reason, however, had to be stated with sufficient definiteness to enable the employee to understand the exact cause for which his removal was sought and to make a proper answer. A mere general statement of inefficiency, misconduct, negligence, or inattention to duty would not be sufficient.

After this declaration few cases of improper removals came to our attention. A far greater number of employees who should have been removed were retained in the service than the number of those removed who ought to have been retained. Appointing officers were very reluctant to make removals which involved hardship.

There were indeed some complaints of improper removals. For instance, Miss Rebecca Taylor was dismissed from the War Department because she had made and published pungent and bitter criticisms of the conduct of that department and of the administration. This was an impropriety which certainly justified dismissal. It is quite evident that the business of no department can be efficiently conducted if those employed in doing the work are allowed to attack the conduct of their superiors in the newspapers. But a great uproar was made on account of the pretended infringement of personal liberty, and right of free speech and of the press, and there was much talk that such a removal was in violation of the civil service law itself. The criticism had no foundation but it had its cheering side. It was delightful to find how many persons who had never before cared for the competitive system were now filled with such eagerness for the enforcement of the law.

The Taylor case was not the only one in which complaints were made. Whenever some employee who had been violating his duty found himself in danger of dismissal he would send his attorney to the Commission and demand all sorts of things. He would want to know whether the civil service law meant anything, would insist that if he could be dismissed the whole competitive system would be destroyed and the overthrow of all free institutions was at hand.   This became quite an old story and the worse the case the more strenuous was the man for the maintenance of what he called his rights.   But cases of improper removals were extremely rare.[1]

PROMOTIONS

Far greater were the evils in regard to promotions.   Although a man's entrance into the classified service might depend upon competitive tests, yet as soon as he was in, the political "pull" was as strong as ever and his promotion frequently depended on patronage.   Members of Congress and others prominent in political life would go to heads of departments and bureaus and ask the promotion of personal or political favorites.   These requests were frequently complied with and the undeserving were advanced over the heads of those who had fairly earned promotion, thus demoralizing

[1] At a later period (on Nov. 17, 1903) President Roosevelt changed the removal rule so as to provide that when the President or head of any department was satisfied that an officer or employee was inefficient or incapacitated his removal might be made without notice but the cause should be stated in writing and filed.   Where misconduct was committed in the view or presence of the President or head of department, the removal might be made summarily and no statement filed.   The department head might, however, in his discretion, require a statement of reasons and a reasonable time for answering them.

This modification was brought about because the President personally saw what he considered an act of misconduct on the streets of Washington and removed the employee at once.   It cannot be said, however, that the change was an improvement.   There was no great hardship in requiring the removing officer to state his reasons and give the employee a chance to be heard and by this means injustice was sometimes prevented.

Accordingly President Taft on Feb. 8, 1912, restored the rule substantially to its former shape.

On August 24th of that year Congress enacted into law the rule which already existed but this had the disadvantage of giving the courts jurisdiction to determine whether the proper procedure was followed and the experience of various States and cities had shown that judicial interference with administrative acts was generally undesirable.

the service and encouraging men to seek political influence. A very proper restriction however was made in a rule adopted by the President on July 3, 1902, which provided that no recommendation for promotion should be considered except when made by the officer under whose supervision the employee was serving, and such recommendation by any other person with the knowledge and consent of the employee should be sufficient cause for debarring him from the promotion, and a repetition of the offence, sufficient cause for removing him from the service. This order was aimed particularly at the interference of Congressmen.

The Commission endeavored for a long time but without success to devise some general promotion regulations. The problem was a difficult one. If promotions were to depend upon records of efficiency it had to be remembered that these records were often very inadequately kept and gave rise to much injustice. The heads of many bureaus and divisions did not want to discriminate among their subordinates and some marked all their employees at the highest figure. In other offices the subordinates were all marked alike but with a lower figure so that injustice was done to the employees of one office when compared with those of another and there was no authority to equalize these records.

Before a general and uniform system of promotion could be adopted the entire service would have to be reclassified so that the different grades as well as the work of persons employed within each special grade could be fairly and justly compared.

The question of promotion examinations was also considered. These examinations could not well test the executive or administrative qualifications required in the position for which the examination was taken but were useful in determining general intelligence as well as a knowledge of the duties of the higher position. We strongly urged that Congress should provide for the reclassification of the entire departmental service and submitted suggestions, but no action was taken and we felt that until this was done we were not justified in prescribing a general plan, but we urged instead that each department should adopt, in coöperation with the Commission, a system of promotions (including examinations where feasible) which would best meet the conditions within that department.

POLITICAL ACTIVITY

Another matter in which the civil service rules were strengthened was by a clearer definition of the offence of political activity and more precise provisions restricting it.[1]

[1] President Cleveland on July 14, 1886, had issued an executive order in which he said:

"The influence of federal officeholders should not be felt in the manipulation of political primary meetings and nominating conventions. The use by these officials of their positions to compass their selection as delegates to political conventions is indecent and unfair; and proper regard for the proprieties and requirements of official place will also prevent their assuming the active conduct of political campaigns.

"Individual interest and activity in political affairs are by no means condemned. Officeholders are neither disfranchised nor forbidden the exercise of political privileges; but their privileges are not enlarged nor is their duty to party increased to pernicious activity by officeholding."

This order was issued at a time when it had been so long the practice for federal officeholders to take a leading part in politics that it could not be impartially enforced. Men were removed for "pernicious activity" when they belonged to the opposite party while if they belonged to the party in power they were not disturbed. By attempting to apply the rule equally to classified and unclassified positions it was found impracticable to give general effect to it at all.

The postal regulations had contained a clause providing that officeholders should not offend by obtrusive partisanship nor assume the active conduct of political campaigns. On April 1, 1902, new postal regulations were issued in which this clause was left out. We called the attention of the President to this omission and quoted from a previous report prepared by Mr. Roosevelt himself on this subject when he was Commissioner. On June 13, 1902, the President replied:

"As the greater includes the less, and as the executive order of President Cleveland of July 14, 1886, is still in force, I hardly think it will be necessary again to change the postal regulations.

"The trouble, of course, comes in the interpretation of this executive order of President Cleveland. After sixteen years' experience it has been found impossible to formulate in precise language any general construction which shall not work either absurdity or injustice. For instance, it is obviously unwise to apply the same rule to the head of a big city federal

LOBBYING BY EMPLOYEES

There was still another kind of influence which about this time began to be exerted by officials in the classified service, particularly in the Post Office Department. Organizations had been established among letter-carriers, clerks, and others for the purpose of bettering their own conditions, securing higher salaries, civil service pensions, and other desirable things. The rural free delivery carriers already had a lobby working for an increase of pay and the general free delivery carriers and postal clerks were also soliciting legislation which would improve their condition.

The danger of such movements was apparent. If public employees were permitted to combine and impose their will upon members of Congress in favor of their special interests they might secure legislation which was opposed to the public welfare. Accordingly, on January 31, 1902, the President

---

office, who may by his actions coerce hundreds of employees, as to a fourth-class postmaster in a small village, who has no employees to coerce and who simply wishes to continue to act with reference to his neighbors as he always has acted.

"As Civil Service Commissioner under Presidents Harrison and Cleveland I found it so impossible satisfactorily to formulate and decide upon questions involved in these matters of so-called pernicious activity that in the Eleventh Report of the Commission I personally drew up the paragraph which you quote. This paragraph was drawn with a view of making a sharp line between the activity allowed to public servants *within* the classified service and those *without* the classified service. The latter under our system are, as a rule, chosen largely with reference to political considerations and, as a rule, are and expect to be changed with the change of parties. In the classified service, however, the choice is made without reference to political considerations and the tenure of office is unaffected by the change of parties. Under these circumstances it is obvious that different standpoints of conduct apply to the two cases. In consideration of fixity of tenure and of appointment in no way due to political considerations, the man in the classified service, while retaining his right to vote as he pleases and to express privately his opinions on all political subjects, 'should not take any active part in political management or in political campaigns, for precisely the same reasons that a judge, an army officer, a regular soldier, or a policeman is debarred from taking such active part.' This of course, applies even more strongly to any conduct on the part of such employee so prejudicial

12

issued an order that all employees serving in any of the Executive Departments were forbidden under penalty of dismissal to solicit, either individually or through associations, an increase of pay or to attempt to influence in their own interests any legislation whatever, save through the heads of the departments under which they served.

This order aroused much indignation among the employees affected, and some members of Congress, anxious to curry favor with these organizations (which were becoming powerful in their respective districts), criticized it sharply.

As the order of the President had been prepared in the office of the Commission I defended it in an interview saying that it was directed against an evil which had led in some cases to the looting of the Treasury at the solicitation of employees. The people in the public service had shorter hours than in private employment; they were, in the lower grades at least, better

---

to good discipline as is implied in a public attack on his or her superior officers or other conduct liable to cause scandal.

"It seemed to me at the time, and I still think that the line thus drawn was wise and proper. After my experience under two Presidents—one of my own political faith and one not—I had become convinced that it was undesirable and impossible to lay down a rule for public officers not in the classified service which should limit their political activity as strictly as we could rightly and properly limit the activity of those in whose choice and retention the element of political considerations did not enter; and afterwards I became convinced that in its actual construction, if there was any pretense of applying it impartially, it inevitably worked unevenly and, as a matter of fact, inevitably produced an impression of hypocrisy in those who asserted that it worked evenly. Officeholders must not use their offices to control political movements, must not neglect their public duties, must not cause public scandal by their activity; but outside of the classified service the effort to go further than this had failed so signally at the time when the Eleventh Report, which you have quoted, was written, and its unwisdom had been so thoroughly demonstrated, that I felt it necessary to try to draw the distinction therein indicated."

This letter was generally published and the principles it announced became the rule of action for the different departments.

Our Commission believed that the standards here adopted were the highest which were practicable at that time and that in enforcing them performance might always keep pace with promise, which would not be true if a more exacting standard were adopted.

paid, yet many were continually importuning Congressmen for laws granting increase of salaries, additional leaves of absence, still shorter hours, and other favors benefiting themselves at the expense of the public. Sometimes they threatened to defeat a Congressman for reëlection if he would not accede to their demands. It certainly would be against good administration in the army and navy if those in the service should be allowed to lobby in their own behalf. What would be thought of an association of captains, lieutenants, and enlisted men engaged in importuning Congressmen for increase of pay? But this would be no more a violation of good discipline than in the civil service. There was nothing in the President's order which prevented employees from presenting their claims through the heads of the departments under which they served and it would be subversive of all order that they should go outside and endeavor to secure favorable action in opposition to these departments.

I was asked what I thought of the claim that the order was a violation of the constitutional right of petition, and I answered:

I think this is about as sensible as to claim that it was violating the right of free speech if a man in the service were to be dismissed because he had called his superior officer a fool or a scoundrel. Of course, all Americans have a right to assemble and petition for a redress of grievances, but they have no inalienable right to hold public office and while they hold such office they have no right to violate the rules of good discipline. I see that one of the Democratic members of Congress speaks of this as an infamous order and calls it a ukase, saying that the President has given material for the campaign which will largely aid this fall in electing a Democratic House. If this be representative of Democratic sentiment I must congratulate the party on having discovered a superb foundation for future success. In these days when the silver plank is a little rickety, when even the project of consigning the Philippines to the devil is not without its difficulties, our Democratic friends have now found a secure and immutable foundation for political success in the sacred right of officeholders to raid the Treasury for their own benefit. I hope these gentlemen will not abandon the ground so skillfully chosen. [1]

---

[1] The President's order did something in restricting open lobbying by officeholders but the evil still remained a serious one. Later, on April 8, 1912, President Taft superseded this order and provided instead that com-

CODIFICATION OF THE RULES

The rules adopted by the Civil Service Commission had received so many amendments at different times that they constituted a rather confused mass of badly arranged provisions and we determined to re-codify the whole. This had been attempted by previous Commissioners but they had found so many points upon which they could not agree that it was said their sessions on the subject were like the meetings of a debating club; nothing was done and the effort was abandoned.

In our case, however, the utmost harmony prevailed, and we had no difficulty in framing, with the valuable assistance of Mr. Doyle, our secretary, a new set of rules, greatly condensed and simplified, which embodied substantially all the provisions of the former rules and the amendments with a few trifling changes. This new "Justinian Code" as we called it was submitted to the heads of the various departments and approved by them and was promulgated by the President in April, 1903. It remained in force for many years with but few alterations.

SPECIAL EXCEPTIONS

Under Section 2 of the Civil Service Act the President was authorized to make special exceptions and to appoint particu-

---

munications to Congress by employees should be transmitted through the heads of departments who should forward them without delay with such comments as they deemed requisite. The Post Office Appropriation Act, approved August 24th of the same year, allowed postal employees to organize and to affiliate with outside organizations which did not impose an obligation to strike and the act declared that their right either individually or collectively to petition or furnish information to Congress should not be denied or interfered with.

The dangers incident to such legislation would be particularly great in time of war, when the entire postal service or that of the War Department or other vital branches of the government might be paralyzed by the combined action of the employees.

I remember that some years after this at an annual meeting of the National Civil Service Reform League in Chicago, a member of one of these organizations denounced Mr. Roosevelt as "the greatest enemy civil service reform ever had." It was not hard to divine the particular act which lay at the foundation of such a judgment.

lar individuals or provide for the appointment of particular classes without examination.

One of the earliest questions which came up for consideration after I became Commissioner was whether it was better to except the place or the individual. Early in November, 1901, we were asked to except from competitive examination a laborer with the duties of coachman in the office of the Assistant Secretary of the Navy. This place had been included in the competitive service by the general blanket order of President Cleveland some years before. I confess it seemed to me rather absurd to require a competitive examination for such a place. Some time before when the Commission had certified for the position of a coachman the three highest names on a skilled labor register of persons who had had experience in that kind of work, it turned out that one of the men had been driving a milk-wagon, the second a hearse, and the third a street-car. We might indeed have instituted a special test for this particular place and have added to the gayety of Washington by a competitive trot down Pennsylvania Avenue, but this alternative did not seem desirable. We thought we ought to let the secretary appoint his own coachman and the question was whether it was better to except the particular man whom the secretary desired to appoint or to except in general the position of coachman. I thought we should except the position generally, but Mr. Proctor, the President of the Commission, who had had much more experience, said to me, "If we except coachmen in general we shall find that every place filled by any man who ever drives a horse will at once become an excepted place. Coachmen will multiply like gooseberries and instead of letting down the rules in one case you will let them down in fifty. Let us just except this one man and have it stop right here." He convinced me. We accordingly recommended to the President that exceptions should be made of particular individuals and not of general classes of places. When each man's name had to be published, with the reasons for the exception, thus exposing to criticism each special case in its most obnoxious form, it was quite certain that the number of such exceptions would never grow so fast as it would if they could be made wholesale by a single stroke of the pen, and where it could only be ascertained after an investigation how many had got in by each exception.   During the year ending June 30, 1902, there were only twenty of these special exceptions, in the following year there were twenty-five.   In most of these cases they were necessary or desirable though there were a few dictated by considerations of benevolence; an appointment, for instance, of a man who had become injured while in the service, to a position which he was able to fill but to which he would not otherwise have been eligible.   I do not remember a single case where the appointment was made for political reasons.

Yet criticism came in abundance.   This thing was represented as a complete overthrow of the competitive principle. It was stated that President Roosevelt had made a larger number of irregular appointments than any of his predecessors, while the fact was that during his whole first term there were some sixty cases of such suspensions of the rules and only thirty-three of these were persons who were allowed to enter the service without examination.   This was less than one twentieth of one per cent of the appointments. They included such exceptions as that of the steward in the White House, two special agents in the Bureau of Corporations, the Superintendent of the Government Hospital for the Insane, and other cases where, on account of special reasons, the application of the rules was considered impracticable, unwise, unjust, or unnecessary.

At a meeting of the National Civil Service Reform League held in Washington in 1904, after I had ceased to be Commissioner, there were serious criticisms made of this method of excepting special individuals.   Mr. Schurz regarded it "as a very dangerous venture in its ulterior consequences, weakening popular confidence and increasing pressure for further exceptions."   Others insisted that if exceptions were made it should be done in accordance with fixed rules; that this had been the former practice; that the civil service system could not be safely administered in any other way, and that the logical consequences of a continuance of special exceptions would be the restoration of the spoils system. There was held up to us for emulation the example of a certain judge who had declared that it was not his duty to administer justice but only the law.

As I was largely responsible for the new practice, I felt bound to defend it. I observed in reply that the example of the judge was hardly applicable to executive action and that I doubted whether it was the highest ideal even for judicial action. It reminded me of the definition given when I was examined for admission to the bar. The examiners asked one of the candidates the question "What is a Court?" and the candidate in his confusion parodied Blackstone's definition and said, "It is a place where *injustice* is judiciously administered." I thought we had better have a President to whom considerations of justice as well as law were not wholly alien. Even in the development of the law, those were not the worst judges by whose judicial discretion that great system of equity jurisprudence was developed out of the special cases "where the law by reason of its universality was deficient." But whether that were a good thing for a judge or not, the executive office was different. Our constitution placed in the hands of our President the pardoning power, which was wholly discretionary. Our laws provided for the punishment of crime. They were universal but would it be said that the pardoning power (even though it might sometimes be abused) should be wholly taken away from our executive? Whether justice, mercy, or expediency demanded its exercise it also supplied a defect in those things where the law by reason of its universality was deficient.

I took an illustration of these special exceptions. One of the instances cited was the appointment of a doorkeeper for the White House on the ground that such doorkeeper "must possess qualifications not ordinarily found in the executive service." It might seem strange that a mere doorkeeper should be specially excepted for this reason but those who remembered the assassination of Garfield and McKinley would realize that for the place of doorkeeper in the White House a man was required with a special knowledge of faces and character and a knowledge of the proper way to act under critical conditions which might require the utmost responsibility. One case after another might be taken and it would be found that there was some good reason for nearly all of them.[1]

The question whether it was better to except a single person or an entire class was not passed upon by the League. I still regard our plan as much the better one.

Of course it is inconsistent with the general principle that appointments should be made by rule and the danger is, just as in the case of pardons, that improper cases will creep in and that men will be appointed from motives of benevolence, friendship, personal convenience, and the like and in some cases this occurs. But such evils are less than the exception of entire classes for the sake of consistency and uniformity which is the inevitable alternative in every case where an exception is really necessary. The important thing is to see that unnecessary exceptions are not made.[2]

The average number of special exceptions annually during Mr. Roosevelt's two administrations was fifty-eight, Mr. Taft's sixty-two, and they did not materially increase since that time, up to the outbreak of the war.

ENFORCEMENT OF THE LAW. INVESTIGATIONS

Important as were the extensions of the classified lists and the changes in the rules, the most important service which the

[1] The Boston *Herald* on December 14, 1904, criticized me for excepting the coachman and not insisting upon the competitive examination, saying it was a case of favoritism, pure and simple. "Mr. Foulke's logical error is in maintaining that a man not eligible to the classified service had to be gotten into it somehow, because some one of influence insisted upon it."

In answer to this article I referred to the time when the Commission had adopted the plan recommended by the *Herald* and certified the driver of the milk wagon, the hearse, and the street car, adding that it was just this sort of hyper-criticism which enfeebled the efforts of the Commission to strengthen the law in public opinion, and that it was stickling for just such trifles in opposition to plain common sense which was calculated to divide the counsels of those who ought to be working together for the advancement of civil service reform.

[2] To accomplish this a valuable suggestion was made by Mr. Choate,

President rendered the reform was by his strict and impartial enforcement of the law. Up to this time the Civil Service Act had been largely regarded as a theoretical statute to be enforced only in cases where it was politically convenient and desirable. It was not until Mr. Roosevelt's administration that offenders were actually taken by the nape of the neck and ejected from the public service for violating this law.[1]

President of the League, at its meeting in Pittsburg, Dec. 17, 1908, and adopted in its resolutions, that the application for a special exception should be first made to and investigated by the Civil Service Commission.

[1] Among the more important cases disposed of were the following:

Charles E. Sapp, Collector, and Leonard Parsons, Deputy Collector of Internal Revenue at Louisville, were both separated from the service (as we have already seen) for collecting campaign funds, and they, together with Joseph Potoning, who had solicited such funds, were afterwards indicted, pleaded guilty, and were sentenced; Sapp and Potoning to a fine of $500 and Parsons to a fine of $200.

Collector Dillon, at El Paso, who had caused frauds to be committed in the examinations in that city, was removed from office.

C. O. Self, a clerk in the office of the Commissioner of Internal Revenue, was dismissed because he refused to furnish to the Commission information and testimony regarding violations of the law in Terre Haute, Indiana.

D. A. Nunn, Collector of Internal Revenue at Nashville, Tennessee, made a clean sweep of the subordinates in his office for political reasons. The Commission recommended his removal and he resigned.

James M. Curley and Thomas F. Curley were convicted of impersonating two candidates at a civil service examination in Boston and were sentenced to two months in jail. It is a rather remarkable commentary upon public opinion in that city that some years afterwards James M. Curley was elected Mayor.

In the office of Appraiser W. F. Wakeman of Brooklyn, examiners had been irregularly chosen, there were many temporary appointments in violation of the rules, and laborers had been assigned to classified duties. On October 29, 1901, the Commission submitted to the President a memorandum of the facts and on December 21st, Wakeman was removed, other causes contributing to his removal. A year later in a letter to the Commission he demanded a public apology and correction of our Nineteenth Report, which referred to his delinquencies, declaring it to be false, misleading, and unjust. We asked him in what respect but received no answer. Accordingly, on January 28, 1903, we addressed him a public letter, stating that the only correction which was desirable was to say that the Nineteenth Report contained a very incomplete presentation of his numerous acts of obstruction which had extended over several years, were

The recommendations of the Commission as to the punishment of offenders were nearly always adopted. In one case

established by repeated investigations, and abundantly shown by the records of the Commission and of the Treasury Department. We specified in detail a number of his violations of the law and thus concluded:

"These cases are shown by the records to which you appeal; at the President's request a statement was furnished to him shortly before your removal and was considered by him in determining whether you should continue in office. It may be that other reasons for your removal which were disconnected with the civil service law were considered still graver and led more directly to your separation from the service, but if so, we should think that you would be the last person to insist that this was the fact. Since you demand a public statement we think you are entitled to it."

One of my earliest cases was an investigation into the fairness of an examination held in June, 1901, for special statistical compiler for the Department of Agriculture. It appeared that the employees in the Division of Statistics were assisted in their preparation for this examination by Mrs. Bertha Burch, stenographer and clerk, in pursuance of instructions from John Hyde, the statistician, to give them all the help in this examination she "legitimately" could. The information she gave them included matters embraced in at least six questions afterwards asked in the examinations. Mr. Hyde admitted it was his desire to avoid a certification from our eligible registers and to secure instead a special examination where employees were aided in their preparation for it by their assignments of work and that he had not expected that any others could pass. We regarded such conditions as unfair to outside competitors. The examination was accordingly set aside.

In some of our investigations of course the charges were not sustained. For instance, on March 10, 1902, T.W. Wittler, a clerk in the Chicago post office, alleged that the postmaster, F. E. Coyne, had twice reduced him in place and salary for political reasons and had then removed him. The investigation proved that the reductions were made because of the lack of harmony between Wittler and his subordinates and that he was afterwards dismissed because he refused to accept his reduced position.

A statement was made to the Commission that Postmaster George H. Roberts had made removals, reductions, and appointments in unclassified positions in the Brooklyn post office for political reasons. I went to Brooklyn and investigated the matter thoroughly, but the evidence did not sufficiently establish the fact.

In other cases there were reasonable grounds for leniency. In May, 1902, I went to Terre Haute and made an investigation of the alleged political coercion of employees and political discrimination in the assignment of storekeeper gaugers to duty, by John R. Bonnell, Collector of

however[1] the evidence was considered insufficient and in another there were extenuating circumstances that led to milder treatment.[2]

There was a case of political assessments in Pennsylvania in which Senator Quay was implicated. A circular had been sent out by the State Republican Committee, of which Mr. Quay was chairman, signed by him, soliciting contributions from office-holders. Commissioner Garfield at once reported the fact to the President, who directed him to inform the Senator that this

---

Internal Revenue. The evidence showed no coercion though it appeared there was some political discrimination in the assignments, which had been made by the collector under a misapprehension as to his rights, he having been recently appointed and unfamiliar with the duties of the place. I thought the circumstances did not indicate a willful violation of the law and did not justify his removal and he was warned that if similar complaints were made in the future serious consequences would follow.

An amusing letter was sent to me upon this subject, from an unknown correspondent at Crawsfordsville, Indiana, as follows: "I do not endorse your decision in the Bonnell case. He violated one of the most important provisions of the law. He lives here and is active in the management of the party and is as much entitled as anyone to be classed as head cook and bottle washer. It is my opinion that you cannot make many such decisions as the Bonnell case without losing your influence as a Civil Service Reformer. Mr. Bonnell may very properly be classed as one who needs to be placed under the restraining influence of the civil service law in office."

To this I answered: "Your views would indicate that hereafter I ought to pay less attention to the evidence and more to the opinion of those who have not heard it. Unfortunately, a habit contracted through some years' experience in practicing in the courts will still prevent my adopting that view, even though I incur the risk of losing my influence. Nor do I understand how it is that Mr. Bonnell needs to be placed under the restraining influence of the civil service law when in office, if according to your judgment in another part of your letter he ought to be kicked out of office at once."

[1] The Commission preferred charges against Park Agnew, Collector of Internal Revenue and Morgan Treat, United States Marshal in Virginia, for being concerned in the solicitation of campaign funds, but upon a hearing before the Attorney-General to whom the matter was referred by the President, it was decided that the evidence was not sufficient to show their participation in the soliciting circular.

[2] The case of Wm. T. Sullivan and Charles L. Doran, post office inspectors at Denver.

request for contributions must be immediately and publicly withdrawn as it was an express violation of the law. It was thought more could be accomplished in this way than by a criminal prosecution which had small chance of success. Quay at once withdrew the circular in a written statement which was generally published and circulated. But afterwards another letter was sent out signed by the treasurer of the committee, and upon the letter head was the name of Quay, showing that he was its chairman. One of these letters came to my notice. I showed it to the President and he sent me to Philadelphia to tell Mr. Quay that this letter, like the other, would have to be withdrawn at once. I did so and Quay said to me: " I won't do it. I would do more for the President than for any man living. I withdrew the previous letter but this one was written when I was off in another part of the State trying to settle the coal strike. I did not know anything about the sending of the letter and therefore I will not withdraw it. I made a fool of myself once to oblige the President and I won't do it again. Let him have me indicted if he will. But," he added significantly, " I hope he won't do that before the election."

I at once communicated this answer to Mr. Roosevelt, who suggested that I lay the matter before the Attorney General to see whether a prosecution could be sustained. Mr. Knox however decided that it would be useless, inasmuch as we were entirely without proof that Mr. Quay had taken any part in sending the latter communication or even knew that it had been sent.

No doubt mistakes were made in some of our investigations and a few like those last mentioned had no results but on the whole those in charge of the various branches of the government became well convinced that the civil service law had to be respected as much as any other and the violations of it became fewer and fewer.

POST OFFICE SCANDALS

While I was on the Commission a serious scandal arose in the Post Office Department involving a considerable number of the officials. Among these was Mr. Beavers, Chief of the Salary and Allowance Division. None of the officials implicated had entered the service through the competitive system and the disclosures formed an impressive commentary on congressional patronage and the interference of Congressmen in the department.

When the charges were first made Congress asked for a report of the facts and Mr. Bristow, then Fourth Assistant Postmaster-General, was directed to conduct an investigation. His report showed that about one hundred and fifty Congressmen had been seeking favors of Mr. Beavers, asking increases of allowances at different post offices, many of which increases were illegal and fraudulent.

Beavers was soon under indictment and there was a large number of Congressmen to whom a certain share of suspicion attached. The constituents of these men began to find fault and the result was a tremendous outcry in the House of Representatives. The report was declared to be a libel on Congress. The men who prepared it were called liars and scoundrels and the Post Office Department in general, including officials who had no hand at all in its preparation, was denounced in unmeasured terms.[1]

When the guilty officials were tried Beavers and some others were convicted and served terms in the penitentiary.

[1] The New York Evening *Post* asked me what I thought of the matter and I said: "Congress wanted a report of the facts and now howls with rage and pain when the consequences of its own demand are found to be so destructive to its peace of mind. In making this uproar it will not have the sympathy of the country. There are, no doubt, Congressmen who have innocently made these requests for favors from the indicted official but the essential fact is that they had no business to be asking such favors at all. Congressmen are sent to Washington for other purposes. . . . Many of the members spend, apparently, about half their time in congressional work and the rest of it 'legging' from one Department to another trying to get a pension here, a promotion there, a transfer yonder, and an increase of allowance somewhere else.

"This business is simply detestable. Congress has an undoubted right, by means of legislation, to control the administrative branches of the government and through its committees to make inquiries, to take testimony, and call on the departments for every possible aid in its legislative

An entertaining episode of my service upon the Commission was a controversy upon the floor of the Senate in respect to the right of a Commissioner publicly to defend his own acts. We had investigated charges of the collection of campaign funds by Joseph Perrault, Surveyor General of Idaho, Banford A. Robb, his chief clerk, and Elmer E. Forshay, his chief draughtsman. Perrault refused to testify. We notified the President. His term had expired and he was not reappointed. Robb resigned, and Forshay was dismissed.

On February 17, 1903, Senator Du Bois from that State charged in the Senate that we had unjustly procured Forshay's removal, since Forshay, he said, had acted under duress, and that we had attempted to conceal the facts and had refused to furnish to him proper information when requested. He introduced a resolution that the Commission send to the Senate a statement of the charges and the evidence. Senator Spooner opposed this resolution on the ground that the Senate could not properly devote its time to inquiring into each case of removal.

The charges were entirely without foundation. The Commission had not refused to furnish any information and Forshay had not been acting under duress. I therefore believed it to be my right and duty, as one of the Commissioners involved, to deny the charges thus unjustly made and I accordingly wrote to Senator Spooner and to two other Senators saying that if not opposed to the public interests I sincerely hoped the Senate would adopt the Du Bois resolution and let us furnish the evidence. In my letter I pointed out various inaccuracies in the remarks of Senator Du Bois and also in a

---

work. But single members of Congress acting in their individual capacity have no right whatever to belabor these departments with personal importunities.

"The wrath of the Congressmen, now that their peccadilloes are to be ventilated, will awaken the laughter rather than the sympathy of the country, and where, as in some cases, the thing is more than a peccadillo, it will arouse the just resentment of their constituents and some of them may very properly be elected to stay at home."

statement of Senator Bacon of Georgia who had said that it
seemed to be a conceded fact that the Commission had unjustly visited its condemnation upon the young man Forshay
and had failed to extend it to the officer under whose command
the violation of the law had been perpetrated—a statement
quite at variance with the facts. My letter was sent by Senator Spooner to the reading desk and read to the Senate by the
secretary. The resolution of Senator Du Bois was accordingly
adopted and we furnished to the Senate the charges and
evidence. A whole special session of the Senate now elapsed
and that body adjourned without making any investigation
or even referring the matter to a committee. Moreover
Senator Du Bois on February 25th had admitted that the
statement made by him in regard to the removal of Forshay,
which was the whole gravamen of the accusation, was incorrect.
Yet Senator Bacon declared that I had no right to address
to individual Senators a letter pointing out these inaccuracies.
He said:

> I am not going to dignify those subordinate officials by entering into a
> controversy with them on this floor as to whether or not what I said was
> correct, or whether what they say in reply is correct. I think it a matter
> of supreme effrontery on the part of these subordinates that they should
> assume to enter into the debates of the Senate in any such way. It is a
> gross, inexcusable breach of the privilege of the Senate.

I accordingly wrote to Senator Spooner on March 19th,
reviewing the facts and adding:

> Thus the paradox is presented, that although the charge was untrue, I
> had no right to point out the particulars in which it was untrue, even in
> letters to individual Senators. In other words, according to Senator Bacon,
> the Senate is not willing to know from the official criticized whether what is
> said on the floor is correct or incorrect, and will not permit men whose con-
> duct is publicly attacked to show that the attack is unwarranted. If his
> position is sound, it would be the duty of executive officers to submit in
> absolute silence to the gravest charges of misconduct or even of crime
> uttered in the most public place in the nation. No self-respecting man could
> hold an administrative office under such conditions. I submit that it is
> not *to my letter* that the epithet of "supreme effrontery" can most fitly
> be applied. . . . I do not believe that any considerable number of Senators
> will insist upon such a doctrine of senatorial *lèse majesté* as will prevent any

officer, however humble the position he may hold, from protecting himself
against unfounded accusations by every lawful means in his power.[1]

CONCLUSION OF OFFICIAL LIFE

For more than a year I had been suffering from an affection
of the heart and my physician had told me that if I continued
to work as I had been doing my life would be greatly shortened.
I was accordingly constrained, in the spring of 1903, to give
up my place on the Commission. I had intended for some
time to do this but at a somewhat later period, resigning to take
part in the presidential campaign of 1904, in which Mr. Roosevelt (whom I determined actively to support) would be a
candidate.[2] My increasing ill health however made it necessary for me to leave sooner than I intended.

[1] The press of the country seemed to take my part. The Washington
correspondent of the New York *Evening Post* remarked: "When one
Senator corrects another's misstatements some days after their utterance, it
is a pretty fair sign that he was belated in learning the truth himself, and
whether in the meantime he ascertained it through the newspapers or from
a book or in a conversation across a dinner table or from a friend's letter,
how is the question affected or the Senator's dignity concerned? To
everyone outside of the sacred four walls of the Senate Chamber such an
assumption seems as comical as the pretensions of the grand Llama of
Tibet. Almost every other petty officeholder, like a Civil Service Commissioner, would have gone in and hid his head after such a dressing down
as Mr. Foulke received that day, but he has a strenuous streak in his composition which makes him slightly uncomfortable when things are moving
too smoothly. Instead of admitting that he had done wrong and deserved
his punishment, he actually assumed that it was his critics who had offended
and that they would hasten as soon as they were cool once more to retract
their assaults upon him. He waited all through the regular session and
all through the special session in vain. Then out he came with his second
letter, addressed like its predecessor to Senator Spooner. Probably whenever his name or that of the Commission comes up next winter in the
Senate he will get his response to this communication in turn. If the
Senators who descanted upon Mr. Foulke's impropriety of conduct expect
thus to move the President to turn him out of office they have poor
memories. No Civil Service Commissioner was ever more given to speak
his mind of the Senators than Mr. Roosevelt." Here the article cited Mr.
Roosevelt's controversies when Commissioner with Senators Gorman,
Plumb, Stewart, Gallinger, Mitchell, and others under similar conditions.
[2] I had previously spoken of this to a number of my friends and naturally

The President was in the West and would not return for a considerable time.   I learned that on a certain date he would come as far east as Kansas and I met him in a little town in the western part of that State where I explained to him my inability to continue the work and gave him my resignation which he accepted with many kindly expressions of regret and friendship.   In a very short time I was on my way to Europe to take treatment at the baths at Nauheim, which I repeated nearly every year until the outbreak of the great war.

For many reasons I was very sorry to quit the service. Life in Washington had been delightful and I could but feel that the competitive system had been making long strides ahead.   In spite of the controversies with various members of Congress, that body had become more tolerant of our work and had given us the additional appropriations necessary to carry it on.   Indeed, the House of Representatives had voted for this in December, 1902, without a dissenting voice.   The National Civil Service Reform League had spoken in warm approval of the progress made.   My resignation was given on April 30th, but at the President's request it was not published

---

the newspapers learned of it, upon which the Washington *Post*, which had always been poking fun at the Commission, published on April 21st an editorial containing the following:

  " We were a long time catching Foulke, and now that we have got him, we shall not let him escape without a struggle.   Who has contributed so much in the same period to the gayety of nations?   Who has rapped fault-finding newspaper editors over the knuckles with the same expansive glee?   Who has jumped into squabbles with a finer indifference to consequences, when he saw a head sticking up that he believed he could hit? Who but he ever put the astute Spooner into a defensive position among his colleagues by so simple a process as writing him a letter which he would publish without reading?   Who ever told the whole Senate what he thought of its authority over the office holding freeman and snapped his fingers in its august face with more unceremonious directness? . . .

  "Nay, nay!. There is still work to be done in Washington which only Foulke can do.   Indiana can take care of herself.   She has been carried before without the aid of civil service reformers.   There is no reason, in view of her record in politics, why Foulke—our Foulke—should immolate himself on the altar of strenuous oratory and leave the Capital of the nation widowed."

nor generally known in order that he might not be unnecessarily pressed in regard to my successor.   Mr. Alford Warriner Cooley was afterwards appointed to the place—a very admirable appointment—and later Mr. H. F. Green was appointed to the position which had already been vacated by Mr. Garfield.[1]

[1] Shortly after I had sailed for Europe a very flattering article on the retiring Commissioner appeared in the New York *Evening Post*, written by its Washington correspondent, Mr. Francis E. Leupp.   And about the same time the New York *Sun*, which for many years had been deriding civil service reform, published the following which, although filled with imaginative material, expressed fairly well the idea of the opponents of the reform concerning the progress made:

> "The butcher, the baker, the candlestick maker
>   Are all on the classified list.
> The watchman and fireman, the cook and the pieman
>   Must do just what we insist.
> The porter and painter, the plumber and waiter
>   Are examined when we demand.
> Oh, we're getting them all, they come at our call,
>   And we're right up behind the band.

"That is one stanza of the 'Anthem of the Civil Service Commission,' also known as 'The Song of the C. S. C.' There are sixteen other stanzas and they are all on the same order and just as good.   They set forth the expansion policy of the Commission and describe as fully as can be done in poetry turned out with a conscientious regard for feet as well as sentiment, the manner in which this particular branch of the government service is practicing a new kind of benevolent assimilation.

" According to the best authority—which is a delicate way of intimating that somebody is afraid of getting hurt if it became known that he let out the secret—the anthem was left to the Civil Service Commission as a legacy by the Hon. William Dudley Foulke—'our Dudley,' as he is proudly and familiarly called in Washington—who resigned his office some months ago in order to tighten the Indiana cinch of the Republican presidential saddle.   As a matter of fact, the announcement of Mr. Foulke's authorship of the 'Song of the C. S. C.' should not occasion even a ripple of surprise.

"Almost all of Mr. Foulke's moments of relaxation and recreation from his arduous duties as a member of the Civil Service Commission were devoted to the discomfiture and undoing of such critics of that body as he considered worthy of his ink and steel.   It was Mr. Foulke who trifled with the dignity of the United States Senate at the last session of Congress, just as his friend, former commissioner, now President Roosevelt did some years ago, and it was Mr. Foulke who damned a torrent of abuse eloquent from the pen of an irate editor with the now famous remark that his critic argued like the man who defined a crab as 'a small red fish that walks backward.' It is true that the editor, in a final letter, rude in tone and chary of words, insisted that a small red fish that went the wrong way had nothing to do with the administration of the civil service laws, but Mr. Foulke's admirers and friends took this as a confession of weakness on the critic's part, and as no high class argument anyhow.

"In the brief intervals when Mr. Foulke was not transacting business nor writing letters, he was thinking up ways and means to extend the powers of the Commission. He was the moving spirit in the blanketing scheme which resulted in general orders from President Roosevelt placing the entire rural free delivery, with its thousands of employees, under the civil service, and celebrated this achievement by twisting a somewhat familiar advertising catch-phrase into the aggressive announcement: 'Anybody! Everybody! Everybody! Anybody! Get examined by the civil service man.'

"Mr. Foulke was also the inventor and elaborator of the extended registry system now in use, which has made the Commission similar to an employment agency on a gigantic scale, with ability to furnish from its eligible list men and women capable of filling any job under the sun, including a selected assortment of mechanics, interpreters, snake catchers, nurses, anthropologists, physicians, hodcarriers, lawyers, bricklayers, brass finishers, and ordinary government clerks.

"In view of the many instances in which Mr. Foulke evinced his versatility and talent, the 'Song of the C. S. C.' hadn't been out very long before it was generally understood that he was the author. And the song itself, expressing as it does, all the ends, aims, hopes, and desires of the Commission and jingling through its sixteen stanzas to a mighty catchy air —Mr. Foulke hasn't been accused of writing the music—had made a great hit with the employees of that particular branch of the government service.

"A Washington citizen heard about the song some days ago and decided to procure a copy. His visit to headquarters was decidedly interesting.

"He arrived at Eighth and E Streets, where the Civil Service building is located, just at lunch time. On a wide ledge, just outside the front door, a colored messenger was sitting, kicking his heels against the bricks and whistling with all the strength of his lungs a catchy but unfamiliar air.

"'What's that?' asked the citizen, who has lived in official Washington so long that he is politely curious and curiously polite from mere force of habit.

"'That's the anthem of this here commishun,' was the reply. 'Ain't it got a shuffle! Suttently do mek my feet itch. I'se been promised a copy of the words this evenin'.'

"The messenger took up the tune where he left off and the visitor entered the building.

"'Good morning,' he said to the elevator man, but that official was otherwise engaged and didn't answer.

"A sheet of paper was fastened to one side of the wire cage on a level with his eyes, and he was singing, in a very audible tone, as he clutched the starting lever from force of habit:

"'The kickers and knockers and growlers, you know,
    May roast us as much as they please,
But they've only a show for the government dough
    If they pass their exams. with ease.
No official nor clerk with a shirk to his work
    Can bluff us with frown or glad hand.
Oh, we're getting them all, they come at our call,
    And we're right up behind the band.'

"'Howdy,' said the elevator man when he had finished. 'That's the twelfth verse,' he added with almost proprietary pride, 'and the rest are all just as good. It ain't no weak wishy-washy stuff about trees and flowers and love and sad sea waves. It's somethin' a feller can understand and sing without feelin' foolish. There ain't nobody but Mr. Foulke can write stuff like that.'

"The elevator man became so interested in describing the merits of the anthem that he took the visitor to the top floor by mistake and had to be punched in the ribs for a reminder. When he let the passenger out and shut the door for the down trip, he was so busy with the thirteenth stanza that he appeared in danger of bringing up with a bump at the basement.

"The visitor was considerably interested and a whole lot amused by this time and thought it possible that Secretary Doyle could settle the authorship of the anthem. Mr. Doyle is an austere individual of some forty-odd winters, who has a severely aquiline nose, a firm mouth, and a firmer jaw, and who is partial to somber-hued raiment of a clerical cut. In the language of the Irish applicant for a government position who, at a recent examination before the Commission, read the Thirteenth Amendment to the Constitution from a page of the Postal Laws and Regulations and was somewhat hastily rejected in consequence, 'Mr. Doyle is a cowld, har-rd man.'

"Consequently the visitor gasped with surprise when, on entering the secretary's private office, he found Mr. Doyle with an expression of intense enjoyment on his aristocratic countenance, beating time with a ruler on his polished desk top and singing, in a voice grown a trifle rusty from disuse:

"'I think we may say, as we work day by day,
    To show what a pupil ain't worth,
That at some future date, just when we won't state,
    We will rule o'er a classified earth.

When everyone here, on this eligible sphere,
    Will greet us with outstretched hand.
Oh, we're getting them all, they come at our call,
    And we're right up behind the band.'

"When Mr. Doyle perceived his astonished visitor, he blushed like a schoolgirl, cleared his throat with an official rasp, frowned severely, and began to muss up some paper on his desk.

"'Good morning,' he said with a remarkable access of dignity. 'What can I do for you this morning, sir?'

"'You might tell me the name of the author of that popular ditty,' answered the citizen.

"Mr. Doyle mussed up some more papers.

"'I really cannot give you the desired information,' he said. 'A copy of that—er—somewhat frivolous composition was left on my desk the other day and I was—er—merely enjoying—I should say, trifling in a moment of relaxation.'

"'Oh,' said the visitor. 'Then you can give me your copy? I should like to have one.'

"'I should be pleased to do so,' returned the secretary, his dignity well in hand, 'but the fact is, I—er—have promised the only one I have to—er—a friend.'

"The visitor decided that he would have to go back and borrow the elevator man's copy of the 'Song of the C. S. C.' and on his way down the hall stopped to pass the time of day with Commissioner Greene. Mr. Greene is rotund and good natured, and on this particular occasion he was standing at the window, drumming with his finger tips on the pane, and singing merrily:

"'When we rule every job on the classified earth,
    We'll turn our attention to Mars,
And when there's a dearth of classified worth
    We'll examine the classified stars.
We're here with our lists and we're here with the jobs,
    And we trust you will understand
That we're getting them all, the great and the small,
    And are right up behind the band.'

"'Mr. Commissioner,' said the visitor, in desperation, 'everybody in the building is singing that infernal song and I want a copy of it. Have you one to spare?'

"'Why, of course,' said Mr. Greene, pulling out a drawer of the desk formerly occupied by Commissioner Foulke. 'Here are half a dozen. Help yourself.'

"The visitor took two neatly typewritten copies of the 'Song of the C. S. C.' and remarked earnestly:

"'Mr. Commissioner, I wish you would tell me who wrote this song.'

"The Commissioner smiled a wide smile, stuck his hands in his pockets, and closed his left eye for a brief space.

"'I'm blessed if I know,' he remarked cheerfully."

CHAPTER XIII

In the fall of 1903, I returned from Europe considerably improved in health and at a meeting of the Council of the League on October 7th, I was again elected a member of that body from which I had resigned when I became Commissioner and was soon working again with my old friends in the same way as before.

I attended the annual meeting at Baltimore, December 10 and 11, 1903, and there delivered an address in a rather triumphant strain on "The Advance of the Competitive System," showing the immense strides which civil service reform had made since the passage of the law and particularly during the administration of President Roosevelt, and pointing out the need of consolidating and strengthening the things we had gained by suitable provisions against superannuation in the service.[1]

But the cause of civil service reform now sustained a serious loss in the death of one of its strongest and ablest supporters, the Hon. John R. Proctor, president of the Commission. He had been present and had taken part in the debates at this Baltimore meeting. He had spoken with a number of others at the dinner given at the close of our session, and on the following day on returning to Washington he had been seized with an attack of angina pectoris and after a few hours of intense suffering he expired. He was an able and upright official, an attractive and lovable companion and a loyal friend, and those of us who attended his funeral at St. John's Church, where the President was one of the chief

[1] This address is given in Appendix VIII.

mourners, realized that at no time since the death of George William Curtis and Dorman B. Eaton had so large a vacancy been left in the ranks of the eminent advocates of civil service reform.

The President appointed to succeed him John C. Black, a veteran who had been seriously wounded in the Civil War and who had been Commissioner of Pensions in a previous administration. Mr. Roosevelt made this choice, I think, largely because he believed that the merit system could be strengthened by the participation of one of the active members of the Grand Army of the Republic in the work of the reform. General Black was a man of great eloquence, of the highest character, and devoted to the competitive system, although his advancing age and his infirmities rendered the services which he was able to perform on behalf of the system less effective than if he had been a younger and more vigorous man.

The presidential campaign of 1904 was now approaching. Mr. Roosevelt had been nominated by the Republican party. to succeed himself and Alton B. Parker was the candidate of the Democratic party.   During the summer of this year I had again gone to Nauheim, Germany.   I returned in September. The Democratic platform which had been adopted at St. Louis contained the following:

The Democratic party stands committed to the principle of Civil Service Reform and we demand its honest, just, and impartial enforcement. We denounce the Republican party for its continuous and sinister encroachments upon the spirit and operation of the Civil Service rules, whereby it has arbitrarily dispensed with examinations for office in the interests of favorites and employed all manner of devices to overreach and set aside the principles upon which the Civil Service was based.

I naturally was indignant at such a declaration and said, in an interview, that a more glaring example of impudent mendacity it would be impossible to find.   The resolution contained two distinct falsehoods: first, that the Democratic party was committed to the reform, whereas eight years before, Mr. Bryan, its candidate, went through the country denouncing the system and the platform, practically demanded its repeal, and within four years that platform was reaffirmed and the same candidate renominated. It was equally false to say that the Republicans had made sinister and continual encroachments on the civil service rules, dispensing with examinations in the interest of favorites and employing devices to overreach the law. At no time since the adoption of the law had the rules been so uniformly enforced and the spirit of the reform so consistently observed.

But all through the campaign the drift toward Roosevelt was unmistakable. The huge Democratic transparencies "Parker and Prudence," the demand for the election of a "safe and sane candidate," and the kaleidoscopic shifting of the issues as presented by the Democrats were all extremely uninspiring and there was little surprise when after the election it was found that Mr. Roosevelt had been chosen by the largest majority ever cast up to that time, for an American President.

In this campaign the New York *World*, one of his strongest opponents, declared that the paramount issue was himself, and as this was undoubtedly the fact, the present may not be an inappropriate place to consider what were the qualities by which he had won the confidence of the American people after nearly four years' experience with his administration.

I.   Conspicuous among these was his daring frankness in thought and speech and action. He did not say one thing and mean another. He had no subtlety or diplomatic finesse. He was not lacking in tact but it was the tact that depended upon good sense and love of fair play. He could "think straight and see clear" and he sought his end by the directest road.

II.   His utter fearlessness, not merely of personal danger but of the consequences to himself from doing the thing he believed to be best for the public welfare. When warned that his intervention in the coal strike would blast his future he set his teeth and said, "Yes, I suppose it ends me, but it is right, and I will do it." But he was by no means as rash as many supposed. In important matters he consulted those he trusted and no man was more willing to change his mind if reasons were given to him which he believed were sound. I have seen him reverse his decision in an instant upon a mere suggestion which he recognized was supported by good grounds. Counsel was always welcome to him from sources which he respected but no effort to control him ever succeeded.

III.   His accurate sense of justice.   He wanted every man to have "a square deal."   When he was Civil Service Commissioner he filled the quotas from the South by announcing that Democrats should have just as good a chance for appointment as Republicans.   I think his support of the civil service system was due principally to the fact that this system encouraged fair play, that under it the farmer's lad and mechanic's son, who had no one to speak for them, had the same chance as the social and political favorite.   It was this spirit that led him to declare "The White House door while I am here shall swing open as easily for the laboring man as for the capitalist and *no easier*."   It was natural that his straightforward way of dealing with men should be misunderstood by politicians, who called it the "honesty racket" and exclaimed, "How well he does it!"

IV.   His immense human sympathy.   He was naturally fond of men.   Although of aristocratic lineage and antecedents, he was instinctively drawn to "the plain people." With the policeman, the locomotive engineer, the cowboy, the mountain guide, he had often a closer sympathy than with members of the exclusive social circle in which he was born and bred.   This sympathy had not the least taint of cant or political motive behind it.   It was a corollary to this feeling that he had an implicit reliance upon the mass of the people.   He used to distrust his own skill in handling political conditions but no man since Lincoln ever had a stronger belief in the honesty and good sense of the American electorate.

V.   His prodigious capacity for hard work.   He could think like lightning and weigh in an instant considerations which with others would require a hundred fold the same period of time.   I have seen him go over a huge pile of correspondence, read some of the letters and correct and sign others with great rapidity, and at the same time discuss with a number of visitors seated around his table complicated questions upon an entirely different subject. He did not work as many hours as some other Presidents, such as Mr. Cleveland, but he had an extraordinary faculty of boiling down the thing he had to do and getting it finished. He actually revelled in his work. "It's a pretty hard job here," he once said to me, "but I'm having a good time of it." He not only worked tremendously himself, he also made everybody under him work in the same way. His knowledge of men was extensive and accurate. No one in America had so wide an acquaintance and knew so well how to lay his hand upon the exact man he needed for the task under consideration. And when he had chosen his agent he trusted him with all the details and demanded only results. He wasted no time on trifles. The moment he arrived at a decision he carried it into instant execution.

VI. His inspiring personality. I certainly never knew anyone who could arouse so much enthusiasm and devotion. Those with whom he was associated would go through fire and water to serve him. He was always ready to give the fullest amount of credit where it was due and was generally proud of the men whom he had gathered around him and indeed of all those who coöperated in his undertakings. He once said to me in the early days of his administration, "I have an admirable Cabinet and I have the right to say so for I did not select it." He had retained the members chosen by McKinley.

VII. His practical nature. He had high ideals but he never sought the unattainable. He would not struggle vainly for the perfect and abstract right when he would lose thereby the good that could be accomplished by seeking something less. He had to make all the parts of this great government work together and he would make them work as nearly right as he could but he would never insist vainly upon things which could not be accomplished. Many considered him erratic, "an uncertain quantity." But he was not uncertain in the least. His conduct in any given case *if you knew all the facts* could be predicted more surely, it seemed to me, than that of any other man I ever knew. When you could tell what was the right thing to do so far as that right thing was reasonably attainable you had your answer to the question. It was this consideration which explains his association with Platt, Quay, and other bosses for which Mr. Schurz and others reproached him. He never refused to coöperate in all measures which he deemed desirable with those whom the people had chosen as their representatives, or to maintain friendly relations with them. It was only when they sought to do something which he thought ought not to be done that he stood in their way.

His affections and his antipathies were strong, his personality was masterful, his home life was ideal, his powers of conversation were brilliant. He was constantly bubbling over with merriment, he had the keenest sense of humor, and would keep the table in roars of laughter. Of the thousand absurdities which took place in his presence not one escaped his penetrating observation. He could enjoy a joke upon himself too and his friends were not afraid of criticizing him. He talked a great deal and upon every possible subject, for his knowledge was encyclopedic.

All these things, with his splendid physique and the spirit of practical optimism by which he epitomized the joy of living, realized to the full the old Roman ideal of the "*mens sana in corpore sano*" and fitted him admirably to be the President of a vigorous, great, and flourishing republic.

FURTHER CHANGES

After Mr. Roosevelt's reëlection he made further extensions in the classified service and introduced improvements in the methods of carrying on the work.[1]

On June 3, 1907, he inserted in the civil service rules the declarations contained in his letter to us on June 13, 1902, forbidding officers and employees in the competitive classified service from taking part in political management or in po-

---

[1] A very valuable improvement had been made shortly after I left the Commission, in consolidating the local civil service boards into districts with an experienced man in charge of each district. In 1904, thirteen such districts were established.

litical campaigns. This gave the Commission power to investigate and report upon all such cases.

In the meantime changes had been going on both in the Commission and in the ranks of the League. On November 6, 1906, Mr. Cooley, the able Commissioner who had succeeded me, resigned to take an important position in the Department of Justice and Mr. John A. McIlhenny of Louisiana, one of Roosevelt's "Rough Riders" in the Spanish War, was appointed on the Commission.

In 1905, Charles J. Bonaparte, chairman of the Council of the League, was made Secretary of the Navy, from which office he was afterwards transferred to the position of Attorney General.

CARL SCHURZ

On May 14th, the League lost by death its former president and most distinguished member, Mr. Carl Schurz. I shall not attempt any complete characterization of this eminent man. While he and Mr. Curtis advocated the reform with equal devotion, their methods were as far apart as the poles. Their temperaments were utterly unlike. With Curtis "sweetness and light" were predominant, with Schurz the odor of brimstone was by no means absent when there was some unscrupulous foe to be assailed. The man who had taken so hazardous and so creditable a part in the Liberal movement in Germany in 1848 brought with him to America a courageous and militant spirit which was now placed wholly at the service of his adopted country. He was the ablest controversialist of his time, matchless in the warfare of debate. His English was as fine as that of any native American. He chose his position philosophically and sustained it by an array of facts and arguments that made it overwhelming. In statement indeed he sometimes exaggerated and spoke often in superlatives. Yet he was always impressive and convincing. His wit was not the delicate and playful humor of Curtis but often grim satire and biting sarcasm. His scathing irony at the conclusion of his second letter to Senator Gallinger, October 1, 1897, in the *Exeter Newsletter* (see Schurz's *Letters and Speeches*, v.,

428) is as fine as anything in Junius. His critics likened him to Mephistopheles, and there were instances of mocking raillery in his speeches and his behavior which made the comparison not an incredible one.[1]

His learning, especially his knowledge of history, sociology, and economics, was extensive and profound. His biographical articles on Lincoln and Webster and his *Life of Henry Clay* were masterly. He cared little for popularity and everything for principle. Indeed his devotion to his own philosophic conclusions was absolute, and at times (as in his support of Bryan upon the issue of anti-imperialism in 1900) it carried him to lengths which many of his friends regretted. Though his personal feelings were strong, his chief aim was to serve his country and mankind, and he will remain in history as an illustrious figure in the social movements and political controversies of his time.

[1] An illustration of this appears in his own reminiscences (vol.ii., pp.82, 83). He had been nominated for Lieut.-Governor of Wisconsin and was beset by office seekers who sought his recommendations. There were several applicants for each place. He asked each of them to meet him at an appointed hour in his hotel. The room was crowded. None knew that the others were coming and he thus addressed them: "You are all worthy citizens fully deserving what you seek. You will admit I cannot make any invidious discrimination between you. All I can do therefore in justice and fairness is to recommend you all for the places you seek on a footing of perfect equality." There was silence, then laughter and an early adjournment. "But," he adds, " I fear I made some enemies on that occasion."

CHAPTER XIV

THE TAFT CAMPAIGN—CHARGES OF COERCION

As the second administration of President Roosevelt drew to a close the question of the political activities of office-holders became more and more prominent and the President was not content, as some of his predecessors had been, to enjoin upon these officials that they must not take an active part in political work and then to let these injunctions remain unheeded and partisan activity go on as before. He encouraged the Commission to make investigations and there were a number of removals, suspensions, and reductions in pay of those who violated the rules. Among the officers removed were the Second Assistant Postmaster-General and the Collectors of Customs in West Virginia and in Port Huron, Michigan. This was the first time when such punishments were inflicted during a political campaign.

Long before the time of the Republican Convention, Mr. Roosevelt had openly expressed his preference for Mr. Taft as the candidate of that party and no doubt many office-holders as well as others were influenced by this fact to support the President's choice. He was bitterly attacked by the friends of the other candidates as well as by the Democrats. It was said that he was virtually selecting the President and that he was coercing his own subordinates. Early in January an Indianapolis paper, supporting the candidacy of Mr. Fairbanks, accused President Roosevelt of using the federal patronage to secure the nomination of Mr. Taft and named particular post offices in which it was charged that this was done.

I at once went to Washington, had an interview with the

President and Mr. Taft upon this subject, and learned that the charge was untrue. Upon my return home I heard of other articles making similar accusations.

On January 17th, the *Indianapolis Star* spoke of the "partial eclipse of our redoubtable Hoosier reformer Mr. William Dudley Foulke, who has never heard of the entire federal administration being harnessed up to the Taft boom." It derided the "hypnosis that had overtaken valiant civil service reformers."

What do they think about the lash from the White House that is being laid about the backs of federal employees in Washington and to the furthest corners of the nation to make them use the government's time and money to impose the President's personal choice upon the National Convention six months hence? They are dumb. They have never heard of it.

I enclosed this article in a letter to Mr. Roosevelt to which he instantly replied:

Will you produce the name of a single man whom I have coerced or influenced? Will you give me the name of any official who has been controlled by the threat or implied threat of dismissal or from whom I have demanded support for Taft? You cannot do so, and as you cannot why do you not repeat this challenge to the newspaper in question? Assert that their words are absolutely false and challenge them to make good.

I rejoiced at the opportunity and at once wrote to the *Star* repeating the challenge. My letter was published on January 24th, with an editorial comment in which it said that it was unfortunate "that my activity had not been more generally known." But my inquiries were unanswered and I asked, "Am I not, therefore, compelled by your own silence to consider your charges against the President as absolutely devoid of foundation?"

This letter the *Star* would not publish though it continued to repeat its general charges. In view of these reiterated complaints it seemed to me that a detailed statement of the President's appointments, the men by whom they were recommended, his reasons and the principles on which he had acted in making them, as well as a statement in regard to coercion, would be the best method of exhibiting the facts, and on February 5th I wrote to the President to that effect. On February 7th he answered:

MY DEAR FOULKE: The statement that I have used the offices in the effort to nominate any presidential candidate is both false and malicious. It is the usual imaginative invention which flows from a desire to say something injurious. Remember that those now making this accusation were busily engaged two months ago in asserting that I was using the offices to secure my own renomination. It is the kind of accusation which for the next few months will be rife. This particular slander will be used until exploded and when exploded those who have used it will promptly use another. Such being the case I almost wonder whether it is worth while answering, but as it is you who ask, why, the answer you shall have.

Mr. Roosevelt here gave an elaborate statement of the character of his appointments and the principles upon which he had acted.[1]

Not an appointment has been made that would not have been made if there had been no presidential contest impending and in no case has there been a deviation from the course that I would have pursued had none of those who actually are candidates for the nomination been candidates: nor has a single officeholder been removed or threatened with removal or coerced in any way to secure his support for any presidential candidate. In fact, the only coercion that I have attempted to exercise was to forbid the officeholders from pushing my own renomination.[2]

---

[1] He stated that he had made within eleven months 1352 appointments subject to confirmation by the Senate. Appointments in the diplomatic, consular, and Indian services were made without regard to politics and in judicial appointments he had conducted independent inquiries through prominent members of the bench or bar. But in the great bulk of the offices, amounting to about 1250, he normally accepted the suggestions of the Congressman of the locality, reserving the right to disregard these if he considered the men unfit. In the South he selected a large number of Democrats. In New York, Pennsylvania, Illinois, Indiana, and Wisconsin an enormous majority of appointees were in each case in favor of the presidential candidate from the State. This had not been true in Ohio and his interference in patronage matters in Ohio had been limited to insisting, as he would insist anywhere else, that opposition to the administration should not be considered as a necessary prerequisite to holding the commission of the President.

[2] More than a year later at the annual meeting of the League on Decem-

14

As time wore on the charge that President Roosevelt was coercing his subordinates gradually crystallized into the criticism that it was very wrong for him to declare any preference whatever among the candidates, trying to dictate the nomination of his successor. "He ought to remain quiet and let the party choose." "The party is wiser than any man in it," etc. In answer to this criticism I spoke at many places to the following effect:

Theodore Roosevelt was a member of the Republican party. He was the leader of that party. If he were to remain silent whose duty was it to speak? Was it to be only the selfish interests that were demanding the power to work their will? Were they to be the only influences entitled to be heard? It was true that hundreds of thousands would follow where he led because they believed that he would lead aright and that he had better knowledge than they. Why not? That was the privilege and prerogative of leadership.

He had done a great work for "the plain people" against the tyranny of capital, the debauchery of spoilscraft, and the abuses of predatory wealth. He had been the leader in the work of regeneration. He caused to be established the Department of Commerce and Labor, and the Bureau of Corporations, which required publicity for the acts of the gigantic combinations that were oppressing the public. He procured the enactment of the pure food law and government inspection of the great sources of our meat supplies. He secured an investigation of the rebates granted by the railroads to mo-

---

ber 9, 1909, after the political prejudices of the campaign of 1908 had become extinguished, the report of the Council of the League contained the following:

"Evidence was wholly lacking to substantiate the charges as to coercion of officeholders by the President in order to secure the nomination of a particular candidate. President Roosevelt allowed his appointment lists for a considerable time prior to the convention to be examined and not only were the appointments made in the usual manner on the recommendation of Senators and Congressmen and others claiming the patronage of offices involved but sometimes those on whose recommendation the appointments were made were notoriously opposed to the candidate whom President Roosevelt was known to favor."

nopolies, and instituted the prosecutions by which they were compelled to halt in their evil career.

He secured the passage of the rate bill preventing unjust discriminations by those who controlled the great arteries of our commerce. He promoted the peace of the world by the settlement of the great war between Russia and Japan. He administered the government of the Philippines for the benefit of the inhabitants, conducting the natives by educational methods into a higher civilization. He began the construction of the Panama Canal. He maintained an efficient and peaceful government for the Cuban Republic under our protection.

And now the question arose: Who was to succeed him in carrying out the measures he had inaugurated? He had declined a renomination and a reëlection, but what man in his place could be indifferent to the future of his country? If he were to hold aloof and say in effect, "I do not care who will succeed me," he would be leaving his great work half accomplished. He had preëminently the right to speak, and those who believed in him would not be slow to accept his counsels as to the choice of a successor.

When the Republican convention was held in June there was a large number of officeholders among the delegates, especially from the South, but these officeholders were greatly divided. A considerable proportion of them advocated other candidates than Mr. Taft, who was however nominated by a large majority.

RESULTS OF ROOSEVELT'S ADMINISTRATION ON THE CIVIL SERVICE

The report of the Civil Service Commission on November 16, 1908, presented in glowing colors the great advance made in the classified system under President Roosevelt. The number of competitive positions had increased from 110,000 on September 14, 1901, to 206,000 in addition to the laborers now registered.

But more was to come. Only two weeks after the date of

this report President Roosevelt after consulting with his successor, Mr. Taft, included 15,488 fourth-class postmasters, being all those in New England, New York, New Jersey, Pennsylvania, Ohio, Indiana, Illinois, Michigan, and Wisconsin.

The classified service had now grown under his administration by more than 116,000 places, a very much greater increase than during any other similar period. When he came into office only 46.2 per cent of the federal civil service was competitive, and when he left it was 66 per cent or two thirds of the whole.

CHAPTER XV

MR. TAFT'S personal inclinations were just as friendly toward the merit system as those of Mr. Roosevelt. It had been established in the Philippine Islands while he was the head of the government there and had been conscientiously administered both in those islands and in the War Department of which he afterwards became the chief. It was with his concurrence that Mr. Roosevelt had extended the rules to the fourth-class post offices north of the Ohio and east of the Mississippi and he completed this work at a later period by including the remaining fourth-class postmasters within the competitive service. He had caused it to be understood that he would veto the Census bill if it provided for the patronage appointment of Census clerks, and he issued, early in his administration, a strict injunction to supervisors and enumerators of the Census to refrain from all political activity under pain of dismissal. On September 30, 1910, he extended the classification to 2237 assistant postmasters in first- and second-class post offices, and to some 1386 clerks in these offices which had not theretofore been included. He repeatedly advocated in his messages to Congress the extension of the system to presidential postmasters and indeed to all administrative officers of every kind except the very small number who determined the political conduct of the government. He also favored legislation to give a secure tenure during efficiency for all purely administrative officials. He kept politics out of the consular service and extended the principles of the merit system to subordinate diplomatic appointments.[1]

[1] This was done by two orders November 26, 1909, and December 23, 1910, providing for entrance and transfer examinations and for promotions

By his courageous veto of one of the great appropriation bills in the summer of 1912 he prevented the fastening on the service of a proposed tenure-of-office act which would have immediately injected politics into the departments in Washington.

But in Mr. Taft's administration of the civil service law there appeared just a little of the same quality which led to disaster in regard to other public questions. He was of a generous nature but not always a good judge of men and he was not infrequently misled by those around him. An instance of this occurred very early in his term when he asked for the resignation of Mr. Henry R. Greene, one of the Civil Service Commissioners. Mr. Greene had been an admirable officer, was well acquainted with the workings of the system, and had done everything possible to enforce the law and promote the principles of the reform. In doing this he had made enemies. These enemies complained to the President and he believed them. He put in place of Mr. Greene, on May 5, 1909, Mr. James T. Williams, Jr., a young newspaper man whose experience and knowledge of the system was by no means as complete as that of the man he supplanted.[1]

An unfortunate exception to Mr. Taft's general attitude toward the civil service was shown in his "Norton letter." A number of Progressive Congressmen had given offense to the President by opposition to his policies in regard to the tariff and other questions and on September 15, 1910, the President's secretary, Mr. Norton, wrote to a leader in Iowa: "While Republican legislation pending in Congress was opposed by certain Republicans, the President felt it to be his duty to the

---

for merit as shown by records of efficiency, and on December 7, 1911, he recommended to Congress the enactment of a law providing for such examinations.

[1] Within a few weeks however Mr. Williams resigned on account of ill health and on May 26, 1909, Wm. R. Washburn was made Commissioner. He had risen from a subordinate position in the Commission where he had been first an examiner and later at the head of the Philippine Civil Service Board. He was thoroughly qualified for this new position which he filled to general satisfaction.

party and to the country to withhold patronage from certain Senators and Congressmen who seemed to be in opposition to the administration's efforts to carry out the promises of the party platform." This letter became public in an unexpected manner and was widely criticized as an attempt to use public offices to influence legislation. It seemed to mean in substance, "Vote as I want in these matters or you shall have no patronage to distribute," which is spoils doctrine pure and simple. Senator Bristow of Kansas and other "insurgents" were "punished" in this way.

President Taft was also unfortunate in another matter. The entire force of post office inspectors had been put under civil service rules and these positions were to be filled by promotion, but now Mr. Robert S. Sharp, an office seeker and political organizer, was excepted from examination and appointed chief inspector and after his appointment, instead of attending to his official duties he remained long in Tennessee organizing the political forces under his control.

Moreover there was a certain laxity in the enforcement of the rules during Mr. Taft's administration. Thus the Commission's report shows that during the year ending June, 1911, temporary appointments had increased more than three thousand and adds:

> A tendency exists on the part of some appointing officers to continue the service of temporary employees either out of sympathy for individuals or because of the supposed needs of the service. If the appointing officers had been keyed up to a proper appreciation of the need of strictly enforcing the law such laxity would hardly have existed.

This same report reveals that in some cases there was long and unnecessary delay in punishing delinquents, for the Commission observes, "Allowing a year or two to pass before action is taken upon a distinct offense is manifestly inimical to good administration."

THE NEAL CASE

In one important case which I personally examined, this long and unnecessary delay was attributable to the President himself. This was the case of Elam Neal, internal revenue collector at Indianapolis. In November, 1911, I received information that Collector Neal had, as far back as 1906, coerced his employees into making political contributions by giving favorable assignments to his subordinate gaugers and storekeepers who had contributed to the Republican campaign fund and by laying off or giving undesirable assignments to those who had declined; that similar discrimination had been shown in favor of those who contributed on behalf of the collector's candidate in the Republican primaries in 1908, and that the Civil Service Commission had investigated the case and found him guilty,[1] saying in their report to President Taft in April, 1909: "The attempt which is shown to have been made by Collector Neal to coerce his subordinates who are in the classified civil service into making political contributions is something which attacks one of the very basic principles of the civil service system."

The Commission recommended that Mr. Neal be suspended without pay for six months.

[1] It seems that early in February, 1909, the case was brought to the attention of the Commission, which at once investigated it, Commissioner Henry F. Greene going personally to Indiana for that purpose. He found that immediately after the campaign of 1906 gaugers Wells, Schooley and James were reduced to positions of storekeepers, having failed to contribute. James was assigned to Hammond, an undesirable situation far from his home. Those who contributed kept their good positions and some were promoted. Collector Neal admitted that he had furnished a list of employees in his district to the Republican State Committee and later had received from some member of the committee a list of those who had contributed which he gave to his chief office deputy who made the assignments. Neal denied the discrimination and said the list was furnished merely as a matter of news and personal interest!

In February, 1908, there was a primary campaign for governor. Schooley, James and Wells supported Watson; the collector supported C. W. Miller. Schooley saw the collector to complain about his assignments. Neal told him that "loyalty meant something more than official loyalty and that it was about time for him to find out that there was a new collector and a new administration."

In the final campaign of 1908, these gaugers having learned their lesson all contributed to the campaign fund and the assignments of every one of them were changed for the better.

The President concurred in this conclusion and so did the Secretary of the Treasury, who wrote to the Commission on July 30, 1909, that the President had authorized him to say that he had made up his mind to adopt its recommendation. Yet although the matter was repeatedly called to his attention the President utterly failed for two years and eight months to take any action in the case![1]

Finally in January, 1912, he wrote: " It is sufficient to invite Mr. Neal's attention to the history of the case, to the leniency that has been shown him, and to the fact that the office as now administered with his full attention to the same is in a condition that must continue or his removal must follow."

Thus after three years' delay Neal was finally permitted to continue in office and escape wholly unpunished![2]

---

[1] A rule the Commission adopted at the President's request, that while cases were pending the files could not be inspected, also led inevitably to the concealment of abuses. In this case the fact that a crime had been committed was concealed for nearly three years by the President's rule and his delay.

[2] The efforts of the Commission to secure some disposition of the case by the President were frequent and pressing.

On April 25, 1910, the Commission wrote to the Secretary of the Treasury calling attention to the fact that nothing had been done. On December 28, 1910, the Commission again earnestly called the Secretary's attention to the case. "It is the view of the Commission that the long delay in the Neal case, which will be two years old in February, 1911, is to the *detriment of the service.*"

Nearly six months more elapsed. On June 7th, the Secretary of the Treasury wrote to President Black of the Civil Service Commission: "I also beg to advise you and the Commission in confidence that the case of Elam Neal of Indianapolis will be disposed of in accordance with your views without further delay." Yet still the months dragged on. In November I went to Washington and interviewed the Secretary of the Treasury, who did not at any time claim that Mr. Neal was not guilty of the charges made against him.

On January 2, 1912, the President wrote the Secretary of the Treasury as follows:

"I have *not examined* fully the papers in the case of the complaint against Collector Neal, but I have examined the correspondence with the Commissioner of Internal Revenue and remember to have examined with much

At the close of Mr. Taft's administration a larger percentage of the executive civil service was in the competitive class than at any previous time but it may be doubted whether the service was as efficient or as free from political influence as during the administration of President Roosevelt.   In 1912, the influence of federal officeholders was strongly felt in the election of delegates to the national convention which met in Chicago and nominated Mr. Taft.   Evidently this convention did not represent the real wishes of the Republican voters since Mr. Roosevelt as the Progressive nominee had an overwhelming plurality among the votes afterwards cast at the election in opposition to the Democratic candidate.   When the election came on Mr. Wilson, the Democratic candidate, was chosen by a large majority of the electoral vote, Mr. Roosevelt was second, while Mr. Taft was third upon the list, receiving the electoral votes of only two States, Vermont and Utah.

---

care the complaints against Collector Neal in 1909.   It did not then seem to me that he ought to be dismissed but I thought he ought to be fined in some way."

Now the only way Neal could be fined would be in a criminal prosecution for violation of the civil service law and the President's words, if they meant anything, meant that Neal ought to be criminally prosecuted and punished for an official act and *yet retain his office undisturbed !*

CHAPTER XVI

THE federal civil service has been the theme of most of the preceding chapters, but during the years which elapsed since the Pendleton law was enacted, progress had been made in the introduction and development of the competitive system in a considerable number of States and in a very large number of the cities of the country.[1]

Wherever the system was submitted to popular suffrage it was approved by an overwhelming vote. The people of Chicago favored it by a majority of over 50,000; in Illinois, the question, "Shall the next General Assembly enact a comprehensive civil service law?" was carried by a majority of over 290,000; and Ohio adopted the civil service provisions in her constitution by a majority of over 100,000.

In the great movement toward the Commission and the Commission Manager forms of city government civil service provisions were very generally incorporated, though these varied greatly in excellence, some of them being quite ineffective.

It was on November 15, 1910, while this movement was going on that I was elected president of the National Municipal

---

[1] New York passed a civil service law in 1883 (the same year the federal statute was enacted), Massachusetts in 1884, Wisconsin and Illinois in 1905, Colorado and New Jersey in 1907, Ohio in 1912 by constitutional provision, Connecticut in 1913, and Kansas in 1915.

In all the foregoing States as well as in many others there were laws either authorizing or directing competitive methods to be applied to some or all of the cities therein. Under these provisions the cities began very generally to adopt the merit system. In 1910 it had been extended to about 100 of these and in 1911 to 217, and the growth has continued since that time.

League at its annual meeting in Buffalo and I began to look at the civil service question more largely from this new angle of State and municipal development, especially the latter.

It was easy to see that some modifications of the federal civil service law were necessary in applying the merit system to cities. The Pendleton act was of the most general character, leaving the development of the system mostly to the President and the Commission. It would be dangerous however to adopt the same plan in cities, where the people when this reform was introduced were commonly quite ignorant of the necessary provisions for eliminating patronage. Where this is so these provisions have to be prescribed in considerable detail in the law itself. The rules adopted by the federal commission were to a large extent the models for State and city laws. Moreover it had been found that where the administration of the law in cities was subject to State control as in New York and Massachusetts the result had been more satisfactory than where the whole system had been under the exclusive control of local civil service commissions. These commissions were generally appointed and removed by the political authority (that is the mayor or council) of the city and the rules which they adopted had to be approved by such authority. Thus the whole administration of the law became subject to the very authority which it was designed to restrain. More independence was necessary for the civil service commission and this could be given by making it subject to the supervision not of the city authorities but of a State commission. Moreover the commissioners ought to be appointed for overlapping terms to ensure continuity and experience, and they should be removable for cause only and after a hearing, so as to be as far as possible free from the control of the political power which appointed them.

Our National Municipal League devoted a considerable portion of its activities to promoting the adoption of effective civil service reform laws for municipalities. During the summer of 1912 this League, which had been invited to hold its annual meeting at Los Angeles by the mayor and council of that city to consider the provisions of a new charter then under consideration, devoted a considerable portion of a session of three days to the question of expert city management and civil service reform as a means of obtaining it. I took this subject as the theme of my annual address and after setting forth the need of experts and the way in which they should be secured, I insisted that the charter ought to provide that under the commissioners chosen to manage the city practically every place should be filled by experts chosen by competitive methods without reference to any kind of politics and insisted that the fewer the exceptions the better the result.[1]

It is curious to note in this connection that with the gradual development of the competitive system the ideas of the public and of civil service reformers in regard to it also developed. It used to be said that the system could not apply to a considerable class of public servants; for instance, not to the labor service, where examinations were impracticable; nor to private secretaries and confidential agents, where personal selection was necessary; nor to places involving pecuniary responsibility since the superior officer should choose the men for whose acts he would be liable; nor to places requiring expert professional or administrative qualifications, since the best men would not apply.

But one by one all these exceptions are now successfully eliminated. Labor registration produces better results than the old system; in confidential places the confidence (which is due to the government and not to the superior) is secured better by competitive tests and by probation than by patronage; official bonds protect the superior in cases of financial

---

[1] A joint committee of the National Municipal League and the National Civil Service Reform League to consider the selection and retention of experts in office presented a report at this meeting in accordance with the foregoing principles which met with general approval.

This report was afterwards presented to the annual meeting of the National Civil Service Reform League held at Milwaukee December 5 and 6, 1912, and was approved by that body also.

At that meeting I delivered an address showing in a practical way the need of expert service in city government, the kinds of competitive examinations used to secure it, and the places to which it could be applied.

responsibility; and expert professional and administrative places of high grade are now filled far more successfully by the competitive system than by the political system which it superseded. For such places there is no pedagogical examination, but a competitive investigation is made of the education and experience of the respective applicants, and experts of the highest character are called in to grade them in the order of merit. When such places as the librarian of the Chicago Public Library, the superintendent of streets of Philadelphia, superintendent of the Syracuse Institution for Feeble Minded Children, superintendents of Indian reservations and other similar positions can be thus successfully filled it can no longer be said that the method is not practical.[1]

In 1913 I was made chairman of a committee of the National Municipal League to prepare a model charter setting forth what we considered the best form of government for the average American city.[2]

Much labor was expended upon this charter and it was nearly three years before the work was completed and approved by a referendum of the League. The form of government proposed provided for the election of a council of a small number of members nominated by petition and elected by a non-partisan ballot. The council was to select a city manager solely on the basis of his executive and administrative qualities and the choice was not to be limited to the inhabitants of the city or State. He was to be appointed for an indefinite period and removed by the council only upon written charges and after a public hearing. He was to be responsible to the council

---

[1] I was asked to discuss this question at the annual meeting of the National Civil Service Reform League in Chicago on December 3, 1914. The address appears in the Appendix IX.

[2] This committee was composed of the following gentlemen: M. N. Baker, Engineering News, New York; Richard S. Childs, Short Ballot Association, New York; Prof. John A. Fairlie, University of Illinois; Mayo Fesler, Civic League, Cleveland; Prof. A. R. Hatton, Western Reserve University, Cleveland; Prof. Herman G. James, University of Texas; A. Lawrence Lowell, President of Harvard University; Prof. William Bennett Munro, Harvard University; Robert Treat Paine, Boston; Delos F. Wilcox, New York City, Clinton Rogers Woodruff, Philadelphia, and myself.

for the proper administration of all municipal affairs and was to make all appointments according to competitive methods.

At the head of each administrative department was a director who might also be chosen by the competitive system if the city so determined, and we provided for a civil service board for the appointment of all other officers, prescribing in considerable detail its powers and methods.

The League's municipal program having now been completed and my own precarious health forbidding longer continuance in the work, I resigned the presidency and Mr. Lawson Purdy of New York, an expert of eminent qualifications upon the problems of city finance and taxation which were now coming to the front, was elected as my successor.

THE PROPOSED MODEL CIVIL SERVICE LAW

The Civil Service Commissioners of the country, federal, State, and municipal, had organized an association to promote improved methods in the competitive system. This association was known as the National Assembly of Civil Service Commissioners and at a meeting in New York in June, 1913, it had appointed a committee to draft a model law and invited the National Civil Service Reform League and the National Municipal League to appoint special committees to confer with its own committee for this purpose. The appointments were made and several conferences were held.

The leading spirit in the preparation of this model law was Mr. Robert Catherwood, who was the president of the Cook County (Illinois) Commission, and was also a member of the Council of the Reform League. He had drafted a bill containing some new and radical features which aroused animated discussions.

According to this bill the commissioners themselves were no longer to be appointed by the political authority of the State or city but by competitive examinations and they were to hold office indefinitely. The bill provided that whenever there was a vacancy in the office of civil service commissioner of any State the governor should appoint a special examining board of three persons; first, a member, secretary, or chief examiner of some civil service commission, second, a man who had been engaged in selecting trained employees for positions involving professional or technical skill, and third, a judge of a court of record. This board was to hold an examination and prepare an eligible list and the governor was to appoint the person standing highest upon that list to the office of commissioner. The State Civil Service Commission was in like manner to conduct examinations for the appointment of municipal civil service commissioners. No commissioner was to be removed except for malfeasance, neglect of duty, or incompetence, and only upon written charges (which might be filed by any citizen) and after an opportunity to be heard by a trial board consisting of two *nisi prius* judges and a third person selected by the two. The decision of this board was to be final.

The commission was to classify the service, fix salaries, and prescribe standards and tests of efficiency. It was to cause charges to be filed against delinquents. No person was to be removed except for cause upon written charges (which however might also be filed by any citizen or taxpayer). Such charges were to be investigated by the commission or by some trial board appointed by that body. The decision was to be final.

There were various meetings of committees and of the Council of the National Civil Service Reform League upon the subject. I urged that at least one member of the commission should be appointed by the executive authority of the State or city, insisting that there were still political duties to be performed by the commission and that it was important to have at least one commissioner appointed for the performance of these duties. I remembered that when I was upon the Civil Service Commission my own duties were mainly political, not in a partisan sense, but for the purpose of upholding the law and the competitive system against opponents in Congress, in the press, and elsewhere; that it was also the duty of the commissioners to advise the President and the departments as to the extent and manner in which the competitive principle should be applied by the law and rules.

I opposed the proposed removal rule strenuously and while agreeing to give the commissioners concurrent power to remove or discipline delinquents I insisted this power should not be entirely taken away from the officers who were responsible for administration and placed wholly in the hands of an independent official over whom they had no control.[1]

As a final result of our discussions a provision was added that nothing in the proposed law should limit the power of any appointing officer to dismiss a subordinate upon filing written reasons and giving the accused notice of the charges against him and an opportunity to answer and file affidavits, but that no trial should be required except in the discretion of the officer making the removal.[2]

---

[1] A brief prepared by me against taking the power of removal from the appointing officer will be found in Appendix X.

[2] The Council of the League also adopted three alternative provisions as to the manner in which commissions should be appointed.

The first of these alternatives for a State commission provided for the appointment of one person only as commissioner, the man who should stand highest on a competitive examination before a board of special examiners.

The second alternative provided for a State commission of three persons to be appointed by the governor for overlapping terms of six years.

The third alternative provided for a State commission of three persons, one to be appointed by the governor to serve during his term of office and the other two appointed by competitive examination. This was the plan I preferred.

As to the local commissions the first alternative provided for one commissioner to be appointed by a competitive examination held by the State commission.

The second alternative, for municipalities having a population of 250,000 or more, created a commission of three persons, one to be appointed by the chief appointing authority of the municipality to serve during his term and the other two to be selected as the result of a competitive examination held by the State Civil Service Commission. Local commissioners were removable after trial by the State commission.

The National Municipal League however was not willing to adopt the principle of selecting the commission by competitive examinations. In the model charter prepared by that League the civil service board was to be chosen by the city council for overlapping terms of six years and any commissioner could be removed by a four-fifths vote after charges and a hearing. Employees could be removed by the city manager or by the head of a department after notice and opportunity to answer but no trial was required.

CHAPTER XVII

THE WILSON ADMINISTRATION

WHATEVER the inconsistencies and shortcomings of the various administrations since the passage of the civil service law, the classified lists had been pretty constantly extended. Only one backward step had been taken and that was when President McKinley had withdrawn from the competitive service some four thousand places included by the "blanket order" of his predecessor Mr. Cleveland.

But during the first term of Mr. Wilson's administration there was again a period of reaction. This was a great surprise to the advocates of civil service reform. The new President had declared himself on many occasions in strong and unmistakable language as a friend of the merit system and at the time of his election he was one of the vice-presidents of the League.

He had indeed resigned after he became President, but had written that his "interest in and sympathy with the work of the Civil Service Reform League had not been and could not be abated." About the time of his inauguration there was the usual scramble for office such as follows the accession of a President belonging to another party and some of the incidents attending this scramble were peculiarly amusing. One of our Indiana Congressmen prepared a list of presidential post offices in his district, giving the names of the occupants and the salary of each. At the left of the sheet a large marginal space was reserved in which to write the names of applicants. The first of these were written in his customary well rounded hand, but as the swarm grew he reduced the size of his handwriting to conserve space. But it was of no use. The man who wrote the Lord's Prayer on a piece of paper no larger than his thumbnail might be able to get it all in, but however fine his chirography, the Congressman could not crowd in the names of all those who wanted these places.

Another Indiana member received the following note from a modest constituent:

KIND SIR & FRIEND: At last the Democratic party is in sight of the clover patch. It has been a long, dreary experience waiting on the outside, so let us not hesitate to enter and take possession of the promised land. I would be glad if you would sound Governor Wilson and see if you can get a place for me that pays well. I wish you would strike for something high up on the list and then if you have to drop, all right.

I would suggest trying for a Cabinet place first. If the Governor won't come across with that appointment touch him a little more lightly, say for a job like commissioner of internal revenue, commissioner of pensions, or something like that. If you can't do any better for me I would be willing to take a job as post office inspector though, of course, it would not be wise to let that be known in advance. Do the best you can for me.

Another wrote:

I have thought over the matter at some length and would not mind being appointed to some nice ambassadorship in a nearby country. Kindly notify me if it is all right.

President Wilson appeared to start well in resisting solicitations. On March 5, 1913, the day after his inauguration, he issued a statement that he deemed it his duty to decline to see applicants for office in person except when he himself invited the interview and that he would deal with applicants through the heads of the several departments. But this announcement merely changed the point of pressure. The members of his Cabinet were swamped with importunities. Senator Tillman found in the Department of State "swarms of hewers of wood and drawers of water. The wild asses of the desert were athirst and hungry. They had broken into the green corn."

LAWS ELIMINATING THE MERIT SYSTEM

The first important inroads into the competitive system were made by Congress but they all met the approval of the Executive. The Democratic national platform of 1912 declared: "The law pertaining to the civil service should be honestly and rigidly enforced to the end that merit and ability should be the standard of appointment and promotion rather than service to a political party." And the resolutions at their conclusion stated, "Our pledges are made to be kept when in office as well as relied upon during the campaign."

Mr. Wilson was supported by a large Democratic majority in both houses of Congress. Any attack by Congress upon the law was surely a violation of the promise and it was well known that the act and rules applied not only to existing positions but also to places created by future legislation.

Yet as soon as the Democratic majority in Congress began to enact important laws it also began to chop off piecemeal the application of the civil service law both to the places which were created by new legislation and also to places which already existed.

A large number of employees were provided to administer the income tax and Congress made all the positions in the field force of this service the subjects of political plunder by taking them out of the operation of the civil service law for two years[1] and providing for appointments under regulations to be made by the Secretary of the Treasury.

The President signed the bill in this form. He would have had the power even under this law to direct the Secretary to provide competitive tests but he did not do so. The Democratic majority next fastened a rider on the Urgent Deficiency Bill removing from the operation of the law deputy revenue collectors and deputy marshals, positions which had long been in the classified service.

Then the employees of the Federal Reserve Board created by the new currency act were excluded from the classified service. Vice-President Marshall gave the casting vote in the Senate in favor of this exclusion.

Next, fourteen important positions of commercial attachés credited to American ministers abroad, positions which ought

[1] After the places had been filled by partisan appointments these appointments at the end of the two years were to be given greater permanency by *then* including them in the classified service.

to be non-political, were removed from the merit system to be made the spoils of party and changed with each change of administration.

By the Trade Commission Bill all the attorneys, special experts, and examiners of that body were excluded from the classified service.

When the Agricultural Credits Bill was enacted the employees were also to be appointed without reference to the civil service law. The President approved all these measures.

SPOILS IN SANTO DOMINGO

In addition to this record of promise-breaking the confidential instructions of Mr. Bryan, Secretary of State, were most illuminating. On the 2d of September, 1914, he sent to Walter W. Vick, then Receiver General of Customs at Santo Domingo, a letter which attracted much attention. Places in the government service were still a little scanty at home. Pickings for the faithful must be found elsewhere, and in what better place than in Santo Domingo where nobody was watching and where "our beloved and oppressed brethren" of the Dominican Republic might be made to pay the piper. The letter contained the following:

Now that you have arrived and acquainted yourself with the situation, can you let me know what positions you have at your disposal with which to reward deserving Democrats. Whenever you desire a suggestion from me in regard to a man for any place down there, call on me. You have had enough experience in politics to know how valuable workers are when the campaign is on, and how difficult it is to find suitable rewards for the deserving. I do not know to what extent a knowledge of the Spanish language is necessary for employees. Let me know what is requisite, together with the salary and when appointments are likely to be made. Sullivan will be down before long and you and he together ought to be able to bring about such reforms as may be necessary there. You will find Sullivan a strong, courageous, reliable fellow. The more I have seen of him, the better satisfied I am that he will fit into the place there and do what is necessary to be done.

Very truly,
W. J. BRYAN.

And accordingly the "strong, courageous, reliable" Sullivan

proceeded to "reform" things by transferring the public funds to a precious group of patriots in control of the "Banco Nacional," an institution described by one of the witnesses as "a joke," and from which these funds afterwards had to be withdrawn and restored to the original depository. A newly created office at "$8000 a year and expenses" was given to a man without experience and other illustrations were shown of Mr. Bryan's altruistic principles towards Santo Domingo. As the result of an investigation Sullivan afterwards had to resign and his predecessor was reappointed.

It was quite natural in view of the disposition of Mr. Bryan as shown by the foregoing correspondence that the most flagrant disregard of the merit principle should be found in the Department of State and this was shown in the appointments made to our foreign embassies.

EMBASSIES TO CAMPAIGN CONTRIBUTORS

There is no higher office at the disposal of the government outside the Cabinet itself than the position of ambassador at the court of a foreign power. The ambassador is the immediate personal representative of the President charged with the duty of maintaining before the other powers of the world the interests and the dignity of the nation.

When Mr. Wilson became President William Rockhill was minister to Turkey. He had been in the diplomatic service for nineteen years, first in the Department of State, then as minister and consul-general to Greece, Roumania, and Servia, then director of the International Bureau of American Republics, then commissioner in connection with the Boxer insurrection, then minister to China in 1905, ambassador to Russia in 1909 and to Constantinople in 1911. There was no more skillful diplomat in America. He had the widest knowledge of international law, was proficient in many foreign languages, including even Chinese, and was admirably equipped for any place in our foreign service. But he was displaced to make room for a man absolutely inexperienced in diplomatic or international affairs, Mr. Henry Morgenthau, a New York lawyer and financier. What was the reason of the appointment of this untried man who had never been distinguished either in politics, letters, or diplomacy?

He had been the chairman of the Democratic Finance Committee in the campaign of 1912 charged with the administration and largely with the collection of the fund raised for the election of Mr. Wilson. He was also one of the largest contributors. According to the report furnished by the Democratic National Committee, as published in the Congressional Record of August 10, 1916 (see page 14,394), he contributed to the McCoombs pre-nomination fund to secure the nomination of Mr. Wilson the sum of $20,000 and then to the general fund for Mr. Wilson's election the further sum of $10,000, or $30,000 in all.

As soon as the new President was warm in his place and Mr. Bryan had become Secretary of State, Mr. Morgenthau's application for his reward was made and on the 4th of September, 1913, he was made ambassador to Turkey.

The embassy to Vienna was bestowed upon another extensive contributor, Mr. Fred. C. Penfield, who had given, according to the same authority, to the McCoombs pre-nomination fund $12,000, and to the fund for Mr. Wilson's election $10,000, being $22,000 in all. Mr. Penfield however had had some previous experience in our foreign service having been vice-consul-general at London and consul in Egypt some twenty years before.

The embassy to Germany was bestowed upon James W. Gerard, who had contributed according to the same authority $13,500 to the Democratic campaign fund. Mr. Gerard, like Mr. Morgenthau, had been absolutely without diplomatic experience. He was chairman of the Democratic campaign committee of New York County for four years and Associate Justice of the Supreme Court of that State from 1908 to 1911. Not a single element of diplomatic qualifications had been shown in his career.

Another man contributed $5000 and was made minister to Uruguay.

Thus the baleful precedents set by President Harrison in the case of Mr. Wanamaker and by President Cleveland in the case of Mr. Van Alen were now followed in greater number under President Wilson.   How much of the responsibility was personal to the President and how much to a Secretary of State who was anxious to reward "deserving Democrats" it is not easy to say.

Out of eleven ambassadors eight were replaced and among thirty-five ministers there were twenty-two changes in less than eight months with the result that other men of long experience were supplanted by those who were wholly untrained.   It is fair to say that some of the new appointments were made because those in the service voluntarily resigned.

It should also be acknowledged that the Wilson administration did far better in the lower diplomatic service and in the consular service than with the ambassadors and ministers. The executive orders promulgated by Presidents Roosevelt and Taft requiring pass examinations for subordinate positions were observed in all but five cases, and in four of these, persons of experience were appointed.

In respect of the consular service the President in general withstood the attacks of the place hunters and in 1915 a bill was passed known as the Stone-Flood Bill which provided for the grading of diplomatic secretaries and consular offices and the assignment of the members of the service to these grades, the President being authorized to transfer employees from one grade to another.   This embodied in legislation the methods introduced by the executive orders of Presidents Roosevelt and Taft.

CIVIL SERVICE COMMISSION REORGANIZED

In regard to the vital matter of the Civil Service Commission Mr. Wilson disappointed expectations.   General John C. Black and William S. Washburn resigned, and the President appointed in place of General Black, Charles M. Gallaway, a newspaper man of South Carolina, former secretary to Senator Smith of that State and clerk of the Commission on Immigration in the Senate.   In place of Mr. Washburn, Herman W.

Craven, of Seattle, Washington, was appointed. Neither of the new commissioners were experienced in civil service matters.

FOURTH-CLASS POST OFFICES

It will be remembered that Mr. Roosevelt before he left the Presidency classified the fourth-class post offices lying east of the Mississippi and north of the Ohio and Potomac, about 15,000 places in all, and President Taft on October 15, 1912, just before the presidential election, classified the remaining post offices, about 36,000 in number.

When these places were classified those who held the positions at the time were "covered" into the service. Naturally the Democrats when they came into power resented the fact that so large a number of postmasters who had entered without examination were now in the competitive class. Fourth-class postmasters are very useful to Congressmen in their political campaigns and the problem apparently arose how best to get the places that were wanted and still leave the classification intact. The method adopted was this. President Wilson on May 7, 1913, promulgated an order that no fourth-class postmaster should be given a competitive status unless he had been appointed as the result of an open competitive examination. From the eligible lists appointments were to be made from among the three highest, the former appointees taking their chances with other competitors. Since there was an average of less than three applicants for these small places the choice among them would give all the latitude necessary for political appointments.

The League doubted the practicability of the competitive examination ordered by President Wilson. The plan would be costly and laborious, involving examinations for many thousands of offices, but *if fairly executed*, it would improve administration. Here was exactly the crux of the matter. Would the plan be fairly executed?

The examinations were held throughout the country at an expense of not far from $100,000 and took nearly two years for their completion. When the eligible lists were made up what was done with them? The Postmaster-General in a public statement, issued November 17, 1913, declared that it was "*his practice to ask the member of Congress in whose district the vacancy exists to advise him relative to the character and fitness of the three eligibles.*"

But Section 10 of the civil service law had provided that no recommendation by any Senator or Representative except as to character or *residence* of the applicant should be *received or considered.* This section was inserted to put an end to the control of appointments by Congressmen, since their recommendations were bound to be largely political and were the source of most of the evils of the whole spoils system.

The League, on January 8th, wrote to the Postmaster-General reminding him that his public statement violated Section 10. He answered that he believed it did not do this and that he was justified in securing information from Congressmen "not in their capacity as members of a political party but as representatives of their districts and of the postal communities interested in the service."

Of this, President Dana of the League aptly remarked that under such a construction a judge prohibited from sitting in a case in which he had an interest might ignore the law and say he was not to sit as a party interested but as an impartial judge. The League asked to have the legality of this position submitted to the Attorney-General, but its request was not granted. It then asked the Civil Service Commission for leave to inspect the eligible lists to see how far the appointments had been made from those who stood highest, but the Commission refused to allow such inspection.

We were not at all convinced by the edifying declarations of the Postmaster-General that it was his purpose that the positions be filled "in accordance with both the letter and the spirit of the law" which at that moment he was violating. It was quite vain to say that "such recommendation must be based solely upon merit and fitness and without reference to political affiliations" and that letters based on political considerations would be returned.[1] Equally unconvincing were

[1] Indeed he afterwards stated that he was not asking "recommendations" at all but merely "information."

his directions to the First Assistant Postmaster-General that he desired the person with the highest rating to be chosen unless good reasons were submitted showing this would "not be to the best interests of the service." It would be a barren intelligence which could not furnish an appropriate and plausible reason when desired. A better way to ascertain whether the appointments were really non-political would be to find out in what per cent of these cases the highest man was actually chosen or the incumbent retained. On this point, Mr. Burleson afterwards made a statement in a speech to the League, December 5, 1916, at New Haven, which on its face was particularly strong. He declared that 66 per cent of the incumbents had been retained and classified, that 30 per cent of the places had been filled by other men whose names stood highest, that in less than 3 per cent of the cases the incumbent had been succeeded by the second eligible and in less than 1 per cent by the third eligible. He further added that of the whole number of appointments made, 89½ per cent were from the eligibles who stood highest. But when Mr. Burleson's figures were analyzed in comparison with those in the report of the Civil Service Commission of November 15, 1916, the results showed something quite different. He had only appointed 29 per cent of the incumbents in cases *where he had any choice at all.* This was considerably less than one third instead of two thirds.[1]

But perhaps they may have been an undesirable lot. A better test will be, did Mr. Burleson really choose the highest

---

[1] The Commission reported (pp. xviii., xxvi.) that the number of certificates upon which the incumbents' names appeared was 7845 but that *in 4947 of these, the incumbent was the only eligible.* The Postmaster-General could do nothing but appoint him. It was only in the remaining 2898 cases therefore that there was any choice.

Now the entire number of incumbents appointed by the Postmaster-General on these certificates was 5565 and the entire number appointed where the incumbent was the only eligible was 4717; therefore the number of incumbents appointed where incumbents were *not* the only eligibles must have been 848. In other words the Postmaster-General in those cases *where he had any choice at all* appointed 848 incumbents or 29 per cent of 2898.

eligibles? Was his claim that he selected 89 per cent of these correct? Here too the figures in the report of the Commission are illuminating and they showed that only 57 per cent of the highest candidates were appointed in cases where there was any choice at all.[1]

In 1906, during President Roosevelt's administration, the appointing officers in nearly 90 per cent of the cases followed the order of the register in making appointments. (See p. 1, 23d Report C. S. Commission.) Now Mr. Burleson followed this order in less than 57 per cent and there is the strongest reason for thinking that a good part of this difference (over 33 per cent) was political plunder.[2]

This political manipulation was particularly bad in Indiana. Congressmen might be told that nothing but merit and fitness should be considered yet they still made partisan selections. Chester C. Hicks, a Republican whose standing was the highest of any candidate in his district, was passed over and Mort Ellis, a Democrat, was recommended by Congressman Moss and received the appointment. Hicks wrote to the Congressman asking why and Mr. Moss replied, April 7, 1914:

[1] In 7441 cases only *one* eligible was secured from each examination. (See 23d Report C. S. Commission p. xxv.) In 2856 cases appointments were made from lists of *two* eligibles. In 1795 of these cases (62.8 per cent) the *first* eligible was appointed. In 3038 there were three eligibles (p. xxvi). In 1561 of these (51.4 per cent) the highest was selected. Thus it appears that out of 5894 cases in which the Postmaster-General had *any choice at all* he selected the highest man in 3357 cases or less than 57 per cent.

[2] Of course there were exceptional cases where the highest man was properly passed over, perhaps because of the location of the office or possibly he might be holding some position which would render him ineligible, and occasionally there were other reasons. The secretary of the League made an investigation early in 1917 (the Postmaster-General having allowed him access to the records of the department) in the States of Massachusetts, Georgia, Texas, and Oregon, and he came to the conclusion that in most of these cases the selection of the lower man was justified by records or papers on file with the Department and that while political influence may have crept in in some cases the record was on the whole to the credit of the Postmaster-General. But in the particular States which happened to be selected the highest man was passed over in less than 34 per cent of the cases while in the average throughout the country he was passed over in more than 43 per cent of the cases; so that these States

"I have followed the invariable custom under all administrations in nominating members of my own party to fill vacancies. I cannot act otherwise unless the department prefers to take the candidate with the highest grade."

Senator Hoke Smith of Georgia wrote to a candidate for appointment, "I have always felt that this being a Democratic administration, appointees should be Democratic. What I wish to know from you candidly is how you have voted in national politics."

These are but illustrations. In the opinion of the President himself the bulk of the postmasters of every class, after three years of his administration, had become Democratic, for at the national convention of these officials held in Washington in the summer of 1916, he said that he was at liberty to talk frankly and freely as his auditors were "virtually all Democrats." This could hardly be so unless the postmasterships had virtually become the subjects of Democratic patronage.

But whether the number of political appointments of fourth-class postmasters was large or small it is plain that they were brought about by the Postmaster-General's clear violation of the law.[1]

---

were not fairly typical, the competitive principle being better observed there than in most other places.

Moreover the grounds for appointment shown by the "records and papers on file" might not in all cases have been the real ones. Congressmen who "recommend" will not often declare openly a political motive when they are told by the Department that if they do so their communications will be returned unconsidered.

Much additional light could be thrown upon the question if it were ascertained in how many cases Republicans had been superseded by Democrats and vice versa. The worst instances of political manipulation (as stated by Mr. Gillette in his speech in Congress on August 18, 1916) (Record, p. 14,550) were in the middle West and no State was chosen from that section when the secretary of the League made his examination.

[1] The officers of the League in the autumn of 1914 had a conference with President Wilson who expressed some surprise that the Postmaster-General had issued a circular stating that the recommendations of Congressmen would be sought. He thought that Mr. Burleson was observing the merit principle and that the outcome would be satisfactory to the League. Yet no change occurred. The recommendations continued to be sought. Meanwhile, Mr. McIlhenny, President of the Commission, made the extra-

RURAL FREE DELIVERY CARRIERS

Many places in the important rural free delivery service, a service employing over forty-three thousand carriers, were also turned over to congressional patronage in the following manner. A joint resolution of Congress extending the appropriation for the postal service for the year ending June 30, 1916, contained this proviso:

That in the discretion of the Postmaster-General the pay of rural carriers who furnish and maintain their own motor vehicles and whose service routes are not less than fifty miles in length, may be fixed at not exceeding $1800 per annum.

Nothing in this resolution contemplated the creation of any new service. These carriers had a peculiarly strong claim to retention because they had purchased their horses and vehicles at their own expense and great numbers had secured admission by competitive methods. But the Postmaster-General, seizing this joint resolution as a ground for abolishing great numbers of rural routes and for creating a so-called new branch, "Motor Rural Carriers," proceeded to make a clean sweep of many hundreds of positions, turning out all the incumbents, no matter how well they had performed their duties, and appointing new men by means of a so-called new examination by the Civil Service Commission, the eligible lists from this new examination being turned over to Congressmen for recommendations in the same manner as had been done in the case of fourth-class postmasters.

The Postmaster-General had the right to promote the men already in the service or add to their compensation. This he did not do but in order to make the political changes he desired he had a new examination. For this purpose it was necessary to secure the coöperation of the Civil Service Commission, and it seems remarkable that the Commission should have acquiesced without a protest.

If an examination were to be held and all the difference

___

ordinary statement that the Postmaster-General was entirely within the law in seeking these recommendations! (Minutes of League's Council meeting of October 9, 1914.)

between these motor carriers and other rural carriers was that they were to drive an automobile instead of a horse, the new examinations ought to have some reference to this new duty. But, on the contrary, the examinations were precisely the same as those for ordinary rural free delivery carriers. There were no competitive tests of any kind as to running a machine.[1] The examination was in spelling, arithmetic, letter-writing, penmanship, copying, and reading addresses. The men already in the service had passed that sort of an examination in the past and had been working six, eight, twelve years in that particular line of duty except that they had used a horse instead of a machine. How could another examination on the same subjects secure better men to operate an automobile? Is it not clear that the real object was merely to get the old men out and put new men in?

And this becomes all the clearer from another fact:

The Commission determined that applicants who had served in the position of regular rural carrier should be given additional credit in the examination.[2]

How fair! But *how much* should it count? The Commission announced, "There will be added to the general average attained in the examination, a credit of *one half of one per cent. for each year's experience* not exceeding a total of six years of such experience, or a maximum of *three per cent.*"! Frankly it would have been more decent to have allowed nothing. For according to the rules of rating announced by the Commission, a single omitted punctuation or a fraction correct but not reduced to the lowest terms will deduct from one to two per cent of the whole while *a year's experience in faithful work counts for one half of one per cent only.* Thus it would require

---

[1] No questions were asked in regard to it except that in the preliminary and declaration sheet (not the examination paper) the applicant had to give a statement of the experience he had in the operation of motor vehicles. But no weight whatever was given in the rating to the answer to this question. The man who furnished the best machine and was most competent to run it had no advantage over the man who furnished the poorest and who was least competent.

[2] Cong. Record, Dec. 14, 1915. Letter of Fourth Assistant Postmaster-General.

from two to four years' experience to make up for that omitted punctuation and no amount of past faithful experience could atone for two or three such mistakes!

But comment cannot add to the irony of this method of covering up the process by which a great branch of the classified service was again consigned to patronage and spoils. After the examinations were held and the new eligible lists made up they were turned over to Democratic Congressmen, who appointed the politicians most serviceable to them in their campaigns.[1]

Such is the history of the political manipulation of the rural free delivery service. It was far worse than if these places had been withdrawn from classification and had been openly

---

[1] To illustrate, let me take the case of my own city of Richmond and of Wayne County, Indiana, in which it is situated. There were eight rural routes starting from this city and there were nine others in the county. In November, 1915, I learned that all these seventeen routes were to be abolished, the carriers dismissed, and new motor routes were to be established in their places.

The postmaster at Richmond, Charles B. Beck, a Democrat, appointed on the recommendation of Finly P. Gray, the Representative from the district, showed me letters from the Department instructing him to discontinue the rural route service from Richmond, giving the names of the eight carriers who were to be discharged and ordering the establishment of four new routes to be served by motor vehicles. The majority of the men dismissed had been carriers for over five years and they had secured admission by competitive examination. New examinations had been held for the position of motor carrier and Mr. Beck informed me that the eligible lists had been sent to Congressman Gray for recommendations and that Mr. Gray had brought these lists and consulted with him as to the appointments. I learned afterwards that Mr. Beck had said to one of the old carriers, "Democrats ought to be in these places, and I will do what I can to get them there." All the new men appointed were Democrats. On December 30, 1915, I inquired of Congressman Gray why he had asked for these lists. He answered that *he had not asked for them at all*, but they had been sent by the Commission at the request of the Department. I at once wrote to the Commission and inquired what were the facts. The Commission in answer enclosed a copy of a letter from Mr. Gray asking for the Wayne County list of eligibles "without delay," also a telegram of November 1st, "Send immediately eligible list rural auto carriers, Wayne County, Indiana," and the list was accordingly sent.

In my conversation with Mr. Gray I reminded him that these places

thrown back into the spoils system. This would have been discreditable but it would have been candid and we could tell by comparison which worked best, patronage or competition, but under Mr. Burleson's illegal manipulation of the lists the evil of the spoils system was attributed to the competitive system itself and the reform was discredited. To make competitive examinations the very means of discrediting the competitive system was injurious to the last degree.

I communicated the foregoing facts to the President in a letter dated January 12, 1916, and on the 17th of that month I received an answer over his personal signature that this letter would have his attention. But if any action was taken by the Chief Executive to stay this prostitution of the service I never heard of it.

---

were in the classified service and that under the law he had no right to make any recommendations nor take any part in these appointments except to furnish information in respect to the residence or character of the applicants. He told me he had found that the characters of every one of the applicants were good. If that were so, his participation in these appointments ought to have ended. He added, however, that he had selected the men who came from the place where the route started since he assumed that people wanted a carrier from their own town. But he did not follow this rule. He recommended Foland of Centerville as carrier on a route starting from Richmond, six miles distant, though there were others on the eligible list from Richmond itself.

Nor did he confine his recommendations to those highest on the list. Logan, a Republican, was higher than Starr, a Democrat, yet Starr was recommended and appointed.

It was clear enough as to these Richmond positions that Mr. Gray, whose recommendations had filled them all with Democrats, got men whom he considered politically useful to him in place of those who had formerly entered by genuine competitive examinations.

To see how these changes worked in individual cases let us take the example of the carrier Joseph Peltz. He had been admitted to the service on competitive examination in 1909, being the highest on the list and passing with a record of 97 per cent. He served faithfully. Postmaster Beck himself told me that Peltz was an efficient carrier. He furnished his own automobile with which he distributed the mail on his route for a salary of $1200. He was dismissed to make place for two Democratic supporters of Congressman Gray who divided his route between them (with some other territory) for a salary of $1800 each. Yet he and the other dismissed carriers had all received from the government a little book of "instructions" which stated:

16

These changes were, however, accompanied with such bad results in many parts of the country that an outcry arose against them and even in Congress speeches were made and resolutions offered denouncing them[1] even by members of the President's own party. The Post Office Department evidently found that the path to patronage was not uniformly lined with primroses and the brakes had to be put on before the rural free delivery service was generally reorganized.

THE COMMISSION CONCEALS ELIGIBLE LISTS

Another abuse was the refusal of the Civil Service Commission to allow an inspection of its eligible lists. The League had been for some years trying in vain to secure access to information showing to what extent the law was violated. On April 13, 1914, the secretary applied for permission to examine the Commission's records as to fourth-class postmasters but the Commission answered that it was compelled

---

"Politics or religious affiliations of applicants are given no consideration nor are political endorsements entertained." "A rural carrier will not be removed except upon written specific charges filed with the Post Office Department of which he shall have full notice nor until he has had an opportunity for defense." Could this carrier be blamed if under these circumstances he considered these assurances of his government a hollow mockery?

The effect, however, of putting inexperienced carriers on routes with which they were unfamiliar in the winter season was quite unexpected to Mr. Gray and startling to the entire community. Mail remained undelivered for days and weeks. Great masses of it were stuffed away in the cellar of the Richmond post office. One or more of the new carriers resigned in disgust, and the entire county was indignant at the abominable service rendered as the result of the peanut politics shown by this peddling of petty patronage at the expense of the community. Day after day the newspapers teemed with complaints. Mr. Gray's responsibility was everywhere recognized and at the next election the voters defeated him. In June, 1917, he again became a candidate, and was defeated at a special election by an overwhelming majority.

[1] In a speech by Mr. Gillette which appears in the Congressional Record of August 16, 1916, these matters were described in detail substantially as given above.

to deny the request "in the interest of public business owing to *congestion of work* in the office."

On December 29, 1915, when I was investigating the appointment of rural carriers in Wayne County, Indiana, I called at the office of the Commission in Washington, and asked leave to inspect these lists for that county to ascertain in what cases the highest man had been selected and whether any political influences dictated the appointments. But after two of its members had orally promised to send me copies, the Commission finally decided they could not be furnished.[1]

In the meantime the Council of the League on January 28th declared that it was interested in terminating a policy of secrecy which gave to Congressmen information for the pur-

[1] I was informed of this in a letter dated January 5, 1916, which gave the following reasons:

"That the practice was found seriously detrimental to the interests of eligibles and of the public service and that little good purpose was served by it. One large corporation indeed dismissed every employee upon his applying for examination. In certain sections of the country eligibles of one social class objected to their names appearing in public on the eligible list, sometimes at low grades as compared with others of a different class, resulting in white Democrats in the South refusing to take the examinations, being chagrined upon finding their names publicly posted. In small communities prying curiosity led to the humiliation of eligibles. The fact that persons were candidates for public employment operated against them in seeking to secure outside employment. . . . The lists were used for advertising, and at times for corrupt purposes; whatever administration was in power was subjected to being harassed by partisan attack and being made the subject of misrepresentation and abuse. . . ."

To this I answered:

"The reasons given in your letter for denying these lists are none of them applicable here. There is no 'large corporation' which will dismiss these applicants for rural carriers' places, nor any 'social class' to ostracize them because their names appear, nor is there any question of 'white Democrats in the South' competing with negroes, nor 'prying curiosity' to 'humiliate the applicants.' The lists will not be used for 'advertising' nor for 'corrupt purposes.' On the contrary the purpose is to expose corruption. If the administration in power should be 'harassed by partisan attacks' it will be only because of the partisan action of its own Post Office Department and its own members of Congress. If this be indeed the reason for your hiding these lists the world ought to know it."

pose of defeating the merit system and declined to give the same information to the League to expose abuses.

In a meeting between members of the Commission and representatives of the League on March 31, 1916, at a dinner given at Washington by John Joy Edson, one of the Council, Commissioner McIlhenny said he could not recede from the decision to refuse access to the records since if this were given it *might lead to criticism of the administration and might seriously embarrass it.*   Commissioner Cravens concurred in this determination.

The League now took up the matter with the President, and on July 3, 1916, sent a memorandum asking him to put an end to this policy of secrecy.

This letter the President answered on July 19th, saying that he had referred the correspondence to the Commission with the suggestion that in their annual report they disclose the method employed in administering the executive order for the examination of fourth-class postmasters, together with the results obtained thereby!

He added:

The Chairman of the Civil Service Commission advises me . . . that his refusal to grant your League access to the civil service records was not based on any fear that the records would lead to criticism of the administration. He states that there is not the slightest apprehension that any proper criticism can be made of the manner in which the Executive Order has been administered and that his refusal to permit general access to the files and the holding of such records as confidential, investigating on their merits all cases of alleged improper action brought to the attention of the Commission, is based upon good administrative practice as is explained in a letter of the Commission to you under date of May 27, 1916, the transmission of which has been delayed.

The Commission's letter declared that it was impracticable that individuals or associations should be permitted at will to search its files and that it was the practice to consider official records as privileged.

The Commission declared, however, that its actions as to its own administrative matters were at all times within the purview of every citizen under reasonable limitations of which the Commission must be the judge.   If it was believed that the Commission was hiding things which should be disclosed it was competent for either House of Congress to make demand for the records and the Commission would then determine its action. The letter further added that the League was a body not known to the law, without power to compel testimony and not responsible to any constituted authority. An investigation by an outside body might be ex parte, partisan, michievous, imperfect, and calculated grossly to mislead the public *and attack and embarrass an administration.* The Commission on the other hand had the legal machinery and experience to conduct such an investigation and its work might be reviewed by the President and a committee of Congress. These were the checks upon maladministration and it was the duty of citizens to seek the betterment of governmental conditions through the processes thus provided. The Commission requested the League to send to it the complaints and charges with reference to fourth-class postmasters and rural carriers for investigation. In other words the Commission would investigate its own delinquencies and those of the department!

This correspondence was communicated to the League at its Council meeting at Stockbridge, Massachusetts, on July 27, 1916, and our reply was sent to President Wilson on August 1st. In it we said:

The transmission of the Commission's letter, as you say, "has been delayed." In fact though dated May 27, 1916, the letter did not arrive until July 22d! The Commission can hardly be congratulated upon its promptness in the dispatch of public business when a letter remains unanswered for more than three months, when a subsequent request for an answer is made in vain, and when an answer is finally sent only after the Commission's delay has been brought to your personal attention. . . .

What the League requests and the Commission refuses, is liberty to inspect the Commission's eligible registers for the position of motor rural carriers and fourth-class postmasters established since May, 1913. The propriety of the Commission's refusal to permit such an inspection involves no considerations which might justify a refusal of leave to inspect "confidential letters or reports from other departments" or "statements or records entrusted to the Commission in confidence" or transcripts of "testimony to the Commission" or of leave to "search at will the files of the National Commission" with which the Commission's letter deals in some detail. It tends merely to confusion to advert to such matters as a ground for the Commission's refusal to permit an examination of the *records of its own administrative acts.*

May we call your attention to the fact that such lists are constantly made public in all parts of the country by State and city civil service commissions ? During the entire existence of the National Civil Service Reform League prior to your administration information as to the public administrative work of the Federal Commission has never been refused to us, except during a short period in the year 1899.

The reasons given by the Commission for this concealment are contradictory and inconsistent. In its letter to the League of April 24, 1914, it says: "This action is necessary in the interests of public business *owing to the congestion of the work in the office.*" Yet after we had waited nearly two years, when it might properly be assumed that this congestion had been overcome, we were told by Mr. McIlhenny, the president of the Commission at our Washington conference on March 31, 1916, that if access were given to these records it might *lead to such criticism of the administration as would seriously embarrass it.* Finally, in its letter received July 22d, the Commission amplifies this ground for its action by stating that an investigation by an outside body may "mislead the public and *attack and embarrass the administration.*" This, therefore, appears as the vital reason for the refusal.

We think you must have overlooked this, for we cannot assume that the President of the United States could permit such a reason to be urged for the concealment of official records concerning official acts or that he would willingly appear to adopt the argument that such concealment is necessary to preserve his administration from attack. . . .

The Commission says in its letter that it believes "the influence of our League in the advancement of the cause of efficient public service is incalculable," yet it refuses us the means of prosecuting our legitimate inquiries, and when we appeal to you from its decision you tell us that you have suggested to the Commission that in its annual report for 1916 it shall disclose the methods employed in administering your executive order of May 7, 1913. It would be a most incompetent body which could not draw up a report furnishing a plausible explanation for even the gravest abuses and we feel sure that neither the League nor the public will remain satisfied with a plan which allows any department or branch of the service to be the only interpreter of its own conduct and denies to the world all access to the evidence by which the truth of its interpretation can be established or refuted.

This letter was generally published and excited widespread comment and condemnation of the Commission.[1] Evidently

[1] See article in New York *Evening Post*, August 9, 1916, St. Louis *Globe-Democrat*, August 13, 1916, Buffalo *News*, August 9, 1916, Philadelphia

wincing under this general disapprobation, the Commissioners on August 15th published an official statement. In this they said:

The Commission has simply adhered to a policy under which it has operated since its establishment in 1883—a policy universal in all Governmental Departments.

The claim of the League that with the exception of a brief period in 1899 the Commission has heretofore extended to the League the general privilege of examining its files cannot be substantiated. While the Commission has often, in its discretion, furnished to the League and to private individuals specific information regarding civil service matters the League has never possessed or exercised the general privilege of inspecting the files and correspondence of the Commission. . . .

A few days later I addressed them the following open letter which was also published pretty generally throughout the country.

I have just read the astounding declaration in your official statement given out last Monday night that in refusing to the National Civil Service Reform League access to your eligible lists "The Commission has simply adhered to a policy under which it has operated since its establishment in 1883."

This declaration is flatly contradicted by the official reports of the Commission itself and by its own public regulations. For instance, in the Sixth Report, p. 3, is the following:

"A most important change in the policy of the Commission was instituted by the adoption on June 29, 1889, of the regulation requiring that the lists of eligibles—that is of those applicants successful in passing the examinations—be made public with the grade of each eligible attached. The adoption of this regulation has already had a most beneficial effect. It is especially desirable that all proceedings under the law should be free from the slightest taint or suspicion of fraud, and it is therefore important that they should be as open as possible."

This report bears the distinguished signatures of Theodore Roosevelt and Governor Hugh S. Thompson, of South Carolina, than whom no more eminent commissioners have ever filled the offices you now occupy. . . . Again you say in your official statement of Monday:

"The claim of the League, that, with the exception of a brief period in 1899, the Commission has heretofore extended the general privilege of examining its files, cannot be substantiated."

Ledger, August 13, 1916, Providence *Journal*, August 10, 1916, and scores of other papers. A particularly pungent editorial appeared August 16th in the New York *Tribune*, entitled "Caught with the Goods."

But the League made no such claim. In its letter to the President it said, "Information as to *the public administrative work* of the Federal Commission has never been refused to us, except during a short period in the year 1899."

The League never asked for access to your confidential files, but only information as to your public administrative work, and as to that you wrote me:

"Its action as to administrative matters was at all times within the purview of every citizen, under reasonable limitation of which the Commission must be the judge, and that its files as to such matters were open to the least scrap of paper to anyone interested either publicly or privately therein."

Are not your lists of eligibles, the results of your public examinations, administrative matters? Yet the Commission has for more than two years refused to the National Civil Service Reform League an inspection of its own eligible lists—at first "owing to the congestion of work in the office," and lastly, lest such an inspection might "embarrass the Administration."

The National Civil Service Reform League asked for this inspection, as I asked for it last winter—when you promised to give it to me, a promise you did not fulfill—for the purpose of determining whether the lists for fourth-class postmasterships or places on the rural free delivery routes had been fraudulently manipulated for political purposes, and if you refuse this on such a ground, is any other conclusion possible except that the administration, protected by your secrecy, is guilty of the fraudulent acts alleged? Can anything but guilt "embarrass" the administration and make necessary the veil of secrecy with which you shroud your own official acts? Will not the President pray to be delivered from apologists and defenders who insist that his administration must not be "embarrassed" by a revelation of the truth?

To this the Commission did not attempt any reply. In November, however, it was announced that the President would reëxamine the matter of the secrecy of these records because, as he said, "That is something I owe the League out of respect for its activities." Up to the present time, however, no change of policy has been announced and the Commissoners who supported this policy of concealment are still in office.

OTHER APPOINTMENTS

The President failed in several conspicuous instances to retain in office men who had risen by merit and demonstrated their efficiency in important places and he appointed politicians to succeed them. Prominent among the former was Postmaster Edward M. Morgan of New York City. His connection with the postal service had extended over thirty-five years. He had gradually risen from the rank of letter-carrier through various grades to this important position to which he had been appointed by President Roosevelt and reappointed by President Taft. Thomas G. Patten, a retired Congressman without administrative experience in the government service, was appointed to the place.

The case of the postmaster of Brooklyn was just as bad. Walter C. Burton was a spoils politician and as civil service commissioner of New York he had done what he could to degrade and debauch the merit system in that State, for which service he was apparently rewarded by this important office. Mr. Wright, an experienced and efficient postmaster at Norfolk, Virginia, was supplanted by a political appointee. A number of similar cases could be given.

There was, however, some gain in other directions, for instance in the position of Chief Post Office Inspector. This position, as we have seen, was excepted from examination by President Taft in 1910, and Robert S. Sharpe, an active politician, had received the appointment. This had given rise to merited criticism. On February 16, 1913 (just before the inauguration of President Wilson), Sharpe resigned, and on May 17th, the President on the recommendation of the Postmaster-General restored the position to the competitive service and promoted J. P. Johnson, inspector in charge of the St. Louis division to the place. The positions of solicitor of the Post Office Department and of first, second, and third assistant Postmasters-General were also filled by men of experience and apparently without regard to political considerations, but the fourth assistant was a political appointment, and it was precisely in this place that the scandal in the rural free delivery service arose.

BURLESON'S SPEECH

An interesting episode occurred at the annual meeting of the League at New Haven on December 5, 1916. The Postmaster-General had declared that the criticisms made by the League were unjust and that we owed him an apology. In order to give him the opportunity to set himself right an invitation was extended to him to speak on this occasion, and he came. The meeting was held in one of the assembly halls of Yale College and President Hadley was chairman. Mr. Richard H. Dana, the president of the League, first delivered his annual address. Mr. Burleson followed in a written speech in defense of his administration and I concluded with some remarks in reply.

The Postmaster-General referred to his first annual report in which he said that the prime consideration should be to recognize efficiency and eliminate partisanship so that ultimately all positions should be included in the classified service. He reminded us that in his Department there were then just seven places not so included, those of the four assistant Postmasters-General, the solicitor and chief inspector for the Department, and his own private secretary; that these appointments had all been made from experienced men and that only one, the fourth assistant, was political.

The question of the fourth-class postmasters, he said, presented a serious problem. Many of these had been selected for purely partisan reasons and then blanketed into the classified service by the orders of former Presidents without any proper tests of qualifications. "What," he asked, "could any one genuinely believing in the merit system do but ask for a revocation of these orders?" He knew this would be misunderstood, but refusing to acquiesce in the degradation of the service he had asked the President to issue the order of May 7, 1913, for a new competitive examination. How could any civil service reformer logically object to this? It was a laudable effort to secure the best men without reference to party affiliations and was in thorough harmony with the civil service law, yet the League had opposed this action as impracticable. It was stated that incumbents belonging to the opposite party were unjustly displaced and that he had invited Congressmen of his own political faith to report on the comparative merit of eligibles. This was a mistake. He had invited no one to report on "comparative" qualifications. All Congressmen were informed that any information permissible under the civil service rules would be considered. They were given every opportunity to speak with reference to the *character* and *residence* of applicants. Congressmen, he said, were not asked to *recommend* candidates nor were any recommendations received or considered.

He also gave in some detail the percentages of incumbents and of the highest eligibles who had been appointed (as given above on pp. 235, 236). The records of the Commission showed why in the few cases indicated the second or third man was chosen in preference to the first but the Commission rightly declined to make this information public because in many cases the record was prejudicial to candidates. But it might be seen by any responsible person who desired to know the Department's reasons for not appointing the first man.

When one of these fourth-class post offices was raised to the presidential grade he informed *the political adviser in the case* that the Department preferred, unless there were substantial reasons to the contrary, to continue the incumbent as a presidential appointee. The same conscientious observance of the civil service law had ruled in the matter of removals. Presidential postmasters appointed by previous administrations had been permitted to serve out their four-year terms except where investigation had shown that they were incompetent or neglectful. A few had been removed for political activity but these cases had been referred by him to the Commission, although no such action had ever previously been taken by any cabinet officer. Mr. Burleson stated that he had opposed the provision to remove assistant postmasters from the classified service and that he had established scientific efficiency records and ratings as a basis for promotions. These were the things that had been done. Whether civil service reformers were moved to praise or censure was for them to determine. In either event he stood by the record.

As to the future he had recommended that *all* postmasters be classified, and, if he could, he would classify every position save that of the Postmaster-General. The ideal system would be one under which every postmaster, if by merit he could earn it, would have within his reach the postmastership of the largest city in the United States.

This address was upon its face a strong presentation of the case of the Postmaster-General and manifestly made a favorable effect upon the audience.

In reply I congratulated the League and the country on the principles he had just expressed and remarked that some explanation was due of the reasons why it had appeared to the League that in the application of those principles he had not observed the requirements of the law.   After expressing our appreciation of the classification of the chief post office inspector I took up the order of May 13, 1913, providing for the examination of the fourth-class postmasters.   In the argument made by the League in regard to that order it had been distinctly stated that if honestly administered and fairly conducted there would be no criticism of the examination but that we did not acquiesce in the propriety of prescribing it *unless political influences were kept out of the appointment after the examination was made.*   I next quoted Section 10 of the law.   The spoils system, I contended, had its root in congressional patronage. Congressmen recommended and their recommendations were followed and thus the spoils of office were divided among them. Therefore Section 10 provided that recommendations should not be received or considered except as to character or residence.   There was no more vital principle anywhere in the civil service law than in Section 10.   The Postmaster-General denied that he had asked for "comparative recommendations" but I quoted his order where he said it was his practice to ask Congressmen to advise him relative to the character and *fitness of the three eligibles.*   That was the thing which the statute said he should not do.   Congressmen had interpreted his request as authorizing political recommendations.

I cited the Hicks case in Indiana, the Hoke Smith case in Georgia where Democrats got the appointments because they were Democrats and Republicans were excluded because they were Republicans.   Whether the percentage was large or small, politics followed and the League had a right to protest.

If the appointments were uniformly made on competitive principles why had the League been unable to secure an examination of the records showing the grades of the eligibles? It was a maxim of jurisprudence that where anyone suppressed evidence, the presumption was against him. We had not asked for confidential records which might injure the character of applicants but only for the *eligible lists* and the Commission had refused inspection.

After approving the Postmaster-General's action in regard to removals I next considered the rural free delivery service. Nothing in the law which authorized an increase in the carrier's pay to $1800 if he used an automobile and served a route of fifty miles justified the Postmaster-General in creating a new service of "motor rural carriers" and abolishing the old service on these routes. As Senator Cummins said in his letter to the Commission:

It might just as well be claimed that when the route is changed from twenty miles to twenty-five miles that a new position had been created, as to claim that when the route is lengthened to fifty miles and necessitates an automobile a new position is brought into existence. . . . While the incoming carriers on motor routes must enter through competition the old carriers lose absolutely a valuable right which was intended to be protected by the civil service law.

I related the experience of my own city of Richmond where all the old carriers, good and bad, had been turned out and where, upon the recommendation of the Congressman, Democrats had been appointed to all the new places. Of course God might have given those particular Democrats the power to pass better examinations than others but unfortunately they did not stand highest on the list.

I criticized the examinations in which the applicants were not graded at all on their ability to run automobiles, the only new duty required, and in which a single omitted punctuation mark would offset a whole year's faithful service.

I closed my remarks with a review of the course of the administration in giving the great ambassadorships to large contributors of campaign funds and called attention to the resolutions of the League passed that very day censuring this practice, and I insisted that no matter what administration was in power the League would remain true to the principles it always advocated.

I noticed that as I proceeded in the discussion the audience (which consisted not only of members of the League but of a large number of students) became greatly interested. I could see them looking at the Postmaster-General with smiles upon their faces. He moved around uneasily in his seat and appeared to be most indignant, talking part of the time very earnestly with Mr. Dana who sat beside him, and as I concluded amid considerable applause and the meeting adjourned, he arose, passed directly in front of me and very close without recognizing my presence, and stalked solemnly and impressively out of the room.

CHAPTER XVIII

WILSON'S SECOND TERM—CONCLUSION

IT will be seen from the foregoing that Mr. Wilson's first term had been mainly reactionary. But unsatisfactory as it was we could not help seeing how much more so it might be if Vice-President Marshall should ever succeed to the office of Chief Executive. In a campaign speech at Terre Haute early in September, 1916, he said:

> Did I say civil service or snivel service? They both mean the same. We found the offices guarded by snivel service and our only regret was that we couldn't pry more of the places loose and fill them with Democrats. If there is any office under the government which a Democrat can't fill I believe that office should be abolished.

When the campaign of 1916 came on attempts were made by the League to secure declarations in favor of the classification of presidential postmasters in the platforms of the various parties but it was unsuccessful. The candidates did better. Mr. Hughes declared that he favored such legislation and Mr. Wilson on November 6th, *the day before election*, wrote to the League to the same effect.

This issue was not prominent in the campaign, which turned mainly upon the absorbing questions resulting from the great struggle in Europe, and Mr. Wilson was chosen by a small majority mainly because he had "kept us out of war."

But after his inauguration things began to improve. Mr. Wilson was personally friendly to the merit system. It had been the pressure of Congress and of party followers which had led to his shortcomings. He now took an important forward step. The Postmaster-General had recommended, as we have seen, the classification of all post offices but Congress had disregarded the recommendations and no law was passed. But the President now determined to take the responsibility himself and on March 31st he issued an executive order providing that whenever a vacancy occurred in the position of postmaster of the first, second, or third class as the result of death, resignation, removal, or on the recommendation of the Postmaster-General the Civil Service Commission should hold an open competitive examination and certify the result thereof to the Postmaster-General, who should submit to the President the name of the highest qualified eligible.

There was one feature of this order which went beyond the general method of appointments adopted for other places. The Commission was to certify to the President not three names but one, the highest, to be nominated for the place. This would exclude the limited opportunity for patronage afforded by the selection of one man out of three. So far it conformed to the best ideals. But on the other hand no provision was made for a new examination whenever the term of an incumbent should expire. The Postmaster-General explained that incumbents who were rendering good service would not be disturbed.

In this order Mr. Wilson and the Postmaster-General were not prepared to take the medicine which they had themselves prescribed in respect to fourth-class postmasters appointed under previous administrations and require *all* in the service to submit to competitive tests. In other words Mr. Wilson having now filled the offices largely with Democrats adopted substantially the same policy of "covering them all in" against which he and his Postmaster-General had objected when they ordered the examination of all fourth-class postmasters and of motor free delivery carriers.

But although consistency was abandoned, civil service reformers have the same reason to rejoice as they had when Cleveland, Harrison, Roosevelt, and Taft made their extensions of the service. The method adopted by the President however was a complete refutation of the Postmaster-General's argument at our League meeting, when he criticized the previous inclusion of the fourth-class postmasterships without requiring an examination.

The number of offices affected was 10,339 and among these were some of the most important in the country. It cannot yet be said that this order is permanent. The Senate has still the right to confirm and may refuse confirmation of presidential nominations made as the result of competitive examinations.

When a Republican administration comes into power will it adopt the President's classification as final or will it follow the example of Mr. Wilson and provide for new examinations of all these places with perhaps the same partisan reconstruction of the service as in the case of fourth-class postmasters and rural free delivery carriers? If so there will be another period of retrogression.

But unless some such backward step be taken hereafter this most important branch of the service will be redeemed from the blight of spoils politics and the President and his Postmaster-General will be entitled to the credit for that most important achievement.

A RETROSPECT

In this survey of the progress of the competitive system, the observer will notice a striking similarity in the conduct of nearly every President. Every one of them since the Pendleton Act has been personally favorable to the system and if left to himself would not only have enforced the law but would have extended its application more rapidly and consistently than was actually done. Yet each was subject to tremendous pressure not only from office seekers but from powerful organizations in his own party, a pressure so overwhelming that perhaps no man could wholly resist it, and the net gain was the resultant of two opposing forces.

In my opinion Mr. Roosevelt was more consistent and energetic than any other President in advancing the reform. But it must be remembered that he followed the administration of a President belonging to his own party and the on-

17

slaught upon the system was not so formidable as in the case, for instance, of Mr. Cleveland whose own supporters had been so long excluded from the patronage during his first administration that they were all but unanimous in their opposition. Mr. Roosevelt had also the advantage of a detailed knowledge of the working of the competitive system acquired by his long experience as commissioner. A great deal of charity will no doubt be extended by history even to the imperfect measure of success attained either in extending the reform or in resisting the attacks upon it. But I have conceived it to be the duty of one who is devoted to the competitive system to judge each administration by the highest practicable standard of achievement and this I have endeavored to do in the foregoing pages.

The general result has been on the whole most gratifying. The classified service has grown from about 14,000 places following the enactment of the law to more than 300,000 places to-day. The law in the main is observed. Political coercion and activity within the service has greatly diminished. The rules have been developed and strengthened and more important than all the need of competitive rather than political methods in determining qualifications for office has gradually permeated the consciousness of our people until their approval of the reform system has become widespread and general.

CONCLUSION

It is now time to close. Another epoch is upon us. In April, 1917, our country passed from the field of diplomacy to the solemn fact of war. We are now participants in the greatest struggle in which mankind was ever engaged. Under these conditions what is to be the fate of the reform? Will this progress toward good administration be submerged in the seething waves of the conflict or will it be realized that the competitive system is even more necessary to secure the efficiency of the nation in this crisis than it was during the piping times of peace? If the great resources of America are to be made effective in this struggle for human liberty, personal and party considerations must be wholly subordinated to patriotic duty. Men must be selected for the civil service on account of merit and because of their fitness for the places to which they are chosen. This can only be done if the competitive system is maintained in its integrity and extended to the vast multitude of new offices which have to be created for the successful prosecution of the war. There never was a time where the efforts of the Reform League were so essential to our national welfare. It is bound to insist with greater energy than ever before that selections made by patronage and political favor shall not be allowed to open the floodgates of corruption, either during the war or reconstruction that shall follow it.

New questions are bound to arise which demand greater effort and energy than those already decided. The absorption by the government of our railways and other industries opens an immense field of new activities which are likely to outlast the war and become part of the permanent policy of a greatly socialized state. In all these new places there will be at first discretionary appointments under political control—that same germ of evil which led to the growth of the spoils system in the past. Can it be eliminated or will the enormously enlarged field of government industries form the great "bribery chest" of future political corruption?

Then when our millions of veterans return from the war and find their places in industrial life largely occupied by others it is natural and inevitable that many of them, especially those disabled in the service, will claim that preference in appointments which these patriotic sacrifices will have so eminently deserved. Can such a claim be resisted? Or can it be recognized in such a way as still to keep our civil service from the baneful influences of favoritism and patronage?

These are among the vital problems which we who are passing from the field of action must leave to those who shall take up the task. God grant to them the clear wisdom and unflagging zeal which characterized George William Curtis and our other eminent leaders in the early days of the reform and to our country the same happy fortune as that which has hitherto conducted it safely and triumphantly through every crisis of its national life.

APPENDIX I

CIVIL SERVICE REFORM[1]

With each new political contest the line of principle dividing the two great parties has been less clearly drawn, the platforms of each of them have become more vague and their candidates less and less the exponents of any definite idea. The matter at issue resolves itself more into the question "who shall have the offices." Everything else seems to be secondary to the distribution of the loaves and fishes. If this continues we can have no healthful Republican government. No party is worthy to rule where the paramount question is the mere possession of power.

The evils which flow from such a system are manifold. The party in power, however corrupt, feels that it has a vast multitude of supporters in every district in the country bound body and soul to its maintenance by motives wholly mercenary and selfish. In every political contest hundreds of thousands on each side support the claims of the parties and their candidates regardless of the principles involved, wholly from the hope of private gain and selfish ambition for office and power. This extends through every grade of society down to the lowest. Parton says "he once knew an apple-woman in Wall Street who had a personal interest in the election of President. If her candidate won her 'old man' would be a porter in a warehouse." Officials are chosen for the party services they have rendered or will render. The government, which ought to be served by the best men in the country, is actually served, to a great extent, by the most mercenary and incompetent. Men whose talents enable them to acquire a competency in private life will not enter a service, the term of which may expire at any time, and which is certain to end whenever a new party comes into power. "At the end of each four years the entire federal patronage (amounting to one hundred and ten thousand offices) is collected into one lot, and the people divide themselves into two parties struggling in name to choose a President but in fact to control this enormous patronage, which the President, when elected, is compelled to distribute. The temptation to fraud, to usurpation, and to corruption, thus created, is beyond calculation. A prize so great, an influence so powerful,

---

[1] An argument delivered before the State Senate of Indiana, February 17, 1885.

thus centralized and put up at short periods, would jeopardize the peace and safety of any nation. No nation can withstand a strife among its own people so general, so intense, and so demoralizing. No contrivance so effectual to embarrass government, to disturb the public peace, to destroy political honesty, and to endanger the common security, was ever before invented." (Report of Committee on Election Frauds, 1879.)

The reform heretofore proposed for these evils has been to turn out the party in power under which they have existed, and fill the places by new men taken from another political organization. The reform which the Democratic party proposes is to turn out Republicans and put in Democrats. The reform which the Republican party will perhaps propose will be to turn out Democrats and put in Republicans. There must be a "rotation in office," in the opinion of all those who are out, while those who are in devote themselves to the perpetuation of patronage and spoils. A moment's thought will show that merely to change an administration is a clumsy way to reform its abuses. It turns out the good as well as the bad; the faithful servant as well as the spoilsman and the sinecurist; the honest officer as well as the jobber. It is like the system of the mother who whipped all her children in turn. It does not encourage merit. The man who does his duty finds that his tenure is no more secure than that of the man who violates it. The fear of removal for corrupt practices may operate in some general and impersonal manner upon the party as a whole, and thus act as some slight restraint, but it does not appeal personally and directly to any individual in the service. Moreover, a reformation accomplished in this manner may be wrought at the sacrifice of some greater principle even than civil service reform, and the time is not distant in the recollection of all of us when those who would have sought reform in this manner must have attained it, if at all, by elevating to power an administration which regarded the war as a failure, the negro as a chattel, and the inflation of our currency and partial repudiation of our debt as national blessings. Reform, even had it then been needed, could not have been had at such a price as that. But even where reform follows a mere change, it is and always must be of the most temporary character. The argument of those who want power is that "a new broom sweeps clean," but a new broom soon becomes old and worn with use. Neither of the two great parties in the country to-day can say that the mere personnel of its adherents is such as to secure it against the temptations of long-continued power. We are not gods, but men; and the party that cries so clamorously for reform when out of office contains within itself as much of human frailty as that which holds for the time the reins of power. Every candid Democrat and every candid Republican will concede this. The party that would weed out abuses to-day will bring forth a plentiful progeny of corruption in a decade. The cry, "turn the rascals out," proceeding alternately from the camps of Israel and Judah, and followed by the mere transfer of spoils, is very edifying, but it gives no hope of permanent improvement. We want something that will apply the remedy at the very approach of the disease, something that works, not transiently and spasmodically, but by a constant, natural law. We do not want a nostrum or opiate which gives mere temporary relief from pain and leaves the source of the malady untouched to attack us with greater violence on the morrow. What we need is a *"vis medicatrix naturæ";* something in the political system which will restore and retain health without external aid; something which shall be present wherever the forces of decay appear to correct them by its own inherent power. The remedy should be as permanent as the evil. It should be addressed to the known weaknesses of human nature, recognizing that these may appear in Democrat and Republican alike.

We must remember that no party ever existed, no, nor any form of government, into which corrupt and selfish motives have not somewhere entered. The question is, what will contract within the closest space the sphere of their activities. Our experience in constitutional restrictions shows that the evils of government are always least where its powers are limited by certain fixed laws; that it is wiser to trust our rights to general preëstablished rules than to leave them to be determined by the irresponsible will of another. Accordingly in general matters of law we leave as little discretion as possible to our judges, our governors, and our political officials. We consider that fixed rules, however imperfect, are better than arbitrary power. Even our own hands as legislators are tied by many stringent provisions of our State and national constitutions. We cannot impair the obligations of contract, nor pass ex post facto laws. We cannot establish a religion, nor create an order of nobility. Why is this? Because it is deemed safer to trust a general rule in these matters than to leave them to be determined by our arbitrary will. The great feature of all Republican institutions is jealousy of arbitrary power. We have eliminated it from many parts of our system. What the civil service reformer asks is that still other limitations should be prescribed. Why is it that an appointing officer should be permitted to act any more arbitrarily in his appointments than in respect of any other official act? Public office is a public trust and he has no more right to bestow it for his personal gratification or for the success of his party than the judge has to take away your property or mine upon personal or party grounds. If you ask then why I want appointments controlled by rules and examinations; why I am not willing to trust the discretion of the executive or even of the Legislature, I answer: "For the same reason that you insist that the judge that passes upon your life, liberty, and property shall be governed by fixed rules of law; for the same reason that you are unwilling to trust his arbitrary discretion to do what to him seems right."

We say that to regulate appointments for office by certain fixed rules, is better than to leave such appointments to the arbitrary discretion of an individual or party, to just the same extent that the reign of law in civil government is better than arbitrary discretion. There are many defects

·n every system of fixed laws. Such systems have their imperfections in the impossibility of adapting perfectly any general rule to the requirements of every individual case. But the blood marks of tyranny which have defaced every page of the world's history show that the imperfections of human nature are such that it is better to trust almost any system of uniform law than the caprice of an individual or collection of individuals; that absolute sovereigns rule for their own aggrandizement and consider the sufferings of their subjects as trivial when weighed in the balance against their own pride and interest. This is no less true of a party than it is of a man; wherever the appointing power is lodged, if it be discretionary, it will in like manner be used for the selfish purposes of the possessor of that power. The further civilization advances the less it leaves to be determined by the caprice of its rulers. Absolutism is an evidence of a low grade of society; and the arbitrary right of appointment to office in a man or a party is a rudimentary form of absolutism still left in a civilization which has, in the main, outgrown it.

If now it be conceded that a system of rules is better than individual discretion, the next question is: What sort of rules must they be? We take it that it is self-evident that the right of appointment to office is a trust; that the duty is to appoint the man best qualified for the office—the one who will best serve the people in his official capacity. The notion that any man or party has a right to an office is erroneous. The right is in the whole people to have the best servants; the right is in the taxpayer to have the best work performed for the money which he is required to pay for it. Taxpayers belong to all parties. You have no right to tax a Republican to pay for services performed for the Democratic party. All pay taxes alike, and the work for which they pay should be work from which they are all to receive a benefit, that is it should be public and not partisan service. It is just as much a crime in principle to appoint to office one unfit to perform its duties, on account of personal or party services, as to devote the public money to personal or campaign uses. If there be any claim to office by any person it is the claim of the fittest person to hold it solely on account of his fitness.

If these conclusions are correct, the only remaining question is: "By what system of general rules can the fitness of men for office be best determined?" It will be hard to think of any system worse than the present one. Capacity for party intrigue (for which offices are now made rewards) ought to be rather a disqualification than a reason for appointment. Prejudice and dishonesty are very frequent companions of partisan zeal and ability. If we selected our officials by lot, and limited their terms of office to two months, as they used to do in the Republic of Florence, we should scarcely fare worse than we do now. We have not even the guarantee of the official responsibility of the appointing officer, for appointments are most commonly made upon the influence of some political friend, which the superior is powerless to resist. He does not even dare remove the subordinate after his unworthiness is known, lest it may give offense. Now no man should fill any office unless he knows enough to perform its duties. This knowledge can be found out in two ways, first by examining him, and secondly by trying him. A man ought not to be a reading clerk who cannot read distinctly, nor an engrossing clerk if he cannot write a good hand, and spell properly. Yet I have known reading clerks who could not read and engrossing clerks who could not write. An hour's examination would easily have exposed these shortcomings. In all matters then, where there are any duties to be performed in which the candidate's fitness can be ascertained by an examination, there ought to be such examination. But this is not enough; we ought to seek not only to obtain a fit man but the very fittest. You cannot tell who the fittest will be until you compare one man with another. Examinations should therefore be competitive. Now the larger the competition the better will be the ability secured. To find out who is the very best, you must give all a chance. This is nothing but simple justice. Every citizen ought to have the right to prove himself the worthest if he can. This is true democratic equality. It recognizes the broad principle that all men are created equal; that they have an equal right to seek any office in the gift of the government; that neither wealth, nor birth, nor influence, nor political opinion can shut the door on them and say: "You cannot enter."

Civil service reform is the cause of the people against the politicians. Let the test be public, like our trials; let the decision of the examiners be open to the criticism of all; let the examination papers be made a matter of public record; let the character of the respective applicants be subject to the scrutiny of their competitors, and we may rest assured that the results of such examination will be, in the main, just. But the duty of the examiners must not be discretionary. It must be confined to making up results from the fixed data furnished by the examination papers, which should always be open to inspection.

But it is not enough that the applicant should be examined. He must also be tried. If he be found unworthy, let him stand aside and give the place to the next upon the list. A period of probation should be imposed, and no officer should receive a permanent appointment until his superior certifies to his proper conduct in the discharge of his duties. There should also be proof of moral character, and limitations as to age and health. When these safeguards are thrown around the service, and promotions are made to depend solely upon the faithful performance of duty, as shown by a record equally public, we have, I think, as good a system as can be devised. We apply to government the great law which nature applies in every gradation of organic life—the survival of the fittest. Of course there are positions in the civil service to which such rules should not apply. All elective offices must remain as they are now and the leaders who direct the policy of the administration should belong to the party in power.

The direct result of the competitive system would thus be the appointment of a much better class of public servants, but its indirect results would be still more important. It would give a new impulse to a thorough education in all the elementary branches required for the public service, and indirectly to education of every description.

But the most important gain would be the removal of one of the main causes of the political corruption which now infects our institutions. The offices at the disposal of party managers constitute a great mass of political capital wherewith to bribe men to perform the baser and more dishonorable party services. It is the glittering prize of some office held before the eyes of the ward politician which animates him in his political bartering. To put these offices beyond the power of patronage, to render them no longer attainable by such means is to wipe out much of the trickery which pervades our political organizations. The purer part of politics will remain; those who work for principle and not for pelf will work as hard as ever. Legitimate party government will not be affected. The higher officers will continue to carry out the policy of their respective parties.

Arbitrary power corrupts its possessor. This is just as true of a party as of a man. The removal of patronage will make both parties purer and cleaner. The demoralizing solicitations which consume the time of legislative and executive officers will cease, and they can devote their undivided energy to matters of public policy and statesmanship. Public economy will be promoted; legislators will no longer vote exorbitant salaries to favor their appointees. Removals without cause will be stopped when vacancies must be filled by competition. The officials, no longer subject to political assessments, nor liable to be arbitrarily removed, will work for lower salaries. They will no longer neglect their official duties for politics, since they will no longer owe their office to political work. Hence the same number of persons can do more and better work. The officers will retain their manhood and independence and will not be required to vote for a person or measure which they do not approve for fear of losing their places. The charge that our best men keep aloof from office because politics is demoralizing will no longer be true. To hold office in the civil service will be creditable, because it will show that the possessor has ability and knowledge. Executive appointments will no longer be influenced by the Legislature, because they will be beyond the power of the Legislature. Politics will become less a trade. Party intrigue will fall more into disrepute, while the general suspicion of corrupt motives which clings to almost every legislative act will in great measure pass away. The bane of modern political life is an accursed hunger for office. It is the common saying "Young men should not go into politics because it ruins them for everything else." The excitement, the intrigue, the passion and ambition attendant upon political life seem to disqualify most men for the duties of business. The temporary character of appointments and the arbitrary removals by which sooner or later nearly all are thrown back into private life are the source of bitter disappointment. Politics wrecks the lives of nearly all who engage in it. In its mad vortex those who enter perish.

Such being its tendency, its baleful influence should be confined within the closest possible limits.

The wisdom of civil service reform is demonstrated, not merely by reason but by experience and historic fact. It is no longer an experiment. It has been tried, and is successful. Its success has been tested, not during a month nor a year, but during a long series of years; in England, in India, in Australia, in Canada, and last of all, in our own Federal Government, and in the Empire State. It has been tried longest and proved most thoroughly in England and her dependencies. Her history in this respect, as in others which have affected our dearest political rights, is pregnant with instruction.

Civil service reform is past its embryonic condition. It is only a question of time until it is introduced into every State and Territory. The country is now ripe for this reform. The thinking people of the nation demand it.

I can see other great measures looming up in the more distant future— great problems in regard to the disposition of wealth—the land question— the labor question. For some of these the world is not yet ready. They must be wrought out in public thought before they can receive definite form in legislation, but this matter has already been developed in a practical shape. It is not a question of the future, but of the present. I do not know what may be the fate of the present bill in this General Assembly, but I know that a similar measure will, at some time, be passed by the Legislat ture of this State, as surely as there is a law of development and growth in human society.

APPENDIX II

WHAT HAVE CIVIL SERVICE REFORMERS A RIGHT TO EXPECT FROM THE REPUBLICAN PARTY?[1]

What have we a right to expect from the Republican party? At a recent meeting of our Indiana Association we had occasion to examine somewhat in detail the precise meaning of the declarations of that party in regard to civil service reform. I desire at the outset to recapitulate in a few brief words the conclusions to which we were led. That party acquired power upon certain definite promises embodied in the national platform. This is the language: "The men who abandoned the Republican party in 1884 and continued to adhere to the Democratic party have deserted not only the cause of honest government, of sound finance, of freedom, of purity of the ballot, but especially have they deserted the cause of reform in the civil service. *We will not fail to keep our pledges* because they have broken theirs, or because their candidate has broken his."

The platform is made, not simply a declaration of policy, but a definite "pledge" (that is the word), which it would be impossible for an administration, acquiring power upon the strength of it, not to regard.

The platform goes on: "We therefore repeat our declaration of 1884, to wit: The reform of the civil service, auspiciously begun under a Republican administration, should be completed by the further extension of the reform system, already established by law, to all the grades of the service to which it is applicable. The spirit and purpose of reform should be observed in all executive appointments, and all laws at variance with the object of existing reform legislation should be repealed, to the end that the dangers to free institutions, which lurk in the power of official patronage, may be wisely and effectively avoided."

General Harrison tells us in his letter of acceptance, that in regard to every subject embraced in the platform, he is in entire agreement with the declarations of the convention. He is therefore in agreement with this pledge, and has made it his own promise.

Now, what is the meaning of these words? They are capable of pretty definite construction.

---

[1] Address delivered at the Conference of Civil Service Reformers, at Baltimore, February 23, 1889.

"The reform should be extended to all grades of the service to which it is applicable." By whom must the extension be made? Undoubtedly by that branch of the government which is now invested with control over executive appointments.

It is the President, and not Congress, to whom we must look for the redemption of this pledge. The promise cannot be fulfilled by a mere approval of reform legislation. The affirmative act of extending the system must be done by the President, in whose hands the power resides. Congress has already enacted legislation which amply authorizes the Executive to make the extensions promised. Section 1753 of the Revised Statutes declares: "The President is authorized to prescribe such regulations for the admission of persons into the civil service of the United States as may best promote the efficiency thereof, and ascertain the fitness of each candidate; . . . and for this purpose he may employ suitable persons to conduct inquiries, and may prescribe their duties. . . ."

The power is plenary. Should Congress be asked to pass new laws extending the system, the answer would be made that the power to do this is already possessed by the Executive.

The President has the right to extend the rules and General Harrison has given his promise that they shall be extended to all grades to which they are applicable.

The next question is: To what grades of the service is the reform system applicable? This also, as to many of these places, is capable of definite ascertainment. The Civil Service Act itself enumerates grades to which it is applicable, and to which it has not yet been extended. The sixth section makes it the duty of the Postmaster-General to classify the public service at each post office where there are fifty persons employed. "And thereafter on the direction of the President to arrange in like classes the persons employed in connection with any other post office."

Under this section there have been brought into the classified service some thirty-seven post offices. The statute recognizes others to which it should be extended. There is no reason why it cannot be extended to all offices where there is a free delivery of letters. There is as much reason for its application there as to the larger places. The duties are substantially the same; the positions are non-political. There is no court in christendom that in construing the promise would deny that the system was applicable to such places. By the terms of the Act, it is the duty of the President to direct this extension. Such extension he has, therefore, definitely agreed to make.

Similar provisions are contained in the Act regarding the employees of collectors, naval officers, surveyors, and appraisers in the customs service and the platform applies to all these places where the rules are not yet extended.

The promise to extend the reform to all places to which it is applicable, certainly includes those grades to which civil service regulations have been successfully applied elsewhere. In such cases experience has shown that the system is applicable. The platform was made with reference to this fact. The men who drafted the platform, and the convention which adopted it, knew that similar provisions had been successfully applied to grades of the service in Massachusetts, New York, and elsewhere, to which they had not yet been extended by the Federal Act, and in promising that the reform should be extended to all grades to which it is applicable, they certainly included these. Let me offer an illustration:—The experience of Massachusetts has shown that it is desirable that the labor service should be placed under the rules. By this means the country will avoid the un-wholesome spectacle of vast numbers of men employed in navy yards and elsewhere, just before election, in order to secure votes and political support.

By the Federal Act, laborers need not be classified, but there is nothing which forbids such classification. The President has the power to make it. It ought to be made, and the platform has substantially promised that it shall be.

The Civil Service Commissioners, without regard to party, have brought to the attention of the President other branches of the service to which the rules may be applied. Among these were the employees of the railway mail service, and many places in the Indian Bureau, in the Labor Bureau, in the War Department, and in the Department of Agriculture. Some of these recommendations have been adopted and the outgoing administration has done no act more important than the inclusion of the railway mail service within the rules. We believe that we have not only the promise of the President-elect that the extensions made shall be maintained, but also that the law shall be applied to those places to which it is not yet extended, but where the unbiased judgment of those best qualified to determine shall declare that it is applicable.

These are some of the places to which it can be definitely affirmed that the Republican party has promised an extension of the reform. In respect to a much wider range of non-political offices such as consulships and fourth-class postmasterships where the ground is more debatable, as to these, we may hopefully await the ripening influences of time and a more progressive public sentiment.

But the promise does not stop at the extension of the rules. "The spirit and purpose of reform should be observed in all executive appointments."

That "spirit and purpose" is, that in non-political offices, men are not to be appointed, rejected, or discharged on account of political services or opinions, but on account of their fitness to perform the duties of office, and that they are not to use their official places for political purposes.

The President-elect, in his letter of acceptance, shows that this is his understanding. He says, "In appointments to every grade and department, fitness and not party service should be the essential and discriminating test, and fidelity and efficiency the only sure tenure of office."

We believe therefore that the spectacle will not be repeated of the appointment of new and untried men to positions for which they have shown no qualifications, on account of the aid given by them to the party or its candidate during the campaign. It will be impossible, for instance, that such a position as a consulship, a place requiring business ability, and a knowledge of the language and usages of the country where the duties are to be performed, shall be filled by a man without business qualifications, ignorant of both language and usages, because such person has been an effective campaign speaker, or useful in the organization of the party in power. Fitness is to be the essential and discriminating test.

But, more than this, the President-elect says: "Only the interest of the public service should suggest removals from office." This means a great deal. It means that the clamor of aspirants and local political sentiment shall not accomplish the removal of that Democratic official who has faithfully performed his duty.

The platform then promises two things: First, an extension of the rules; and, secondly, the application of reform principles to places outside the rules. While the latter is wider in its scope, and harder to carry out, I am inclined to think the extension of the classified service is the more important of the two. If improvement in the personnel of the service is to depend upon the whim of those in power, the benefit is likely to be fleeting. Let the President-elect be ever so firm in withstanding party pressure, yet the good which flows from this may come to an end when the administration goes out; or, at least, with the downfall of the party in power. Let a reform President be followed by a spoilsman, and all that has been won will be lost. But if the rules are extended, the gain is more likely to be lasting. The widening of the classified service is a recognition of the great principle that *law* is to be substituted for personal pleasure, and this is the main point. In the history of absolute governments, rulers, good and bad, follow each other like shade and sunshine, across the field. But when law is put in the place of arbitrary power, something has been gained for all time. The step backward is seldom taken. Free institutions spread and the reign of law becomes lasting from the continued proofs of its beneficent character. So is it in our reform. For myself, I attach the greatest importance to the modest but permanent gain of the extension of the classified service. The history of the growth of reform in England shows us that the betterment of the service outside the rules will not by any means keep pace with the extension of the classified system. After the reform had been introduced into most of the departments of government, the few offices where the patronage system remained were worse than ever, until the wretched service in these places had its good effect in a demand for the further extension of the classification and the utter overthrow of the old system became inevitable.

So will it be with us. Where the two systems stand side by side for comparison, the fittest will survive. Let us then bend our energies mainly to this point. Let us rather forgive unworthy appointments disconnected with the classified service than overlook an evasion of the law. Let us insist that within the stronghold of the Civil Service Act, none shall enter by whose hand it can be delivered to the enemy. Let no man be permitted to carry out this law who is not in sympathy with its purposes.

General Harrison says: "The law should have the aid of a friendly interpretation, and be faithfully and vigorously enforced." This cannot be done, if men who are not in favor of it, men who, like Postmaster Aquilla Jones, say that they despise it—if such as these are appointed to carry it out. If spoilsmen are to be chosen for the service of the government, we must insist, as a vital matter, that they be excluded from places which involve the selection of employees under the Civil Service Act. General Harrison says: "All appointments under this law should be absolutely free from partisan considerations," but this can never be if those clothed with the power of making such appointments are themselves warped by the prejudices of the spoils system.

But the promise of the Republican platform does not stop with the executive branch of government. "All laws at variance with the object of existing reform legislation should be repealed." What does this mean? The object of reform legislation is to make the tenure of these offices dependent upon fitness and the faithful performance of duty. The law which provides that it shall depend upon any other fact is at variance with this. The act which makes places subject to change every four years, notwithstanding the fitness of the incumbent, gives a pretext for the removal of good men upon the ground that their term has expired, and thus encourages the appointment of those who are inexperienced and often incompetent.

The promise of the platform, if it refers to anything, refers to this law. Since both Houses of Congress are to be controlled by the same party as the executive branch of the government, we have a right to expect in fulfillment of this promise that this Act shall be repealed.

So far as future conduct can be foretold by past life and character, we have in the uprightness and honesty everywhere conceded to General Harrison, the strongest ground for belief that when once his word is out, the last jot and tittle will be fulfilled. When he tells us that fitness will be the test and that he will advance the reform, we may feel sure that worthy men will fill the offices and that the reform will move ahead. The highest motives urge him to the accomplishment of his promise. The plainest dictates of honor and good faith imperiously demand it. Duty to the state requires it in behalf of good government, and duty to himself requires it because his word is given.

With Mr. Cleveland, the comparison between promise and performance was most effectively made. Every shortcoming was noted; every gap between word and deed was laid bare in the plainest language possible. Every case where Mr. Cleveland failed to come up to his own standards of duty was thrown into the balance against him in a closely contested election. And I think we may say that the weight of these shortcomings was enough to turn the scale.

A President may be a spoilsman, believing it to be right, and still retain the respect of the world, but a President who is in any degree a spoilsman after his own words have declared that the spoils system is wrong must forfeit in some degree the confidence of the people. Such would be the fate of the incoming administration, so far as it would repeat the shortcomings of the one which is now taking its leave. The pressure of office seekers will be enormous; it will be constant and inexorable, but that very pressure furnishes the strongest inducement for the widest possible extension of the classified service. The pressure can be relieved only by the substitution of an automatic system for that arbitrary discretion which every office seeker will insist ought to be exercised in his own favor. The great engine of the civil service is becoming too large and complicated for all its movements to be controlled by the personal will of the engineer. The governor and the safety-valve must be self-regulating. The authority of the President must be reserved for more important things than the distribution of subordinate places.

The new administration is beckoned toward reform not only by the command of duty, but even by the finger of ambition. So far as mere office is concerned, the President has reached the summit of all hope. There is no prize glittering before him fairer in promise than that which he already holds. Yet office, whether high or low, is little more than opportunity. Even the Presidency is only that greater and higher shaft upon the marble of which are yet to be inscribed those acts which shall pass into history. A President with a just conception of his opportunity will work, not for ease or present popularity, not for the perpetuation of power for four years more—his effort will be directed to the doing of that which shall last for all time. The *monumentum ære perennius* is the one goal ahead.

In what way can the incoming administration best become the benefactor of humanity? In what way better than by eliminating the great danger which hangs over our republican institutions, that lust of office which is corruptly nourished by the spoils of office?

As the advocate of a protective tariff the efforts of the new administration will be mainly conservative. It has no new fields to conquer. There is little to distinguish it from its predecessors; it must shine by reflected light. And the credit or blame will be mainly due, not to the President but to Congress, upon which the burden of legislation rests. But with civil service reform the problem is to bring to a successful issue the question in which the efforts of Grant and Hayes, Arthur and Cleveland, have resulted in a most halting and imperfect measure of success. The man who shall complete this reform and work it into the fabric of our government as the jury system is ingrained in our institutions, this man will deserve and receive the lasting gratitude of posterity. And the credit will be due, not to

18

Congress, but to the President alone. In his hand the power resides to extend this reform.

Should General Harrison succeed in establishing civil service reform upon a permanent basis, he will have added a new and lasting course in the construction of that fabric of liberty, the foundations whereof our fathers laid and our brothers cemented with their lives. It will rise—for it is still far from finished—more symmetrically and more solidly for this new support. Other great questions, such as those affecting the relations of labor and capital, are still to come. The work upon them cannot be safely done until the lower courses are securely laid—civil service reform must precede any other reform. The laws of social gravitation demand it. Happy among his contemporaries and blessed for all time will be the President whose hand is strong enough to work the reform of the civil service solidly and permanently into the fabric of our institutions!

Men call us dreamers and impracticable, as they called the antislavery agitators of thirty years ago. But when we build our dreams upon the necessities of our political life, the fulfillment draws nigh even while the vision lasts.

When Walpole distributed his bribes and his offices, when Parliament was rotten with a corruption which permeated and degraded every class of society, what a wild dream to forecast a time when political activity could be nourished by healthier nutriment than the love of money and the spoils of office, when men would struggle for principle and not for place! But lo! the cloud is scattered and the statecraft of our great mother-commonwealth is no longer soiled with the debauchery of spoils and bribes, the remnants of which still linger among her progeny of States across the sea; and while we dream of the same better time approaching, lo, before our very eyes, the vision turns into a living reality.

APPENDIX III

THE REFORM OF THE CIVIL SERVICE[1]

The principles underlying civil service reform are as clearly demonstrable as any in political economy. They start from the same axioms of self-interest, which, while not the sole motives of human action, are still apt to play a leading part. Just as men will buy in the cheapest market and sell in the dearest (and from this starting-point so much of political economy takes its rise),so it is a necessary consequence of the spoils system that men, in the distribution of offices, will pay the highest price for support of the greatest political value. As commercial value is measured by dollars, political value is measured by votes. The rules of political economy have many exceptions. In experience the "parallax and refraction" (if I may so term them) of the special surroundings make the actual result somewhat different in every case from the theoretical result. Personal preferences, as well as ignorance of surrounding conditions, make it perhaps untrue in ninety-nine cases out of a hundred that men actually buy in the very cheapest market and sell in the dearest. But this law is, nevertheless, the law of all trade. So it is true in the market of politics, which the spoils system represents, that the vote value of every appointment is the normal standard toward which every appointment gravitates. Personal or special considerations may control, just as friendship may lead a man to trade at a neighbor's store and pay a litttle higher price for what he buys. Men have mistaken notions of the political value of a claimant for office, just as they have mistaken notions of the commercial value of the goods they buy. But the laws of trade and of spoils politics are essentially the same.

The more elaborately commercial society is developed and the more generally commercial intelligence is diffused, the more closely is the general economic rule observed and the less do personal considerations affect the matter of barter and exchange. So, in politics, the larger and more complicated the interests, the greater the number of votes, and the greater the certainty of the motives which act upon these votes to cast them one way or the other, just so much more closely will this political rule of barter and sale approach the actual and proved reality. In the primitive stages of republican government men consider more the quality of the man to be

---

[1] Address at the Social Science Congress, Saratoga, September 3, 1891.

appointed than in its later and more impersonal stages. In earlier days we acted upon the theory of personal discretion in the selection of officeholders. The President was supposed to have some knowledge of the postmasters and collectors whose names were submitted to the Senate; and, when postmasters and collectors were few, this theory was not unreasonable. In the early days of the steam-engine the valve was turned on by the personal action of the engineer; but, as the machinery became more highly developed and complicated, automatic action was found to be necessary. So has it been in our government. When the number of postmasters increased to forty thousand, personal selection was no longer possible. These things must now be done by system. What shall the system be?

The development of the spoils system in American politics has been attributed to Andrew Jackson, to Martin Van Buren, to Aaron Burr. It is not due to any man. If Andrew Jackson, Martin Van Buren, and Aaron Burr had never lived, it would still have been engrafted, at some time or other, in some form or other, into American institutions, in the absence of some other definite system established by law. So long as appointments were left to the personal discretion of an officer selected by universal suffrage the spoils system was a necessary result. The vote value of the man could not be disregarded when he sought office from those whom he had helped to power. But, just so surely as the spoils system was the product of natural law, just so certain is it to-day that its abolition is a necessity, born from the evils which it inflicts.

No one will deny that party government is a necessary phase of popular government. Party government in the political world exercises much the same function that competition does in the commercial world, that war does in the physical world, and that the struggle for existence does in the organic world. It is part of the great development of nature through the survival of the strongest and fittest. Where all men vote, the strongest must conquer at the ballot-box by essentially the same rules that armies conquer in war. The temptation is powerful to use all means, lawful or unlawful, according to the Decalogue and the Golden Rule or against them, to defeat the enemy. In earlier times and among the lower types of humanity, the love of booty was a powerful motive with the man of war. The right to despoil his enemy was never questioned. But it has gradually dawned upon the consciousness of the civilized world that this right of plunder not only inflicts unnecessary hardship upon the conquered but that it is the greatest weakness of the conquering army. How many have been the battles lost where, after the first onslaught, the victorious troops, instead of securing the fruits of their victory, devoted themselves to plunder, and have in their turn been overcome and despoiled? The military world recognizes that the courage of the soldier must be sustained by some other motive than the hope of spoil, and that to allow an army to devote itself to plunder is to corrupt and ruin it. This is true none the less in politics than in war. In nearly every instance patronage is a source of weakness rather than strength. The number of the disappointed is always greater than the number of the successful. Even the man who receives the coveted plum is apt to prove ungrateful. The corrupting influence of plunder is such that the honor said to exist among thieves cannot be trusted. President Arthur had the patronage, yet he could not secure a renomination. President Cleveland had the patronage yet it contributed probably more than anything else to his defeat. President Harrison has had the patronage, yet the success of the Republican party in 1888 was converted in 1890 into the most disastrous defeat in its history.

The analogy between the spoils of war and the spoils of office goes far. In the division of booty among chiefs and men, the share of each was determined by the war value of the man. The chief was to have one fifth or one tenth of the whole, then came the greater warriors, while the common men must content themselves with but little. So in politics the place to which a man is entitled depends upon his political value. The man who raises or distributes a small campaign fund gets a small place, while the man who raises his hundreds of thousands may even hope for a seat in the Cabinet. The small speaker in the country district may aspire to a country post-office. But the great leader whom all flock to hear may perhaps become a premier. The question which, after all, determines the office to be given and the man to have it is, "How many votes is he worth?"

Now, it is evident that under such a system as this there is no relation of fitness between the man and the duties he is required to perform, unless those duties are political. If his duty is to spread the principles of his party and win votes for it, of course the best politician will be the best man for the place; but, if the duties are purely administrative or financial, the man whose excellence lies in neither of these fields of action will very likely be a bad man for the place. In all non-political offices we are sure, under such a system, not to get the best service but a poor service. Skill in managing a caucus has no relation to skill in adjusting the accounts of the Treasury Department. The man who can best "whoop up the boys" by promises of patronage is not always the best guardian of public funds. Indeed, the particular kind of politician whose vote value is the most easily determined, and the results of whose labors are the most palpable, is generally the one who is disqualified for responsible office. The influences which determine the conduct of the conscientious, independent voter are not so immediately traceable to the particular action of any one man as are the votes of the venal "floaters" to the man who divides them into blocks of five or who raises the money to corrupt them The venal politician is, upon the immediate face of things, a more valuable man than the more remote agent who merely convinces the intelligence of an unknown number of proselytes. Hence he is apt to secure a better place, unless the fear of public indignation following the discovery of his methods makes his appointment impossible. So it often happens that a few votes in the convention which makes the nomination are more important than a vast number of votes at the popular election.   Hence we find that the support of delegates is especially sought for by candidates and that great numbers of those who have thrown their influence for the nominee in convention are to be found among the successful aspirants for office.

Another thing which results is a political hierarchy, or, as Mr. Lucius B. Swift more accurately calls it, a system of feudalism in officeholding, in which the respective rank and power of the man are often quite different from that prescribed by the Constitution and laws.   According to the latter, the President and members of the Cabinet make the appointments; the head of a department or bureau is generally authorized to appoint the officers who serve under him, and he is responsible for their conduct, dismissing them if they prove inefficient.   Yet in point of fact, we find that appointments are not made in any such way.   A member of Congress or political boss of the State, the district, or the city is really the appointing power.   Sometimes, like Senator Quay, he holds an office which is purely legislative, involving no such duties as the distribution of patronage; sometimes, he holds no office at all.   These gentlemen, the greater barons of politics, divide their possessions among the lesser lords, the county chairmen, and political bosses; and these again apportion their allotments among the leaders in townships and wards, who, in their turn, divide their little holdings among their own thralls and hustlers.   In each case, service and fealty are due, not to the head of the office, not to the government itself, but to the particular source from which the appointment comes.   The result is that the men appointed—inasmuch as they do not owe their places to any qualifications for the work to be done, and do not expect to retain them by virtue of their industry or fidelity, but on account of their influence with the men who appointed them—often neglect their duties and devote themselves to political work quite inconsistent with those duties.   This system has all the vices and lawlessness of feudalism, and those additional weaknesses which spring from the unstable and uncertain tenure upon which these offices are held.   The man who nominally makes the appointments—the head of the office or department—does not dare to make removals for incompetency, lest he should offend the powerful "influence" which stands behind the incompetent man.   The "influence" on the other hand cares little for the manner in which his vassal performs the duties of his office, so long as the personal or political service to himself is satisfactory.   There is thus a divided responsibility, the duties are neglected, and there is nowhere any power to apply the remedy. . . .

[Mr. Foulke now proceeded to consider the appropriateness of the competitive system as a remedy.   The theoretical arguments in favor of that system were given and finally its practical results were set forth as follows.

The wisdom of civil service reform is demonstrated not merely by reason but by actual experience.   Mr. Dorman B. Eaton, in his report to the President concerning the civil service in Great Britain, has shown the beneficial results of the establishment of that system in the mother-country in a historic argument no longer to be refuted. In our own republic the evidence is equally satisfactory. Civil service rules have been applied to about thirty thousand offices in the federal government, something less than one fifth of the whole in mere number, but something considerably more than this in the salaries drawn, and in the importance and responsibility of the places. The more widely extended the classified service, the better its results appear to be. Men who have had special opportunities for comparing the new system with the old in the management of administrative departments of the government (such as Mr. Windom, late Secretary of the Treasury) speak most emphatically of the improved service and the general beneficial results of the competitive system. It would be a sheer impossibility to cast the numerous places in the classified service in the various departments in Washington back into the muddy pool of political patronage. The business of the government could not endure the strain.

The manner in which the spoils system works, as contrasted with the merit system, is very clearly shown by the number and character of removals under each, when a new administration comes into power. I had occasion to examine quite extensively the number and character of removals of presidential postmasters (offices which have not been brought under the rules) during the first year of the present administration.

The statement made by Mr. Clarkson, First Assistant Postmaster-General, showed that the entire number of changes among presidential postmasters during this year was more than 64 per cent of the whole. A great number of the so-called resignations we found to be compulsory. The men removed were in nearly every instance Democrats, and their successors Republicans, and in most cases where the cause was specifically investigated, the reason of the removal was found to be political. An investigation conducted by the Civil Service Commissioners shows that in the unclassified offices the great majority of those in office during one administration were removed during the next, the evident purpose of this being to provide places for their successors for political reasons; while in the classified service, where the successor was appointed upon his merit, and not as a matter of patronage, the average number of changes have been less than 20 per cent during the same period. The comparative workings of this system cannot better be shown than by these figures.

The sum total of the whole matter is this; the service is better, more permanent, and more economical, political removals are eliminated, and the corrupting influence of these political prizes upon caucuses, conventions, and elections is removed, just in the proportion that civil service reform has supplanted the system of patronage and spoils.

APPENDIX IV

SECRET SESSIONS OF THE SENATE[1]

If we were looking for a gauge of the liberality and democratic character of any particular government, we could find a pretty accurate one in the publicity with which its proceedings were conducted. Just in the proportion that open administration takes the place of secret intrigue do we find the institutions of a community free, liberal, and beneficent. Secrecy is the cloak of despotism. It is only that which is fair and just to all men which can bear the full light of day. It was the robber baron who needed the secret torture-chamber and the oubliette to inspire awe and shroud his villainy. It was the tyranny of the Bourbons which made use of the *lettres de cachet* and the iron mask. It was the usurpation of the Stuarts which needed the star chamber. It is in Russia that the political offender who questions the beneficence of autocracy is tried by a military commission behind closed doors or sent to Siberia by secret administrative order.

Wherever freedom prevails, whether in the Athenian Agora, the Swiss Canton, or the American Republic, trials are held in the light of day, the accused may confront his accuser, and the conduct of the rulers is subject to open scrutiny. The world believes that when men seek to cover their official conduct with the irresponsibility of secret proceedings it is because their action will not bear investigation, that they "love darkness rather than light because their deeds are evil."

It is in view of these general principles that we are called upon to examine Rule 38 of the Senate of the United States, which reads as follows:

"All information communicated or remarks made by a Senator, when acting upon nominations, concerning the character and qualifications of the persons nominated, also any votes upon nominations, shall be kept secret. If, however, charges shall be made against a person nominated the Committee may in its discretion notify such nominee thereof, but the name of the person making such charges shall not be disclosed.

"Senators who violate this rule are liable to expulsion."

In other parliamentary and congressional proceedings the evolution

---

[1] An address delivered at the League Meeting in Buffalo, September 30, 1891.

from secrecy to publicity has corresponded with the growth of popular institutions. In the times of aristocratic privilege and royal prerogative Parliament sat in secret. It was a contempt and a crime to publish the debates or the votes. The right of a member to report his own speeches was denied. In 1641 Sir Edward Deering was expelled and sent to prison for this offense. As late as 1747 the editor of the *Gentleman's Magazine* was brought to the bar for reporting the proceedings of the House of Commons. But when the press of Great Britain locked horns with parliamentary privilege, the latter had to give way and sessions became open to the public. So, too, our early colonial legislatures transacted their business behind closed doors, and it was the General Court of Massachusetts, a commonwealth whose ear has always been the first to catch the notes from the bugle of liberty, which first allowed publicity to its own debates on motion of Mr. Otis in 1766.

The Articles of Confederation required Congress (which appointed all federal civil and naval officers) to publish "for the information of the people" a complete journal of its proceedings, saving only the parts relating to "treaties, alliances, and military operations, which require secrecy." It was recognized then that ordinary civil appointments did not require secrecy. When the Constitution was adopted it provided that each House should publish a journal of its proceedings "excepting only such as might, in its judgment, require secrecy." It was not considered that the confirmation of civil appointments rested upon any other basis than legislative proceedings. Hamilton, in the *Federalist*, assumes that confirmations will be public and contrasts the Senate with the New York Council of Appointments "shut up in a private apartment and impenetrable to the public eye" and adds, "every such Council will be a conclave in which cabal and intrigue will have their full scope."

The two Houses of Congress first met in March, 1789, but both were without a quorum until April. Then the House of Representatives, the more popular branch of Congress (and this is another indication how surely publicity follows popular institutions) opened its doors to the world. The Senate, which claimed to represent the States only and not the people, held its sessions in private, and for four years resolutions proposing publicity were defeated. In 1793 the responsibility of the Senate to public opinion began to be recognized and the doors were opened. During this time, however, there was no injunction of secrecy laid upon Senators. They might tell all about the proceedings if they wanted to. In 1800, the first rule *requiring* secrecy was adopted, but it applied only to confidential communications from the President and to treaties pending in the Senate. It was not until 1820, after the patronage and office-trading introduced by Aaron Burr and Martin Van Buren had become incorporated into New York politics, the very year that the four-years' term of office was created which gave to the Senate such increased power over civil appointments and opened the way to infinite intrigue and corruption, that "secrecy became necessary" and the action of Senators upon executive nominations was withheld from the public. And it is in accordance with the logic of history that Marcy's celebrated saying, "to the victor belong the spoils of the enemy," was uttered in one of these secret sessions. Many efforts were made to remove the injunction of secrecy, but they failed. One was attempted by Senator Chase and supported by Sumner, who declared that these sessions ought to be like the house which the old Roman desired made of transparent material that the world might know all that was done therein. But it was not until 1867, when the first Tenure of Office act was passed forbidding the President to remove or suspend any officer without reporting the reasons to the Senate and securing its consent, that it was found necessary to secure the secrecy of these executive sessions by threats of expulsion against any Senator who should disclose them.

Bear in mind that this rule of the Senate is no requirement of the Constitution nor even of a public statute passed by both Houses of Congress and approved by the President. It is the mere private arbitrary regulation of one branch of the federal legislature. It was itself adopted in secret session. In addition to the general guarantees of public trial, free speech, and a free press, which are in effect rendered nugatory by secret sessions, as to all matters there considered, it provides that each House shall publish a journal of its proceedings "except such parts as may, in its judgment, require secrecy." It is only where secrecy is necessary that it is to be allowed, and while the respective Houses are to be the judges of this necessity, they have at least no moral right to impose it without good cause upon a whole domain of congressional action.

There is strong reason to doubt whether the power of confirmation given to the Senate by the Constitution has been beneficial to the country. If it could have been exercised in the manner designed, the Senate giving to the President the benefit of its disinterested counsel and informing him of the qualifications and disqualifications of the men whom he proposed to appoint, of course this limited power would be a salutary check upon bad appointments. But like the Electoral College, the power of confirmation has operated in quite a different way from that intended and it has had much to do with the formation of that injurious system of office patronage which goes by the name of "Courtesy of the Senate," a system which has been developed by perfectly natural laws out of the constitutional power of confirmation. Naturally the Senator from a particular State will know more of the qualifications of the proposed appointee from that State than any other member of the Senate. Naturally the other members will defer to his judgment in the absence of better means of information. The two causes—selfishness and lack of information—combine to cast the responsibility for appointments within particular States upon the Senators who represent those States. This secures an "equitable" partition of patronage. It depends for its consummation upon a very simple principle, "You vote for my man and I will vote for yours." Each Senator has friends to reward and enemies to punish. He will not be slow to communicate to the Executive the name of the man who will be most acceptable to him, and even to hint that no other name will be acceptable at all either to himself or his fellow-Senators. The President is unwilling to send in nominations for the idle purpose of having them rejected. Hence the views of each Senator upon the nominations to be made within his State have great weight. His *previous* "advice and consent" is really the thing that determines the appointment, not the advice and consent of the whole body after the nomination is sent in. The result is that it is not the President who actually makes appointments, but the Senators distributing patronage in their respective States.

The courtesy was always, in substance, says Mr. Eaton, a corrupt barter of duty and honor for power and patronage.

Appointments are often made upon condition that the Senator making the appointment and the Senators coöperating with him should control subordinate places under the appointee. The henchmen of these Senators are thus made clerks, messengers, and spittoon-cleaners to the public at large.

This system of courtesy is a natural development of the practice of confirmations by the Senate, when aided by the irresponsibility of secret sessions.

The people know nothing of the various proceedings leading to an appointment. The obligations of the Senator toward the applicant for office may sometimes be of the most criminally secret character. The intrigues for his nomination, the "pressure" brought upon the President to secure it, can never be divulged, and when it is sent to the Senate the statement of qualifications vouched for by the Senator in question can never be known nor refuted by the public.

The evils which are thus directly traceable to the secret sessions, or distinctly aided by them, are the following:

1st. They encourage bargains between Senators and they have been greatly responsible for the system of "Senatorial Courtesy" described above. They have converted members whose duties were legislative and advisory into active office seekers and corrupt dispensers of patronage, thus interfering with the proper discharge of their functions, demoralizing the Senate, and leading to the neglect of its more important duties.

2d. They impair the confidence of the people in the Senate as well as in individual Senators. Secrecy inevitably begets suspicion. Even where the motive of confirmation or rejection is a fair one, if there be any ground of criticism, the worst will be inferred. A bargain will be presumed even where it does not exist and unworthy motives are sure to be imputed. Senators will be accused by a disappointed office seeker even if they had nothing to do with his rejection. Senators will be suspected of corruptly supporting a bad man who in fact voted against him. Propriety and impropriety, innocence and guilt will be confounded. The Senator unjustly suspected cannot protect himself. He cannot tell the truth in his defense. The good may lose the esteem of their constituents and the bad retain a popularity wholly undeserved, while the entire body is weakened and discredited in popular regard.

3d. These secret sessions encourage the unworthy to apply for office by the promise that their shortcomings shall not be exposed nor subjected to public scrutiny, and they lead to the confirmation of bad men either from ignorance or to "please a brother Senator," without the people being able to fix the responsibility for the vote or statement on any particular Senator. In like manner these secret sessions defeat good nominations by political intrigues. False statements may be used with impunity to screen the guilty and attack the innocent.

In this connection the question naturally arises: Why did legislative sessions become public? It was undoubtedly owing to the demand of the people to be informed as to the conduct of their representatives regarding matters which affected them and thus to fix the responsibility for official action. But have the people no interest in the question who shall be the officers to administer the laws? Is the Senate no longer a representative body when it confirms nominations? Are there not as much fraud and venality in executive appointments as in legislation? Often indeed the policy of the government is outlined by a particular appointment. For instance the Indian policy by the appointment of an Indian Commissioner, and civil service reform by the appointment of a Postmaster-General. Have the people no right to hear the Senate's discussions of these matters?

The Senate rule, in addition to the injunction of secrecy, contains this remarkable clause: "If, however, charges shall be made against a person nominated, the Committee may, in its discretion, notify such nominee thereof, but the name of the person making such charges shall not be disclosed." This sentence is valuable for the light it throws upon the character of the rule requiring secrecy. Charges are to be heard against men in their absence, and except for this provision, they are to take no part in the exoneration of themselves. Accusations of every kind will be preferred of incompetency, imbecility, drunkenness, immorality, and crime. Charges will be made by personal enemies, by competing aspirants for the same office, against the worthy and the unworthy, the skillful and the incompetent, the good and the bad. A man has fairly won his nomination to the Senate by a life of integrity, by special skill in the work to which he is to be appointed; a career of usefulness and honor is open to him, and some assassin of character who hopes to profit by the lie sends to the Committee the charge that he is a drunkard or an embezzler, and in secret without a word of explanation, the doors of opportunity are shut in his face. May not the consequences to him be just as grave as if he were defendant in a civil suit, or indeed in many forms of even criminal prosecution? Now change the case and suppose this were a proceeding at law. What would we think of the safeguards thrown around the person, property, or reputation of a defendant who was protected by a law providing that the court trying and passing judgment upon him in secret might, at its discretion, notify him of the charges against him; but the name of the person making such charges should not be disclosed? Must not the Grand Jury when they bring their bill not only notify the accused of the precise charge but endorse the names of the witnesses upon it? Cannot the defendant confront these witnesses? Must not the name of the plaintiff, as well as the character and circumstances of the claim, appear in every civil suit? Our inheritance of Anglo-Saxon instinct tells us that nothing less than this is fair play, that nothing less is necessary to protect either property rights or the sacredness of human character. When Torquemada was Inquisitor the rules of his tribunal prescribed substantially that if charges were made, the Holy Office might at its discretion notify the accused what they were, but the name of the person making them should not be disclosed. When the Council of Ten consigned the innocent to a shameful death from motives of State policy, they might at their discretion notify the accused of the charge against him, but the accuser who dropped his nameless accusation into the lion's mouth was not disclosed. Yet to-day we are living not in the Dark Ages but at the close of the nineteenth century. This is not the Spain of Ferdinand and Charles the Fifth and Philip the Second, but it is free America. This is not the secret tribunal of Venice which has passed into history loaded with the execrations of mankind. It is the Senate of the United States, whose halls have echoed the voices of Clay and Webster, Sumner and Chase! The common opinion of the world consigns the anonymous informer to the contempt of his fellows. Yet here are charges invited by the protection of obscurity where conviction may follow because they are to remain anonymous. Your heart and mine tell us that it would be better to have bad men in office than to resort to such procedure as this to weed them out. But true charges are not the ones most readily stifled by publicity nor is falsehood most easily suppressed by the immunity of secrecy.

Let the Senate conform to the ideals of republican institutions; let the Senators have the courage publicly to be true to the trusts committed to them. Then and not till then will the fading respect which our people have accorded to that august legislative assembly be rehabilitated and it will become indeed that which our hopes and fancies once believed it, an impenetrable bulwark of liberty.

APPENDIX V

HARRISON'S CIVIL SERVICE RECORD

MR. CHAIRMAN AND GENTLEMEN:

I would speak to you to-night not so much of the general issues of the campaign which is upon us as of that single one to which I have specially given my heart and my labor during the past eight years, the reform of the civil service.

But I cannot enter upon this theme without first bringing to your minds the cloud that has so lately fallen upon us. The great leader of civil service reform is no more. That voice which could speak to us, as none other can to-day, speaks now to the great multitude of the immortals; that hand which wrote, as no other can write which has survived it, will no longer be the inspiration of our work, nor the just critic of our success or failure.

Since the assassination of Lincoln the cause of honest government and popular institutions has hardly sustained a heavier loss from the ranks of civil life than in the death of George William Curtis. He was born for the highest triumphs of literature. All that he said, all that he wrote, was redolent with that native artistic instinct that gave him a place among the foremost where the English tongue is spoken. But this he subordinated to the demands of patriotic duty.

Most charming to all who knew him in social intercourse, it was ever his aim to make his personality a means for the advancement of the public good. He loved his country as few men have ever loved it. He consecrated to its service all his abundant gifts. The allurements of office and power he could cast aside, but he clung always and immovably to the highest convictions of duty.

He was so gentle that we, who were more swayed by prejudice and passion, sometimes wondered whether he was stern enough in denouncing the iniquities around him, but when we thought again, it was not only his charity but his inexorable justice which demanded that due credit should be given for all that was good whenever wickedness was laid bare by his calm and unflinching criticism. He was the Aristides of these latter days, the embodiment of patriotic rectitude. His place cannot be filled. There is no man who can put on the armor he has cast aside, no single champion who can wield his sword and do battle as he did for the cause of free institutions. And yet his memory is an inspiration that shall drive from our hearts all thought of relinquishing the struggle.

He saw the reform to which he had dedicated so much of his life only in part accomplished. It is our duty to see that it does not falter in its progress, to do as bravely as we can, that which we would do if his voice and his presence were with us to cheer us to the victory that we know is coming.

The cause which he stood for is so great and good that it shall live and grow even without his leadership, and we who are left have only to bend our shoulders to a heavier burden and carry it to its consummation. Let us accept the task, and, as apostles of this great gospel, let us diffuse to the uttermost parts of our country, the message that he gave us, until the old heathenism of spoils politics shall be utterly exterminated.

I am about to discuss this evening the conduct of the present Republican administration since it came into power in respect to the civil service.

Four years ago I voted for Benjamin Harrison, but I feel no embarrassment to-night on that account. Mr. Cleveland, as some of us thought in Indiana, had not filled the measure of his promises in regard to civil service reform. The obstacles in his path were enormous; the impossibility of keeping his party together except by concessions was evident. Still we were disposed to measure him by the absolute standard of duty, and, judged by this standard, he had fallen short of realizing his own ideals. He had stood for a long time a bulwark against the plunderers of public service, but breaches had been made in the defenses, and an Indiana civil service reformer, who sees the worst of spoils politics at his very door, is not lenient.

We had known Mr. Harrison well. Both in public declarations and private talk he had given us the fullest assurance of his sympathy. He had said: "I am an advocate of civil service reform. My brief experience at Washington has led me to utter the wish, with an emphasis I do not often use, that I might be forever relieved of any connection with the distribution of public patronage. I covet for myself the free and unpurchased support of my fellow-citizens." His private and public life, as far as it could be observed by those around him, was clean and honorable; the promises of the party made in the words that George William Curtis had penned supplemented by his own expressions of equal significance, were all that we could ask. We believed him and we supported him. Now we have had the proof of four years' trial. His administration and that of Mr. Cleveland can be laid side by side.

Mr. Harrison's word was not made good, his promises have not been fulfilled. Upon the abandoned pledge, upon his violated faith and not upon our inconsistency, must rest the responsibility for our defection.

"The reform of the civil service [says the platform of 1888], auspiciously begun under a Republican administration, should be completed by the further extension of the reform system already established by law to all grades of service to which it is applicable."

The only extensions of the classified service made by Mr. Harrison in pursuance of this promise of the platform were to about seven hundred teachers and superintendents in the Indian Bureau, less than two hundred in the Fish Commission, and a few employees in the Patent Office. The entire number of such extensions is not far from one thousand.

But there are more than one hundred thousand places in the federal civil service which still remain unclassified.

Secretary Tracy has, indeed, provided for a registration of laborers in the Navy Department, under a system quite similar to the classified service, although it is not embraced within the rules or placed under control of the Civil Service Commissioners, and it would be discretionary for any subsequent Secretary of the Navy to abolish his regulations. With these exceptions there has been absolutely nothing done by the present administration in performance of its promise that the reform system should be extended to all the branches of the classified service to which it is applicable.

The civil service law itself provided that it should apply to all post offices and custom house offices having fifty or more employees, and that it should be extended to other post offices and custom houses having less than fifty employees, whenever so ordered by the President. The law itself designated these custom houses and post offices as places to which it was applicable.

After the accession of President Harrison to office, his own Civil Service Commissioners reported, recommending its extension to post offices having twenty-five employees or more, and afterwards, in 1891, to custom houses and internal revenue districts in which there are twenty-five or more employed, as well as to clerks in the navy yards, to the employees of the District of Columbia, to the mints and sub-treasuries, and to all free delivery post offices.

Yet during his entire term, President Harrison has utterly failed to extend it to any of these places. A clearer violation of the written promise of the party could not be imagined.

If there was any branch of the service where appointments should have depended upon the fitness of the appointee, as proved by examination and probation, and not upon patronage and political favor it was the Census Bureau. It was the plain duty of those in charge of this bureau to give to the people the exact facts as to all matters inquired of, unwarped by political bias. If the promise of the Republican platform had any significance at all, it meant that the President would extend this competitive system to the clerks of the Census Bureau, when that bureau should be established. Mr. Harrison, in concurring with and adopting the platform, distinctly made this promise his own. His Civil Service Commissioners advised this extension also. The President refused to make it. The Census Bureau has been used as a partisan machine and the result of the work has been greatly discredited.

In his inaugural, President Harrison declared: "Heads of departments, bureaus, and other public offices having any duty connected therewith, will be expected to enforce the civil service law fully and without evasion." How far, then, has the law been enforced?

The Civil Service Commission, whose duty it is to care for this, is composed of three members, two of whom must belong to opposite political parties. When the present administration came into power, Charles Lyman, a Republican, was the sole acting Commissioner. Mr. Harrison then appointed Theodore Roosevelt, a Republican, and Governor Hugh S. Thompson, a Democrat, a man who had been selected for the place by Mr. Cleveland before he went out of office. These were excellent men, who determined to enforce the law impartially, so far as they had the power. They could see that examinations were fairly conducted and they did. But they could not remove any officer who violated the law, they could not personally conduct prosecutions, they could merely investigate, report, and recommend. The rest lay with the President, the Cabinet officers, and their subordinates, and these have utterly failed in many important instances to sustain the Commission in their efforts.

Take, for example, the Baltimore post office. Commissioner Roosevelt heard that this office was being used to influence a primary election on March 30, 1891, and he went to Baltimore personally to investigate the matter. His report contains the following:

"The primaries held on March 30th were marked by a bitter contest between two factions of the Republican party.

"As a whole, the contest was marked by great fraud and no little violence. Many of the witnesses of each faction testified that the leaders of the opposite faction in their ward had voted repeaters, Democrats and men living outside of the ward, in great numbers. . . . Accusations of ballot-box stuffing were freely made, with much appearance of justification. A number of fights took place. In many wards there were several arrests. In one or two cases so many men were arrested that the police patrol wagons could not accommodate them. In several cases the Judges of the Election were themselves among those arrested. . . ."

As to the post office and marshal's office, Mr. Roosevelt reports, "The evidence seems to be perfectly clear that both these offices were used with the purpose of interfering with or controlling the result of the primary election, and that there was a systematic, though sometimes indirect, effort made to assess the government employees, in both, for political purposes," and he recommended the dismissal of some twenty culprits. "It is evident," he adds, "from the testimony, that the non-classified service in the Baltimore post office, as is the case with the non-classified service in almost every patronage office, was treated as a bribery chest, from which to reward

19

influential ward workers who were useful, or likely to be useful, to the faction in power. . . .

"Mr. Johnson (the Baltimore postmaster) has filled the entire unclassified and half the classified service with Republican ward workers, and has permitted the post office to be turned into a machine to influence primary elections."

Copies of this report were sent on August 4, 1891, to the President, to Postmaster-General Wanamaker, to Mr. Foster, Secretary of the Treasury, and to Mr. Miller, Attorney General. Although the report was delivered in person by one of the clerks of the Commission, the Attorney General stated that he never knew anything of it until nine months after, when the matter was investigated by Congress. The Solicitor General had never looked upon the testimony as calling for action! Secretary Foster says: "Upon inquiry at the department, I find that probably, about the time that this report was printed, a copy was sent to the department. It so happened that I never saw it and we cannot find it at the department."

Postmaster-General Wanamaker, however, saw the copy which was sent to him. But not a single one of the violators of the laws was removed or punished for his misconduct.

On April 19, 1892, the House of Representatives instructed its Select Committee on Civil Service Reform to inquire whether these men were still in office or whether any of them had been prosecuted.

Mr. Wanamaker admitted to the committee that they were all still in the government service. He had another investigation made by some post-office inspectors of his own, who reported in the following December (four months afterwards) that: "After hearing the evidence from all the witnesses and the accused and giving the whole subject thoughtful study and consideration, we are of the opinion that the facts do not justify the dismissal of the twenty-one men or of any for violation of the civil service law, as charged."

The key to this disgraceful business is found in the fact that at the Minneapolis Convention, Postmaster Johnson led a club from Baltimore, and that he and his lawbreaking subordinates were among the most active and influential of the supporters of Harrison for renomination.

In many other cases contributions were shamelessly demanded from officeholders in plain violation of law, and no man has been punished for it.

The blackmailing of government employees went on two years ago and is going on to-day as flagrantly as in the time of Congressman Hubbell.

Thus has the President enforced the law and his own regulations made in pursuance of its provisions.

Another part of the promise in the Republican platform was this: "All laws at variance with the object of existing reform legislation should be repealed."

The Republican party has been in power for four years, for two years it had control of the Senate, the House of Representatives, and the executive branch of the government, yet no bill has been passed to repeal any law at variance with the reform legislation referred to in the platform. There has been not the slightest pretense of even attempting to fulfill this explicit promise of the platform.

Another declaration of the Republican platform is: "The spirit and purpose of the reform should be observed in all executive appointments."

This spirit and purpose was to make appointments depend upon proved worth and not upon political considerations.

The man who has the most extensive appointing power in the civil service is the First Assistant Postmaster-General. Into his hands are committed all changes in fourth-class postmasterships, not far from fifty thousand in number. Whom does the President select to do this work?

He appoints J. S. Clarkson, a politician of the same class as Quay, Platt, and Dudley. Mr. Clarkson has declared in his speeches as well as in published articles, his contempt for this reform. Men do not gather grapes of thorns, nor figs of thistles, nor could the President hope for the redemption of his promises by such an agent. Under Clarkson's administration political executions have gone on at a more rapid rate than ever before, and the entire service, including all desirable fourth-class postmasterships, has been substantially changed for political reasons.

Shortly after Mr. Harrison's inauguration he appointed Joel B. Erhardt, a Republican politician, Collector of the Port of New York. Erhardt turned out to be an efficient man, and enforced the civil service regulations so faithfully that the politicians were dissatisfied. But after a while he resigned, and he thus tells the reason of his resignation.

"I have resigned because the Collector has been reduced to a position where he is no longer an independent officer with authority commensurate with his responsibility. My duties are necessarily performed through about fifteen hundred employees. I am not willing to be responsible for their conduct unless I can have proper authority over them. The recent policy of the Treasury Department has been to control the details of the customs administration at the port of New York from Washington, at the dictation of a private individual having no official responsibility. The Collector is practically deprived of power and control, while he is left subject to all responsibility. The office is no longer independent, and I am. Therefore we have separated."

The private individual referred to was Mr. Thomas C. Platt, the Republican boss of the State of New York. In place of Erhardt, Mr. Harrison appointed Mr. Fassett, Platt's man, Collector. Fassett said when he was appointed that he had no knowledge of the duties of the place.

When Mr. Fassett was sworn in a San Domingo cutlass, of barbaric origin, was presented to him emblematic of the spoils system, and with the following legend:

"This cutlass is an instrument of torture to be used in beheading Democrats. Use it quickly and success is assured for the Republican party.

"Republican directions: Use daily, morning, noon, and night, until every Democratic head is severed. Sure cure for Democratic headache."

Fassett had scarcely taken the oath of office when he left the city to take charge of the Platt division in a quarrel in Chemung County. He soon resigned the place, however, to be candidate for Governor, for which office he was defeated by a large majority.

[A large number of disreputable appointments were now enumerated, among them Flanagan of Texas, a man who passed into immortality by his declaration at the National Convention of 1888, "What are we here for if not for the offices?" Instances were given of the appointment of thugs, defaulters, men indicted for crimes against the ballot, official conspirators, and other men of unsavory reputation.]

But by far the most flagrant abuse of civil service principles made by the present administration has been shown by the manner in which Mr. Harrison secured his renomination at Minneapolis. Unless the people can be protected against the interference of the executive in an effort to secure his own renomination, popular government is a sham and a failure. An honorable President does not actively seek his own renomination. Should he seek it, he is bound to do so by means outside of his official control. To force himself upon his own party as its candidate, through the agency of his own appointees to office, is simply to Mexicanize our government. He might just as well do it through the army.

Before the conventions met which selected the delegates to Minneapolis, Harrison officeholders were hurrying around the country employing every political method to secure delegates instructed for the President or favorable to his renomination. Every convention possible they attended in large force, and took the most prominent part in packing these bodies in his favor.

These efforts were successful mainly through the lack of any other available man for the place. Mr. Blaine had written a letter to Mr. Clarkson, saying that his name would not be presented, and so many pledges and instructions were secured for Mr. Harrison that it was afterwards impossible to change the result. To use the words of Mr. Lucius B. Swift, who was in 1888 a strong supporter of Mr. Harrison, "The successful candidate was successful because through his henchmen he had the convention literally by the throat. One hundred and forty place-holders, at the least estimate, had votes. On the best authority, at least 3000 other place-holders gathered around and bore down opposition. All these were led by a place-holder who makes $30,000 or $40,000 a year out of his place, and came specially from London for this purpose. The whole was superintended by the President, who had wires connecting the White House with the convention, and who, as the Indianapolis *Journal* puts it, was busy sending and receiving communications from the seat of war. It is to be hoped that our United States government has now reached its lowest point of degradation. It would not seem that political pirates or buccaneers could get, or would want, greater power."

It was currently reported and believed that many of the Southern delegates, even though instructed for Harrison, had to be bought and re-bought several times. The bulk of them finally voted for the renomination of the President.

Here is a message from Washington sent by Mr. Foster, the Secretary of the Treasury, to the Utah member of the Republican National Committee:

"Whatever you can do for us at Minneapolis will be duly appreciated and gratefully remembered in Washington."

Among the place-holders who swarmed to Minneapolis were: Land Commissioner Carter, Assistant Postmaster-General Rathbone, United States Marshal Ransdell, Fourth Auditor Lynch, and Register Bruce who led the Washington contingent. Postmaster Johnson led a club from Baltimore. The President's brother, United States Marshal Carter Harrison, had charge of the Tennessee delegation. Postmaster Thompson and his assistants, Wallace, Patterson, and Woodward, and United States Marshal Dunlap, Pension Agent Ensley, Collector Hildebrand, and United States District Attorney Chambers headed the Indianapolis place-holders, while those of New York were led by Postmaster Van Cott, Naval Officer Willis, and Collector Hendricks. This was the way throughout the United States.

[The scandals connected with the appointment and administration of Postmaster-General Wanamaker were here given in detail.]

Not only is Wanamaker richly rewarded for his diligence in securing financial aid, but others were taken care of in proportion to the value of their financial services. Thus Allen Thorndike Rice of the *North American Review* contributes $15,000 and becomes Minister to Russia.

I once listened to the rather frank complaint of an eminent Republican who declared that he gave $30,000 to the campaign fund and all he asked was one office for a friend. "They promised it to me," he said, "but when the time came they postponed and took it back, and at last, when I got the place, I was madder than if they had not given it to me at all."

So it appears that the campaign contributor demands not only a giver of places in return for his contribution, but a prompt and cheerful giver, who will not hesitate upon such paltry considerations as the character and qualifications of the man to be appointed.

If claim to office is to be based upon the amount of one's contribution to the campaign fund, why would it not be well to have a price current of the offices of the country, Cabinet positions to be rated at their hundreds of thousands, foreign missions at their tens of thousands, and consulships and post offices at their thousands and hundreds respectively?

What more effective way of levying assessments for political purposes?

If politics is to become a matter of commerce, why not make the market rates as definite and as easily accessible as possible to all bidders? Let us have a great bucket shop, an office exchange, where the bids and offers for various positions may be readily reported upon a ticker, and where all men may have an equal chance of giving the required consideration for any place of honor and profit in the State. If the last mission to Russia was worth $15,000 how much shall the next mission bring? If $400,000 shall secure the Postmaster-Generalship, what shall be the market rate for the office of Secretary of State?

These things mean something more than the mass of our people seem to think. They mean the degradation of public virtue. They mean unworthiness for that system of popular government which our fathers laid in patriotism, and which their descendants threaten to overwhelm by venality. Pecuniary corruption is the most dangerous enemy of republican government.

These considerations seem to me clearly to point out the duty and probable course of the independent voter in this campaign. And, unless I am greatly mistaken, this election will depend more than any previous one upon the unbought, intelligent, independent vote.

APPENDIX VI

PLATFORMS AND PROMISES[1]

When Deacon Smith said to Deacon Jones, "You don't suppose, Deacon that those little stories, sort of lies like, which you and I *tell in the way of trade* will ever be counted against us in the great day of judgment?" he gave utterance to a sentiment which common opinion has attributed to most of the professors of statesmanship from the time of Machiavelli down to the days of John Wanamaker.

Personally, some of these men do what they promise. But politically, repudiation of their word is not to be reckoned against them in the great day. And so it has come to pass that a political platform is held to be as untrustworthy as an epitaph and that a man whom you could safely leave alone with a bushel of uncounted gold pieces in the dark, can by no means be relied upon not to turn much of his official power and influence to the private gain of his party and perhaps of himself.

It is the purpose of this paper to consider the declarations of the two great parties and their candidates, as well as some of the more recent discrepancies between promise and performance in regard to civil service reform.

The reform itself, at least so far as the competitive system is concerned, is of comparatively recent origin. Little was known of it in America until some time after the war. The Republican platform of 1864 declared: "We regard as worthy of public confidence and official trust those only who cordially endorse the principles proclaimed in these resolutions." None but Republicans must be appointed to office. There was no distinction between political and non-political places. But in considering this platform, the standards of to-day cannot be applied. The time was critical. The principle was that of the old command: "Put none but Americans on guard to-night." A non-partisan civil service was an unknown thing. The Democratic platform said nothing on the subject. The issues were quite foreign to this reform.

In the Grant and Seymour campaign of 1868, the Democracy demanded a reform of abuses, the expulsion of corrupt men, and the abrogation of

---

[1] Paper read, April 26, 1893, at the annual meeting of the Reform League in New York City.

useless offices, and denounced Congress for stripping the President of his constitutional power of appointment even of members of his own Cabinet.

The Republicans, on the other hand, attacked President Johnson for turning the public patronage into an engine of wholesale corruption. The declarations were general in character and had little reference to what is now known as civil service reform.

In the Grant and Greeley campaign of 1872, the abuses of administration had become serious. The Democratic platform waxed eloquent in denunciation of them saying:

"The civil service of the government has become a mere instrument of partisan tyranny and personal ambition, and an object of selfish greed. It is a scandal and reproach upon free institutions and breeds a demoralization dangerous to the perpetuity of republican government. We therefore regard a thorough reform of the civil service as one of the most pressing necessities of the hour, and insist that honesty, capacity, and fidelity constitute the only valid claim to public employment, that the offices of the government cease to be a matter of arbitrary favoritism and patronage, and that public station again become a post of honor. To this end it is imperatively required that no President shall be a candidate for reëlection."

This declaration is quite comprehensive. If it were fully carried out there would be an excellent civil service. But no specific means except the one-term limitation was suggested for its accomplishment. The reform was still to be brought about by the vague, spasmodic, and ephemeral process of turning bad men out and putting good men in their places —a thing which all have favored from the dawn of history but which few have ever seen accomplished.

The Republican platform declared:

"Any system of civil service reform in which the subordinate positions of the government are considered rewards for mere party zeal is fatally demoralizing, and we therefore favor a reform of the system by laws which will abolish the evils of patronage and make honesty, efficiency, and fidelity the essential qualifications for public position without practically creating a life tenure of office."

The Republican platform went beyond the Democratic. This reform was to be brought about by a general law. That was a great step. Yet still the suggestion was far from complete. What kind of a law was this to be? How should honesty, efficiency, and fidelity be made the essential qualifications for public position? The platform does not inform us. Such a law would be immensely desirable, but how should the bill be drawn?

During the next four years there was another decided advance. The first Civil Service Commission appointed by President Grant, of which George William Curtis was the distinguished head, reported the satisfactory results of the competitive system so far as it had been tried. In 1874 the President transmitted this report to Congress with favorable comments, but Congress refused an appropriation. Public sentiment, however, had grown, and in the Tilden and Hayes campaign of 1876, the Democratic platform made a distinct declaration against a clean sweep, against the appointment of men for mere party considerations, against the dispensing of patronage for political purposes. These resolutions—which will be considered hereafter—derive additional importance from the fact that they were reiterated in the platform of last year and constitute in great measure the standard of duty established for the present administration.

The Republican platform of 1876 lagged far behind. It merely said:

"We rejoice in the quickened conscience of the people concerning political affairs, and will hold all public officers to a rigid responsibility and engage that the prosecution and punishment of all who betray official trusts shall be speedy, thorough, and unsparing."

Here was no rule of appointment, no exclusion of political considerations—nothing but a promise to prosecute those who violated the criminal law. But during the administration of President Hayes, Mr. Dorman B. Eaton presented his admirable report upon the history of the civil service in Great Britain. The Jay Commission had shown the advantages of the competitive system in the New York custom house. Mr. James had established the reform in the New York post office.

In 1880—the Garfield and Hancock campaign—the Democratic platform promised a thorough reform of the civil service without, however, stating what that was to be.

The Republican platform was more definite. The convention adopted the declaration of President Hayes that the reform of the civil service should be thorough, radical, and complete.

"To this end it demands the coöperation of the legislative with the executive department of the government, and that Congress shall so legislate that fitness ascertained by proper practical tests shall admit to the public service."

This declaration acquires additional meaning from the fact that the particular reform to which President Hayes referred was the one providing for a Civil Service Commission and for competitive examinations. The demand for the coöperation of the legislature meant that the classified system should be established by law, and it was in pursuance of this platform that the federal Civil Service Act was passed during the following Presidential term.

But it is with the platforms and promises of candidates since that time that we have principally to deal to-day.

In 1884 the competitive system had just been established. In the Republican convention of that year was the greatest of all civil service reformers, Mr. George William Curtis. To his hand was entrusted the drafting of the resolution. From his skillful pen there came the fullest, completest, and most definite declaration upon this subject which has ever found place in any political platform:

"The reform of the civil service, auspiciously begun under a Republican administration, should be completed by the further extension of the reform system already established by law to all grades of the service to which it is applicable. The spirit and purpose of reform should be observed in all executive appointments. All laws at variance with the objects of existing reform legislation should be repealed to the end that the dangers to free institutions which lurk in the power of official patronage may be wisely and effectively avoided."

Here there was nothing left out and there was no ambiguity. It was the particular reform begun by the federal civil service law which should be extended. The language was so certain that it would not be difficult for an honest and candid man to determine by fair and just construction what it meant in any given case, either within the classified service or elsewhere.

The Democratic platform of 1884, on the other hand, was distinctly weaker than several of its predecessors. All that it said was, "We favor honest civil service reform." Now, civil service reform with an adjective is an object of suspicion. The qualification indicates something different from the thing already set on foot. There is no spoilsman, no party hack, who does not vociferously proclaim his devotion to *honest* civil service reform, *real* civil service reform, *genuine* civil service reform— indeed, any kind of a variation from the unqualified thing to which this National League is devoted. That single phrase was all that the new Democratic President could adduce in support of his efforts.

Upon the face of the platforms the Republican party would have been entitled to the undivided support of all reformers. But the candidates were Mr. Blaine and Mr. Cleveland. Mr. Blaine said many good things in his letter of acceptance. If the mere declarations of the platform and candidate had been conclusive, the election of Mr. Blaine should certainly have been satisfactory to civil service reformers. But there was a large number of men devoted to this cause who deeply distrusted the Republican candidate. Although many supported him, yet others, and some of the most eminent, preferred a man who, upon a weaker platform and with a declaration less explicit, gave, as they believed, better assurances in his past record. These were the words in which Mr. Cleveland accepted the nomination:

"The selection and retention of subordinates in government employment should depend upon their ascertained fitness and the value of their work, and they should be neither expected nor allowed to do questionable party service."

This was but one of many declarations then made by Mr. Cleveland in favor of civil service reform. He was far in advance of his party and for some time he resisted with firmness the importunities of spoilsmen. Yet as time went on and pressure was continued there were serious breaches made in the defenses. He promised the enforcement of the Pendleton law; yet in Indiana, in Maryland, in Chicago, in the Philadelphia post office, and in other conspicuous instances, that law was signally evaded and nullified. He declared that removals would not be made on partisan grounds during the terms for which the incumbents were appointed; yet the displacement of such employees to make room for Democrats was well-nigh universal. Thousands were removed upon secret charges, which were not seldom false, preferred often by irresponsible and interested parties, and these men were so dismissed without opportunity for defense, denial, or explanation. Officials should be taught, he said, that efficiency, fitness, and devotion to public duty were the conditions of their continuance in office. Yet the offices were largely filled by the unscrupulous politicians whom he had himself denounced. Republicans forfeited their places for offensive partisanship, yet offensive Democratic partisans were retained. Places were given out as the booty of Congressmen in disregard of fitness, and federal officeholders continued to manipulate conventions. Some few extensions of the classified service were made during Mr. Cleveland's term, yet it was not until he had been defeated in the election of 1888 that a really important extension was made by him—that which included the railway mail service, embracing some six thousand employees.

In 1888, when the Democratic party was in power, the Democratic platform was practically silent. It merely affirmed the very debatable proposition that honest reform in the civil service had been inaugurated and maintained by President Cleveland.

In that year the Republicans, as we all remember, repeated the admirable declaration of 1884, with the vituperative addition that the Mugwumps had deserted pretty much everything that was good and especially civil service reform, and with the tautological assurance, "We will not fail to keep our pledges because they have broken theirs or because their candidate has broken his." Subsequent events would indicate that in this, the party did "protest too much," and doubts may well be entertained whether an agreement not to break one's word adds to the value of the original promise.

Four years ago, at the conference in Baltimore, I took occasion to discuss the meaning of the promises then made and what we might expect in the fulfillment of them. As a matter of the construction of plain English words there could be little doubt as to their interpretation. As a matter of prophecy, the accuracy of my conclusions was not supernatural. According to the platform the reform was to be extended to all grades of the service to which it was applicable. It was applicable to post offices and custom houses having less than twenty-five employees. The law itself said that, yet the President extended it to no such custom houses and to no such post offices until after he had been defeated for reëlection. It was applicable to the Census Bureau yet the President refused so to extend it. It was applicable to the entire labor service of the government, Massachusetts has demonstrated that, yet with one very honorable exception in the navy yards—which, however, have not yet been embraced with the civil service rules—the President failed to extend to any part of this service the principles of classification.

Mr. Harrison said the law should have the aid of a friendly interpretation and be faithfully enforced; yet political assessments went on in violation of law at Baltimore and elsewhere, unreproved and unpunished, over the protests of the President's own Commissioners. The spirit and purpose of reform were to be observed in all executive appointments, "fitness, and not party service, was to be the essential and discriminating test, fidelity and efficiency the only sure tenure of office, and only the interests of the public service should suggest removals," yet Mr. Clarkson's guillotine ran at a speed unexampled in history. Such names as David Martin, Governor Warmouth, and Stephen B. Elkins showed the wide range of that "fitness" which was the essential test, and the presence of the place-holders at Minneapolis the kind of fidelity and efficiency which gave sure tenure to office.

The workmen in the navy yards and a few hundred places in the Indian service and under the Fish Commission were all that Mr. Harrison gave us in fulfillment of his extensive engagements until after the election of 1892. It is when an administration is *in extremis* that its heart turns toward reform. It was amid disheartening surroundings in 1883 that the Republican party favored the enactment of the civil service law. It was after his defeat in 1888 that Mr. Cleveland classified the railway mail service. It was after the writ of ejectment was served last November that President Harrison included all free delivery offices.

Our chief executives are not wholly unlike that other distinguished ruler with whom the affliction of disease was a condition precedent to his desire to assume the sacerdotal office. In a civil service reform sense it may be said of more than one of our Presidents that nothing in his official life became him like the leaving of it. The retiring administration resembles the swan: it sings the sweetest in the hour of its passing. And so may it continue to be until the time when it shall be no longer necessary for the people to decree the death of the singer before they can hope to listen to the music.

In the last campaign the respective situations cÍ the two parties were reversed. It was the Republicans who were stricken dumb by the paralysis of office-holding; it was the Democracy which lifted up its voice like one crying in the wilderness. For it is with parties as with Presidents—there is no greater incentive to the culture of self-sacrificing patriotism than exclusion from the table of patronage. Public virtue resides principally in the party out of power. "Sweet are the uses of adversity." It is sorrow that chastens and purifies the soul.

It is largely in recognition of this fact that Indiana civil service reformers are so often found in the ranks of the opposition. We want to be in the company of those who stand most for political rectitude.

But to return to the platforms of 1892. In the Republican convention

Mr. Foraker was chairman of the platform committee. Under such midwifery it was hardly to be expected that the declaration in favor of civil service reform should be lusty or stalwart. It merely expressed the contentment of those who held the places, who did not wish to be annoyed with the fanaticism of impracticable reformers: "We commend the spirit and evidence of reform in the civil service and the wise and consistent enforcement by the Republican party of the laws regulating the same."

It was the exiled Democracy that could see much more clearly that things were not going on as they ought to go. And as theirs is the platform intended for the guidance of the present administration, it will be well for us to consider, somewhat in detail, the meaning of its language, and what we have a right to expect from a fair reading of its terms taken in connection with the declarations of Mr. Cleveland since it was adopted. I will premise that this is not done in any spirit of prophecy. We have had both words and acts from the same sources before, and we know that they have not always kept step together.

The outlook in retrospect is not always so comforting as that which fancy pictures for the future. "Retrospect," as President Harrison informed us, "will be a safer basis of judgment than promises."

The question is simply this: What have we the *right to expect* from the platform? "Public office," it says, "is a public trust." If it be this, it cannot be used to pay personal or party debts. It can neither be made a family perquisite, nor a fund for the reward of those who have rendered efficient service in conventions and campaigns. It is the administration of the office for the benefit of the people which must alone be considered, otherwise the trust will not be performed. A trustee cannot deal either personally or as a member of a firm or corporation with the trust property. A President cannot so deal with the offices either for himself or for his party.

"We reaffirm," so says the platform, "the declaration of the Democratic National Convention of 1876 for the reform of the civil service, and we call for the honest enforcement of all laws regulating the same." The enforcement of such laws cannot be expected if men who have the appointing power in the classified service are themselves unfriendly to the law, and, like the late Aquilla Jones, say that they "despise it." The law cannot be enforced unless the Commissioners are men of unflinching integrity, earnest purpose, ability, energy, and enthusiasm. But this is not enough. The law cannot be enforced if other officers of the government fail to do their duty in regard to it. It cannot be enforced if the Department of Justice fail to prosecute those who violate its penal provisions. It cannot be enforced if Cabinet officers, heads of divisions, postmasters, collectors, and all other officers in charge of classified subordinates fail to remove the men who violate it. If the Postmaster-General and the Secretary of the Treasury should, like their predecessors, retain in service men who by their own confession are guilty of collecting prohibited political assessments, it cannot be enforced.   The party has promised, then, that this thing will not be done.

The platform of 1876, referred to in these resolutions, declares, "Reform is necessary in the civil service; experience proves that efficient, economical conduct of the government business is not possible if the civil service be subject to change in every election, be a prize fought for at the ballot-box, be a brief reward of party zeal, instead of posts of honor, assigned for proved competency and held for fidelity in the public employ." We are therefore to have no "clean sweep." The civil service is not to be subject to change as the mere result of the election, and we are no longer to see the participants in the political contest rewarded by the offices. That is what the platform means. These places are to be posts of honor assigned for proved competency. How shall this competency be proven? Within the classified service by examinations and probation; and outside of that service is there any better proof than experience? And yet we find that the President looks with disfavor upon applications of persons who held office under his former administration for reappointment to their old places. No doubt in some cases this disfavor is justified. But is not the rule which excludes the good as well as the bad rather inconsistent with the platform? The declaration goes further; the place must not only be assigned for proved competency, but must be held for fidelity. If this rule is observed, no man who has been thoroughly faithful to his trust will be removed or supplanted. There is no question of any four-years term in this; fidelity is to be the criterion of retention.

The platform of 1876 says something even more important: "The dispensing of patronage should neither be a tax upon the time of our public men nor the instrument of their ambition." If this be carried out in letter and spirit, Democratic Congressmen can no longer seek reëlection by apportioning federal offices in their respective districts. The Postmaster-General will no longer regard as conclusive the recommendation of a Congressman, nor indeed as valuable in any other sense than as giving information of the qualifications of the man to be appointed. The domain of public office is no longer to be held upon feudal tenures by the congressional barons and divided among their henchmen. It is no longer to be a tax upon the time of Representatives in Congress nor the instrument of their ambition. When patronage shall be abolished as completely as this platform calls for, we shall have passed the turning point in civil service reform.

But, even thus early in the administration, the proof multiplies that this obligation is little regarded. The President and the members of the Cabinet are spending most of their time with the office seekers. Congressmen belabor them with importunities, bringing in applicants in droves and platoons, twenty at a time. The fourth-class post offices are being filled at the rate of thirty thousand a year. There have been one or two trifling misunderstandings between Congressmen and Mr. Maxwell, but as a rule, the

Congressmen have had their way. They are as busy in the distribution of offices as ever. Postmasters must be faithful to their trust, but not for more than four years. At the end of that time, good or bad, they go. Still there is some gain in this.

We all know that mistakes will be made even by the best of administrations. The great difficulty here is not the occasional error, but the system resorted to which gives rise to this error. Except for political reasons no man in his senses would consider that Daniel W. Voorhees is of all men in Indiana best fitted to give testimony as to the qualifications for office of Indiana citizens. And this has manifestly been the source from which a number of such appointments came.

We now come to the declaration of the platform of 1892 which refers to the Minneapolis convention as an object lesson of the evils of the spoils system: "The nomination of the President as in the recent Republican convention, by delegations composed largely of his appointees holding office at his pleasure, is a scandalous satire upon our free institutions and a startling illustration of the methods by which a President may gratify his ambition."

These words necessarily imply that the Democratic party will not repeat such a precedent. But the platform goes further: "We denounce a policy under which federal officeholders usurp the control of party conventions in the States." This has been done from time almost immemorial under both parties. The Democracy assures us by its denunciation that it is now to cease. Officeholders shall no longer renominate the Congressmen to whom they owe their places. Yet, if this is not to be done, why are Democratic Congressmen bestirring themselves in such wearisome fashion to get places for the men who have already aided them?

The platform closes as follows: "We pledge the Democratic party to the reform of these and all other abuses which threaten individual liberty and local self-government." This contract is a pretty large one. When the party shall have performed it, the party will have deserved well of the Republic.

The platform, if fairly carried out, means a great deal. It means probably much more than many of those who voted for it intended. Many who supported it will no doubt be found foremost in the attempt to overturn its promises. It was on the whole a better platform than many of us expected, and yet it is decidedly inferior to the Republican declarations of 1884 and 1888. It does not specifically demand the extension of the classified system. It does not directly require a repeal of the four-years term of office. Its most important propositions were embodied by mere reference to the platform of 1876. Many who voted for it were no doubt ignorant of the precise nature of the promises they were supporting. They were willing to endorse what a previous Democratic convention had done, even if they did not know exactly what that was. It is by necessary inference rather than by direct allegation that the most important parts of this platform are valuable. The Democracy could not have offered a more stinging criticism upon the conduct of their opponents than to have repeated *ipsissimis verbis* the declarations of 1884 and 1888 They did something less than this, but still enough, under fair construction, to give an immense impetus to the reform.

But more valuable than the platform expressions, the Democratic party has elected a President who, in spite of very great previous shortcomings, has still shown a strong desire and no small amount of persistent energy on behalf of a reformed civil service. In his previous administration he withstood for a long time a pressure which few would have resisted so well. In spite of much inconsistent conduct I do not doubt that the personal sentiments of both of the last Presidents were friendly, or that, if left entirely alone, they would have done much more than they did do on behalf of civil service reform. The immediate influences upon a President are immensely strong in favor of the spoils system. The pressure for place among those who throng the antechambers of the White House is calculated to shut out a fair view of the general perspective of public opinion beyond.

President Cleveland in his present term, reëlected after defeat and with no hope of future renomination, has great advantages. He cannot be unconscious of the fact that his great strength with the people is due more to his resistance to the spoilsmen than to his concessions to them. Nowhere was his consciousness of this more clearly portrayed than in his conduct at the Tammany banquet when, in the midst of a campaign, he refused to make any pledges in regard to the distribution of the patronage. He never did anything which more strengthened him with the people of this country. He can hardly fail to remember that the successful campaigns of the Democratic party were the campaigns in which it had given the strongest assurances of civil service reform. Under these circumstances it is safe to believe that although the promises of the platform will not be wholly fulfilled yet much will be done to remove portions of the public service from the patronage system which has dishonored our institutions. Maxwell, the logical successor of Clarkson, is still hard at work, but the removals are not quite half so numerous as they were four years ago. No raiser of campaign funds has yet received the recognition of a Cabinet appointment. There is strong reason to believe that when the time is ripe the classified service will be extended. Secrecy, which for a moment threatened to obscure changes in the Post Office Department, was speedily discarded. Removal on ex-parte charges that the public were not permitted to see or know was perhaps one of the very greatest of the abuses in Mr. Cleveland's former administration. It has not ceased, but has been confined to smaller places only. Wherever it appears, and under whatever circumstances, it is a crying evil which demands redress. There can be no just removal upon any charges which the accused is not permitted to see. In all these matters public opinion, to which, if it be just and impartial, Mr.

Cleveland is responsive, should be set to work. His friends should be as fearless in criticism as his antagonists. They have, I think, not always been so. As civil service reformers it is our duty to be as free from the cult or worship of any man as from that of any political organization.

Such are the declarations of the several parties and their candidates since the day when civil service reform was first talked of down to the date of these presents. Performance, as yet, does not wholly keep step with promises. It is a little like the clock for which its owner apologized by saying, "It is a good clock if you only understand it. When it strikes ten and the hands point to three, then you may know that it is a quarter past seven." But, whether the clock be fast or slow, time advances surely and constantly. And so does civil service reform. Because parties have not lived up to their platforms will it do to say that these are meaningless? The general advance shows that there is a deep meaning in them. Platforms have outgrown the period of hostility and indifference, and, in response to the force of public sentiment, parties are willing to promise anything, often more than they can perform.

Because Presidents have failed to live up to their own standards of duty, must we, therefore, believe that reform itself has faltered? Its growth has been constant and irresistible, and in the old, illogical, practical Anglo-Saxon way, by compromise. Each President has made a compromise with Satan by which Satan has lost a little territory. Let this go on long enough and the Satan of spoils politics will not have an acre left. The growth has perhaps been more healthy because it has not been too fast. It has followed the analogies of nature: first the blade, then the ear, and after that the full corn in the ear. The best work of humanity has been done in just this way. So it was with slavery: first exclusion from the Territories, next the proclamation, then the Constitutional amendment.

The important thing for us is to observe what have been the lines of this growth. Nearly all the progress we can see and measure has come about through the classified service. This began with about fifteen thousand places, now considerably more than forty thousand are embraced in it. It has twice received most valuable bequests from the last wills and testaments of departing administrations. To the extension of this system should our efforts be chiefly directed.

John and Maria were crossing a stream. The current was swift and the ford was deep. John drove a strong bay horse and a little sorrel mare. The sorrel lagged behind and he belabored her with useless blows. Maria took him by the shoulder. "John," she said, "whip the strong horse." He did so and they reached the bank. Let us whip the strong horse. Let us urge forward the classified service.

APPENDIX VII

ARE PRESIDENTIAL APPOINTMENTS FOR SALE ?[1]

Among the supporters of Mr. Cleveland last year, there was no one whose influence was more potent and valuable than Mr. Whitney, formerly Secretary of the Navy, and Mr. Cleveland's warm personal friend. During the campaign, Mr. J. J. Van Alen, a gentleman of large fortune, whom Mr. Whitney "knew very well," contributed some fifty thousand dollars to the Democratic fund, and after Mr. Cleveland's election he promptly applied for the office of Minister to Italy. Mr. Van Alen was without experience in public affairs. He had not been distinguished in politics, letters, or diplomacy. As early as April last, it was known to some of Mr. Cleveland's best friends that Mr. Van Alen had given this money and wanted this place, and the President was warned of the scandal which would follow such an appointment. This was then understood to be "Mr. Whitney's one request of the administration." On June 20th, Mr. Whitney confirmed the fact in his letter to Mr. Cleveland. "This, as you know," he wrote, "is the first time you have been approached by me on the subject of appointments." Mr. Whitney reserves himself for great occasions. After some delay, and with apparent reluctance, the nomination was sent to the Senate and confirmed.

What is the meaning of this transaction? Why did Mr. Van Alen give the money? Why was he appointed? Men do not contribute fifty thousand dollars for nothing. This money might have been given "freely and from an interest in the success of the party," as Mr. Whitney puts it, or it might have been given with the expectation of some personal return. If it were contributed unselfishly, Mr. Van Alen's devotion to his party is very great, so great that we cannot but wonder why he should so soon ask for an office, the giving of which would bring scandal upon the party "whose success he so earnestly desired," and why he should not, as unselfishly, relieve the President of embarrassment by withdrawing his claim after that scandal had become current. Such sums are not given from disinterested motives if followed at once by personal claims. Whatever may have been the form of the words or the silence which accompanied the gift, Mr. Van Alen expected its equivalent. He gave the money because he looked for the office.

---

[1] Reprinted from the *Forum*, December, 1893.

And the conclusion is irresistible, that he got the office because he gave the money. There was some reason for the appointment. What was it? Was it the eminent services of Mr. Van Alen? He was unknown to public life. Was it his fitness for the place? What is it that qualifies a man for the post of foreign minister? What must he do? In the first place he must represent his country. He must stand for America in the presence of the world. He must illustrate republican government, as Franklin did at the court of France. To do this he must understand and love the institutions of his country. He must be able to show their excellence as James Russell Lowell did in his admirable address on "Democracy." He must have the diplomatic talent to uphold the interests of his country as Charles Francis Adams did during our late war. He must possess dignity and courage in the midst of excitement and danger as Washburne did during the struggle between Germany and France. He must combine skill and delicacy, as Mr. Van Alen's predecessor, Albert G. Porter, did in the late difficulty occasioned by the riots at New Orleans, when Baron Fava, the Italian Minister at Washington, was hastily recalled. Mr. Porter had little experience when sent to Rome, but he had on many occasions manifested the diplomatic talent so needful in such emergencies. These are the qualities required of an American minister, when we need a minister at all. In what way had Mr. Van Alen shown that he possessed them? If he had done anything to demonstrate his fitness for this place, would not Mr. Whitney in a letter designed as a justification of the appointment, have given some fact in support of the opinion that he was "in every way adapted to the position"? The conclusion is irresistible that fitness was not the ground of his selection.

Was he appointed as a reward for political services? If so, what were they? Has anything been specified except the fifty thousand dollars?

Was the place given because Mr. Whitney pressed the appointment, and in liquidation of the President's obligation to his friend? Very likely. We can well understand that Mr. Whitney's importunities would be hard to refuse, especially when he makes but one request. Perhaps the hardest duty of a public officer is to reject, in the administration of his trust, the claims of personal gratitude. By no other channel do unfitness and incompetency more readily creep into the public service. Say, then, that this was the cause. But the question still remains, Why did Mr. Whitney request this appointment? The public reasons for the choice were wanting. His own letter in which he denied that he had promised the place points, clearly to the motive. "There is," wrote Mr. Whitney, "additional reason for appointing him, in that, as the result of that very generous and cordial support of the party in the late campaign when friends were few and calls were great, he has been accused of dishonorable bargaining." Can anyone doubt that Mr. Whitney's obligation to the man who had furnished fifty thousand dollars "when friends were few and calls were great" was the real ground of his insistence? It makes no difference whether there was any contract or not. Instead of suing in covenant upon the bond, Mr. Van Alen brings his action in assumpsit on the promise implied by the rendering of these most valuable services. And it is upon this count that judgment is confessed. He has drawn a sight draft for the office and the consideration is fifty thousand dollars. In the last analysis it is evident that he got the office because he gave the money.

If this be so, what is the full meaning of the transaction? It means that money, mere money, will secure even from our Chief Executive, one of the highest and most honorable places in the gift of the government. Mr. Van Alen is not the possessor of those other personal or political qualities which can be thrown into such a transaction to make it sweet. The selection cannot be justified even by such poor reasons as were used in the case of Mr. Wanamaker where business experience and ability were urged as the reason for his appointment to a business office, and the real motive for the choice was thus obscured. In the Van Alen case we are confronted with corruption in its most naked form. The President has told us that dollars alone, when given to the right person, at the right time, are sufficient to secure as high a place as that of Minister to Italy. We are informed that the mission to Rome is for sale, and the President ought not to wonder if we resent the insult. It will not do to lay this at the door of anyone else. We cannot relieve the President upon the plea of lack of ordinary information. He made this appointment with his eyes open and against the protests of his friends; and the people, whose offices are thus given over to the methods of the auction mart, must hang their heads in shame.

We have had to witness a great many instances of the corrupt use of patronage. Offices, high and low, have been divided among party bosses, and services, often discreditable, rendered to political organizations, have been rewarded by public place and paid for out of the treasury of the State. We have seen a code of morality which even in the army has become extinct revived in times of peace under republican government. Our political sensibilities have become so blunted that we have almost come to believe it right that the victor should carry off the spoils. In our municipalities, bargains are made and money buys the place and we pay little heed to it. Our State legislatures have been corrupted and men have won their way through the power of the dollar even to the Senate of the United States. But until very recent years we have had no reason to believe that the sanctuary of our Federal Executive had been invaded by the defiling influence of gold. It is this last step which indicates only too clearly the direction in which our political morality is moving. The appointments of Mr. Wanamaker and Mr. Van Alen are two long steps downward and backward towards the abyss from which free government can never rise. The descent must be stopped before it is too late.

A little more than four years ago, a successful Philadelphia shopkeeper, upon the instance of Mr. Quay, Chairman of the Republican National Committee, collected a fund of several hundred thousand dollars for campaign purposes. He was rewarded with the Postmaster-Generalship and the price for that office was then established. The public outcry at that iniquity was loud and long. It was one of the strongest reasons urged against the reëlection of Mr. Harrison. In the *Democratic Campaign Text-book* of the last campaign (page 189) is the statement, "Perhaps the most disgraceful act committed by President Harrison was the appointment of Mr. Wanamaker as Postmaster-General." The most sinister feature of the Van Alen appointment is that it comes from the administration of a party pledged to the reform of such abuses and that there is no alternative left to the voters of our country except that between the party which is responsible for Mr. Wanamaker and the party which is responsible for Mr. Van Alen.

What is the essential nature of such appointments? It is set forth in our text-books upon criminal law. In Bacon's *Abridgment* (Officers and Offices, F) we find:

"The taking or giving of a reward for offices of a public nature is said to be bribery. 'And surely,' says Hawkins, 'nothing can be more palpably prejudicial to the good of the public than to have places of the highest concernment, on the due execution whereof the happiness of both king and people doth depend, disposed of, not to those who are most able to execute them, but to those who are most able to pay for them; nor can anything be a greater discouragement to industry and virtue, than to see those places of trust and honour, which ought to be the rewards of those who by their industry and diligence have qualified themselves for them, conferred on those who have no other recommendation, but that of being the highest bidders; neither can anything be a greater temptation to officers to abuse their power by bribery and extortion, and other acts of injustice, than the consideration of the great expense they were at in gaining their places, and the necessity of sometimes straining a point to make their bargain answer their expectations.'"

This is quoted by Russell (*On Crimes*, i., p. 214), who adds:

"The buying and selling of such offices has therefore been considered an offense *malum per se* and indictable at common law."

Thus spoke the rugged intellect of our ancestors. The reasons are as sound now as they were then. The evil is just as great, nay greater, in a government of the people than in one of privilege and rank. Shall it be said that we have so far fallen off from our ideals that the sale of such places shall pass without our earnest remonstrance? It is not pleasant to think that our Chief Magistrate has done a thing which falls so close to the definition of the crime of bribery that it involves all the public injury and moral wrong so clearly described as the essential quality of the guilty act. It is not hard to foresee the consequences of such a precedent. No matter how widespread political debauchery may become, every form of it always begins with a single instance. The common law itself is merely the accumulation of precedents, "that wilderness of single instances" which has grown into jurisprudence. When the example set in this case shall become the rule and it is known that money will buy the place, that the big contributor will get the big office, what will follow?

The ruin of our public service is perhaps the first and most palpable result. No man who buys an office is ever worthy of it. What security is there that the purchaser of a foreign mission will not be base enough to sell his country? No man can fill a place which he has bought without dishonor to the land he represents. The self-respecting American must blush if he is compelled to meet him. A diplomatic service is worse than useless if it is to be the means of disseminating this reputation for our country. It is especially humiliating to reflect that in the land where Fabricius rejected the bribes of Pyrrhus, we are to have the living evidence that our republic has taken so little warning from the example of that which finally led to the decline and overthrow of the great republic of antiquity.

But the most fatal consequence of such appointments is the debasement of the suffrage and the general corruption of the people. There is strong reason to believe that the money secured by some of these vast campaign contributions was designed for this very purpose. The distribution of the funds raised by Mr. Wanamaker among the "blocks of five" is an instance. But whether this be so or not, why should the voter who sees office bestowed for money hesitate to take money for his vote? Why should men love a country where gold buys preferment and where the great offices are confined to the wealthy? Why should they die for it? What inspiration would there be in the great names of our history if we believed that the men who bore them were capable of an act like this? Why should men seek anything but gold, if gold alone is to open every avenue of honor? What sort of human beings will be developed under such a regimen? What other issue is there to-day fraught with results so full of ultimate peril to popular government? The cloud may seem small but it is laden with bolts of destruction. Other questions—the tariff, the currency—occupy more of our attention but they are less vital in their consequences. We may not live to see the results of this corruption, but it is a sad inheritance to leave to our children. If we measure these things as they will be measured in history, other questions which are so absorbing now will fade into nothing by the side of this. We may cripple our commerce or our manufactures by a vicious economical policy, but the material resources of our people are well-nigh inexhaustible and we will soon rally after temporary discomfort. From pestilence, famine, and war we can rise in renewed strength. It is only when the heart fails, when public spirit languishes, that our case is indeed desperate.

APPENDIX VIII

THE ADVANCE OF THE COMPETITIVE SYSTEM[1]

The steady advance made by the competitive system in the federal civil service during the period of a single generation has been quite unique in the history of reform. For it was no longer ago than 1867 that the agitation in favor of this system was first begun by the report of the Hon. Thomas A. Jenckes, of Rhode Island, to the House of Representatives, accompanied by a bill to regulate the civil service.

In 1871, the first step was taken toward reform. An act was passed authorizing the President to prescribe rules for admission to the civil service. President Grant appointed Mr. George William Curtis, with six other gentleman, as the first "Advisory Board," and rules were adopted, classifying the service, and providing for competitive examinations.

But great opposition soon developed. Congress failed to make an appropriation for the support of the Board, and in 1875 the President abandoned the system.

In 1876 President Hayes was elected upon a platform containing a strong plank advocating civil service reform, and he promised in his letter of acceptance that the reform should be "thorough, radical, and complete." In some departments competitive examinations were instituted, notably in the Department of the Interior, where Mr. Carl Schurz had been appointed Secretary, and in 1879 similar examinations were established in the New York custom house and the New York post office. They showed such good results that they formed a valuable object lesson in advancing the reform and in 1883 the Pendleton civil service law was enacted.

There was on several occasions afterwards considerable backsliding in the affection of Congress for civil service reform, but the law was never repealed and under it gradual extensions of the classified system were made as times were ripe for them—the railway mail service, under Mr. Cleveland; the free delivery service, under President Harrison; pretty much everything left in the departments under Mr. Cleveland's so-called "blanket" order, during his second term; the Philippine service under Mr. McKinley; the rural free delivery, the census, the Spanish war service, as well as the

---

[1] A paper read before the Annual Meeting of the National Civil Service Reform League held at Baltimore, December 10, 1903.

registration of laborers, under President Roosevelt. Some of these accessions have been made as legacies of dying administrations, and sometimes they have been apples of discord to the survivors. But with Theodore Roosevelt the time came at last when a President found it possible to make extensions to the competitive system at the very beginning of his official life.

Thus it is that in twenty years the classified service has grown nearly ninefold, from fourteen thousand places when the law was passed to one hundred and twenty-five thousand places to-day, and that even outside the competitive service comparatively few changes are made at the expiration of the four-year periods. Public opinion, which indulgently acquiesced in a clean sweep in years gone by, now resents the dismissal of a single postmistress for political reasons. Outside the consular service and the postmasterships, the great bulk of all classifiable places is under the competitive system.

Even our opponents recognize the conquests we have made. The New York *Sun* celebrates them in a lyric inspired by an afflatus undoubtedly divine, a lyric which it calls "The Civil Service Anthem," or "Song of the C. S. C.," and which is supposed to have emanated from the Commission itself.

The statement of the origin of this poem may not be literally accurate, but, like other unauthentic documents, it is historical in the sense that it portrays the attitude of mind of the source from which it emanates.

Our adversaries attribute to us a spirit of jubilation at our successes, and they do well, for in the federal service we have traversed at least three fourths of the distance from the starting point to the goal of the utmost possible achievement. While other reforms still linger in the valley, we have climbed at least to the shoulder of the mountain.

But there is one thing we are beginning to miss; we no longer march to the inspiring music furnished by the yells of the enemy. The cries of "Pharisee," "Snivel Service," and "Emasculated Reform," uttered by the virile advocates of plunder, come more and more seldom to our ears. More and more faint grow the sounds of their rage, defiance, and despair, until to-day a little rattling in the throat, preceding final dissolution, is almost all that we can hear. So rare are the expressions of reprobation that I for one feel inclined to treasure them as curiosities. I recall in particular, that during the special session of the Senate last spring, a Senator entered my room whose brows were furrowed by Jovian corrugations. He was mad all over. I asked him what I could do for him. He answered, "I have come to the conclusion that this civil service business is a fraud." I asked him in what respect. He said, "I had some clerks in the Census Office, and among them a lady in whom I am interested. When Director Merriam was about to make his dismissals, he told me I could keep two, and I gave him the name of this clerk with one other. But she had been ordered to be vaccinated; she was not well; there was a noise in the neighborhood where she was doing her work, and she was not able to do it as satisfactorily as others, and so she was dropped, and I can't get a place for her anywhere." I told him that the Census Bureau at that time was not in the classified service; and that for what was done the civil service law at least was not responsible. He seemed a little surprised at this statement, then he began on a new tack. He said that promotions within the service were managed by a ring composed of the heads of divisions; that they promoted their friends and relatives, and that a Senator couldn't get any promotion for anybody. I asked him if he did not think that the heads of the divisions under whom the clerks were working could judge better as to the respective efficiency of these clerks than persons upon the outside. He said the heads of divisions did not determine the question upon efficiency at all; they promoted their favorites. I asked him how he knew this, but he did not tell me, except that he knew one man in the War Department who was a very good clerk and had got no promotion. I asked him how he could tell that there were not other clerks still better. He said that was impossible; this clerk was as good as any man could be. He added that the reason he wanted a place for this lady was because she came from his own town and had two children to support. The Senator departed in great discontent, and I reflected for a moment on the logic of the preference he desired. If the residence of the lady in the same town as the Senator constituted a good reason for preferring her, such reason ought to be applied to other cases, and I was wondering how much the efficiency of the civil service would gain by a regulation providing that appointments should first be given to ladies residing in the same towns as Senators. The character of the logic displayed by legislators who make such demands leads one to wonder that our laws are half as good as they are. I must not, of course, reveal the identity of the gentleman in question, yet a certain natural association of ideas leads me to observe that he is now under indictment for securing the appointment of a postmaster for a pecuniary consideration.

It is with pardonable pride that the National Civil Service Reform League may look back on the part it has taken in this advance of the competitive system. And we must remind our adversaries that the evils which they prophesied have not attended its coming. No officeholding aristocracy of tide-waiters and letter-carriers has trampled American manhood under its iron heel; we have not bent the knee to an hereditary sovereign as the result of our adopting so monarchical a system; the man who is not a college graduate has still some opportunities for employment, and there is still interest in political issues and great public questions, though the citizen is not so often paid for this interest by the plum of an office for which he is not qualified. Is there anyone who will look back to-day upon the clean sweep made with each incoming administration in the past, and tell us that the adoption of the competitive system has not marked a distinct gain in our political life?

If we compare the progress of civil service reform with that of other measures which have occupied the public mind during the same period, we can see how swift and steady has been the advance.

Efforts have been made to secure the reform of our city governments, yet after each attempt the wave has receded almost as far as it had advanced.

Laws were passed more than a dozen years ago to prohibit combinations of capital in trusts and monopolies. Yet in spite of these laws such combinations have been growing in a greatly accelerated ratio.

At every recurring election there has been great talk of reforms and changes in the tariff, yet the essential principles of our tariff legislation, whatever the difference of schedules, have been very little affected.

Repeated political convulsions have shaken the country in regard to the currency, and yet the changes made in actual legislation have been trifling. The mountains have groaned in labor and hardly a mouse has been born.

Many enthusiastic souls believed that efforts to substitute arbitration for war were reaching a golden consummation in the establishment of the Hague tribunal, but more recent events make it seem as if the time were almost as distant now as when the prophet spoke, in which swords should be turned into plowshares, and spears into pruning hooks, in which nation should not take up arms against nation, neither should they learn war any more.

In contrast with these failures to better the condition of the world the competitive system has made a progress which is astonishing, and it has done this, although it has not been the leading issue in any campaign, and although it has not been supported by the personal interest of any particular group, or section of the community. No vast protected industries or labor unions have ever combined in its advocacy, no class even, like the disfranchised, clamoring for equal rights. The tongues of demagogues, the vested interests of political patronage, and the inertia of a vicious system long established were all against us. We could not awaken sympathy, like the early abolitionists, by picturing the oppression of the helpless, the scourge and chain and auction block, the separation of families, the long flight for liberty across forests and morasses under the guidance of the north star. The competitive system is to most persons a dry and uninteresting subject; no vast multitudes assemble to hear its discussion and be swayed by the passions which it arouses. Its advocates have had no other motives than that honest work-a-day patriotism which is willing to renounce the most brilliant fields of conflict and victory, and is content with the modest kind of celebrity which follows more unobtrusive endeavor. Yet perhaps this very weakness has been part of our strength, for our good faith at least was impregnable, when even our adversaries could attribute to us no selfish motives.

What then have been the causes of our phenomenal success? Very prominent, certainly, among these have been the support of advocates of eminence and character. Even before the competitive plan was developed, the greatest voices in American history denounced and reprobated in burning words the evils of patronage. That trinity of eloquence in the golden age of the Senate, Daniel Webster, Henry Clay, and John C. Calhoun, however divergent the views of its members on other subjects, was united in this, that it saw in the spoils system, inaugurated by Andrew Jackson, one of the gravest dangers to free institutions. From that time on we have had at the service of our reform, the tongues and the pens of the ablest in eloquence and statesmanship, that America has produced. In the early days we had the voice of James A. Garfield in the House of Representatives, of Carl Schurz in the Senate, and on the platform the incomparable advocacy of George William Curtis. His words as president of this League have given the country an inspiration which has long outlasted his life. Listen to-day to the divine fire that burns in his sentences:

"Gentlemen, the stars in their courses fought against Sisera. But they fight for us. The desire of good government, of honest politics, of parties which shall be legitimate agencies of great policies; all the high instincts of good citizenship; all the lofty impulses of American patriotism, are the 'sweet influences' that favor reform.

"Sir Philip Sidney wrote to his brother upon his travels, 'Whenever you hear of a good war, go to it.' That is the call which we have heard and obeyed. And a good war it has been, and is. Everywhere, indeed, there are signs of an alert and adroit hostility. They are the shots of outposts that foretell the battle. But everywhere, also, there are signs of the advance of the whole line, the inspiring harbingers of victory. Never was the prospect fairer. If the shadows still linger, the dawn is deepening— the dawn that announces our sun of Austerlitz."

We have also been favored by the pen of a distinguished statesman. The work on the "Civil Service of Great Britain," by Dorman B. Eaton, is as convincing a treatise, from a practical standpoint, as was ever issued in support of a great public measure.

Another powerful influence which has wrought in favor of the reform is that of the press. While there have been dissenting opinions, the judgment of the court of journalism has been delivered with greater unanimity in our favor than upon any other subject that I know. So overwhelming, indeed, is the sentiment to-day that an article, recently appearing in a Chicago paper, in favor of returning to the patronage system seemed, indeed, like the voice of one crying in the wilderness, but without hope of preparing the way for its gospel of demoralization.

Not only has the competitive system had eloquent advocates, but it has had most skillful artificers. The men who framed the Federal Civil Service Act created a mechanism of marvelous adaptability and efficiency for accomplishing the end they had in view. I regard that act as one of the most skillfully devised statutes ever passed by a legislative body. Twenty years have now elapsed since the law was enacted, and except for the limitations excluding laborers and officers confirmed by the Senate from its provisions, I do not know a single particular in which I greatly care to see it amended. Even the reform can go on without further legislative action. In these respects beauty of the law is that it contains within itself provisions for the growth of the competitive system by mere act of the President and the Commission without further congressional enactment. In some respects it adapts itself even better to the conditions of the service to-day than when it first became a law. For instance, the provision that none but men in the civil service should act as local examiners was inconvenient so long as these men were partisans appointed for partisan reasons. But now that the non-partisan character of the service has become general this difficulty no longer exists. It was once supposed that the law was defective in not providing for taking testimony in investigations by the Commission, but this defect was readily amended by a recent executive order. It was feared that it was defective in not providing for the withholding of salaries from those illegally appointed; but all that was needed was a President willing to adopt a rule that such salaries should not be paid, and the evil disappeared as if by magic. Some feared that the law was faulty in that it did not provide for the interposition of the courts, yet recent events have shown that such interposition is not an unmixed blessing, and that under an executive friendly to the law the best administration may be had without outside interference. Indeed there is very little which cannot be done under the present law by a President who is friendly to the system. His limitations are found rather in political exigencies and in the state of public opinion than in the limitations of law, or constitutional right.

I say then that the law is a marvel of legislative skill. The first rules adopted by Mr. Dorman B. Eaton and his fellow-commissioners were framed with equal sagacity. The work began modestly. The competitive system was applied at first to fourteen thousand places only, places to which it was most evidently applicable, where scholastic tests seemed so palpably proper that little objection could be made, places in the departments and the larger offices where personal selections were most difficult, and where the need of the new method was most apparent. The system of civil service jurisprudence, if I may so call it, which has grown up from the rules, has not always been a model of foresight, clearness, or condensation. It was seldom that more than a month or two passed without some new amendment. The various changes made have now been condensed and systematized in the recent "Justinian code," framed by the Commission, which, as I learn from Mr. Doyle, has not needed the scratch of a pen for nearly eight months!

Not only has the competitive system been skillfully devised, but it has in general been well administered, for Dorman B. Eaton, Governor Thompson, John R. Proctor, and, most eminent of all, Theodore Roosevelt have been Civil Service Commissioners. And there has been a peculiar fitness in the character of the leadership, that of Dorman B. Eaton in the formative period, and that of Theodore Roosevelt in the militant period of the reform.

The progress of the competitive system in the federal service depends mainly upon the President. The President's action, on the other hand, must depend in great measure upon the support he receives from Congress and from the people. Since the passage of the civil service law, our Presidents have all been personally friendly to the competitive system, although sometimes when they were overcome by party pressure there have been serious lapses and wide gaps between profession and performance.

President Arthur, who was in office when the law was passed, had been a manipulator of local party patronage, but throughout his term he displayed considerable sympathy with the new law, by approving its provisions, appointing efficient commissioners, and giving them consistent support. President Cleveland, a firm friend of the merit system, took office under peculiar difficulties. The appetite of his party for spoils, after the exclusion of a quarter of a century, was insatiable; he withstood it bravely in many instances, and he maintained the law within its limited field of operation at that time, but outside the classified service there was a pretty clean sweep of the offices, and the system of removal on secret charges of "offensive partisanship" furnished a means of evasion of civil service reform principles which cast a certain discredit upon the merit system. President Harrison entered office under the strongest pledges of his party and himself, both to extend the system and apply its principles in all executive appointments; he was, however, much more subject to political influence than his predecessor, and the clean sweep was again repeated. He made extensions of the classified service it is true, but the most important one (the free delivery offices) was only effected at the last moment, after he had been defeated for reëlection. President Cleveland in his second term did more for the competitive system than had ever been accomplished up to that time, particularly in the extensive additions to the service made by him in his so-called blanket order, which became subject to such bitter criticism when the Republicans again came into power.

It is considered by many that there was a retrogression under President McKinley. The order which he made exempting from examinations some thousands of the positions which had been included by Mr. Cleveland was greatly to be regretted. In point of fact, however, the excepted positions were not so numerous as was supposed at the time, either by the Departments or the Civil Service Commission, many of these places were not actually thrown back into patronage, and the general personnel of the administration was so favorable to the merit system when President Roosevelt entered upon the duties of chief executive that no radical changes were required. And President McKinley performed the inestimable service of initiating the competitive system in the Philippine Islands, thus preserving these dependencies from the dangers of exploitation and patronage.

Concerning the present administration, I have been so closely identified with it, that I hardly feel at liberty to speak. I may, however, call your attention to the figures just compiled by Mr. Kiggins, the Chief Examiner of the Civil Service Commission, figures which astonished me beyond measure when I saw them. During the year ending June 30, 1902, the Commission had examined 59,318 persons, and had made 12,894 appointments to competitive places. That was then our high-water mark. During the year ending June 30, 1903, 109,829 persons were examined and 39,646 competitive appointments were made, more than three times as many as the year before. I had felt during the year that we were making progress, but I had never dreamed we were doing half so well as that.

If a tree be known by its fruits the administration of President Roosevelt must be pronounced prolific, in regard to civil service reform.

The competitive system has been fortunate in its advocates, in its organizers and in its administrators, and in the friendship of our Chief Executives, but it has been still more fortunate in itself, in its essential nature and in the irresistible logic, which declares its excellence to every impartial understanding. The principles underlying that system have been more completely demonstrated than any political issue of the time. They are more conclusive than the arguments in favor of protection or free trade, of the gold or the silver standard, of universal or restricted suffrage, of prohibition or license, of war or arbitration. And not only is the system impregnable in right reason, but it is essentially the most practical of all reforms. It has vindicated itself by its results. Where the competitive and patronage systems existed in the departments side by side the world could see which tree produced the better fruit, and the competitive system thrives by the plain law of the survival of the fittest.

But the question recurs, how safe are we to-day? Since the advance of the reform has depended so largely upon the will of the President, since the rules may be changed or repealed by executive order, since every place in the service may be excepted from examination, are we not constantly in danger of losing all we have gained? The platform upon which Mr. Bryan was nominated looked ominous for civil service reform. How far are we at the mercy of an unfriendly administration?

Of course there is a risk in the election of a President who regards the competitive system with an evil eye. But I believe the time has now passed when that system is in danger of total extermination by executive action. Custom, if it be well fixed, is quite as strong with us as law. The growth of the patronage system itself shows this. The custom of party conventions has nullified even the constitutional provision for the Electoral College. But now this inertia of habit, which it was once so hard for us to overcome, will be our ally for the maintenance of our reform. Any President who, without cause, might attempt the overthrow of the competitive system, would open such floodgates of confusion and incompetency as would sweep his administration into the bottomless abyss. Every breach made in the dikes is bound to cause him greater embarrassment than advantage, and the law of political self-preservation can be counted upon to see to it that these breaches shall be few.

But it is incumbent upon us to watch carefully the growth of our reform, to see that no parasites accumulate upon its branches to stifle its natural and healthy development. I feel impelled to call attention particularly to one feature of our system: its tendency to permanency of tenure, and to consider whether any evils lurk in that tendency; and if so, how they can best be eradicated. It may be said that the civil service law does not provide for any permanency at all, and this is true. It is undoubtedly the right and the duty of every superior officer to dismiss his subordinates whenever they cease to be efficient. But the fact that there is no fixed term, and no temptation to remove a man in order to get his place for another, accompanied with the very human reluctance of all in authority to cause personal distress to those who are dependent upon them, leads naturally to a greater continuity of tenure than exists under the system of rotation in office. And if this tendency be unrestrained, it may in time develop certain evils of superannuation in government employees which will inevitably be attributed to the competitive system. The superannuation which now exists cannot be justly laid at the doors of that system, since the old employees now in the service came in not by competition but by patronage. The amount of superannuation at present is not great. Three investigations have shown that the number of persons in the service over seventy years of age is only about two per cent. Yet in some particular departments, notably in the Treasury, it is very perceptible; and we can hardly doubt that it is likely to grow greater as the years go by.

Now there is an easy remedy to remove the dangers of superannuation for the future, just as effective as the competitive system was in removing the evils of patronage in the past. It is to require that each person entering the civil service hereafter shall, during his period of probation and before absolute appointment, take out a policy in some responsible company, providing for a sufficient annuity when he reaches a certain age and is separated from the government service, or in case of physical disability prior to that time. The government could properly require the deposit of securities from such company, to insure the payment of the annuity. while the premiums could be secured by deductions from salaries. This system would, by a law of natural selection, encourage appointments of such as are physically best qualified for their work, and least likely soon to become disabled and superannuated, since such persons would have an advantage in the matter of premiums. The more difficult question would remain, however, how to provide against the superannuation of those who are now in the service, who have taken no such security against the infirmities of age. These can be provided for in two ways; first, by a government allowance, or secondly, by a system of suitable reductions, giving to those who have outlived their usefulness less pay and lighter work, the reductions to be made either as the result of examinations in regard to their ability to perform their duties, or as the result of the showing of comparative records of efficiency.

I believe that it is high time for the League in these days of its prosperity to forestall the reproach which may be made hereafter, that we have permitted barnacles to grow or remain upon the fair vessel we have so auspiciously launched upon the waters of political life.

Let us improve these days of sunshine by making the amplest provision for the security of the fabric which our hands have aided in erecting, that it may at all times be strong as well as fair, able forever to resist the storms, and to keep safely within its chambers the treasure of good government for future generations.

APPENDIX IX

CITY GOVERNMENT BY EXPERTS UNDER THE COMPETITIVE SYSTEM[1]

We do not know much about expert management in America. Our people are particularly versatile. They can change their occupations very readily. That was one of the exigencies of our pioneer days. But in the complex conditions which now surround city life in America it is necessary that our municipalities shall be managed by persons who have attained high skill by experience.

There were always indeed some places in which we employed experts. You could not very well construct city buildings without an architect, nor a sewer or street system without an engineer. There had to be some kind of a doctor in the health department, and some kind of a lawyer—generally a pretty poor one—in the department of law, but outside of such places any man could do anything. What was the necessity of talking about an expert at the head of the street cleaning department? Get a lot of street sweepers—unskilled laborers—let them pile the dust and the dirt in the street and shovel it into a cart, and then cart it away to the dump pile. Any man could do that, and the politician who controlled a certain election district or precinct was the man who would get the office, and it didn't make any difference whether he knew anything about street sweeping or not. But the street sweeping department requires an expert as much as the department of law or the department of health. In the first place, there is a very close relation between the cleaning of our streets and the health of our inhabitants, especially in the slum districts of the city, where the dust from the street is blown into the houses and breeds contagion and death. It is very important that the head of the street cleaning department should be in close touch with the health department. In the next place, it is well known now that from sixty to ninety per cent of the dirt of our cities can be prevented from accumulating on our streets at all, and the man at the head of the street cleaning department ought to know just what things are necessary to keep the dirt off the street. And then there is a very close relation also with the building department, because the build-

---

[1] Address at the Annual Meeting of the National Civil Service Reform League, December 3, 1914.

ings that are adjoining the street and the excavations that are made have a great deal to do with the cleanliness or the filth of our streets, and the head of the department should know how to provide as far as possible against the streets becoming unnecessarily dirty in that way, and he should know also how to take away ice and snow in the winter time.

I know a head of a street cleaning department, in a certain city not very far from where I happen to live, who, when the alleys of the city got choked up in the winter by filth which made them impassable, said there was no use in the world trying to clean them until the snow and ice had melted! That was his idea of the performance of his duty.

Now, in Germany nobody ever thinks of putting at the head of a department like that an unskilled man. The man must not only be a *Baumeister* but as a general thing he is a professional expert with a university training. In Dresden the present head is instructor to the Royal Technical College of Saxony, and he has a laboratory and does scientific work in the administration of the street cleaning department.

The head of this department must know the various appliances which are used for sweeping and for flushing, and which he can use to the best effect; and the cost of cleaning one hundred square feet of street—whether he can do it more cheaply by flushing or by hand work or by machinery. You go to a German city and the street cleaning doesn't begin until about eleven o'clock at night, when everybody is in bed. Then they come out—first the sprinkler and then the sweeper, and after that the carts to take the dirt away; and in the morning all is absolutely clean. Look at the condition of the streets of our cities and compare it with the conditions of the streets in German cities, or those in Scandinavia, which are as clean as any floor in your home. You can see that one is the result of expert management and the other is the result of the management of an unskilled man.

Take the health department. Everybody knows that infant mortality is caused very largely by trouble with the milk or other food and under Doctor Goler in Rochester the infant mortality was diminished more than one half in a single year, because there was an expert in charge of that department. It is to be said to the credit of the present Dayton management that the infant mortality in that city had been diminished in one year forty per cent by reason of having experts in charge.

Then take the building department. Our loss in America from fires every year is more than one quarter of a billion of dollars. The loss by fire per capita in Germany is 28 cents, in England 33 cents, in America $2.25. Now, that difference is an unnecessary loss.

While I was in Berlin on one occasion a fire broke out right opposite the hotel where we were and there was a little fire engine that came up; it looked ridiculously small. The fire was on the third floor of the building and I saw people on the floor above looking out of the window unconcernedly at the flames below and others, on the floor below, looking out with considerable curiosity at the flames above—not in the least alarmed, because they knew the fire never could reach their floor; and it did not. In a little while it was put out. Why? The building was actually fireproof. How can a German city do that while an American city cannot do it? Because the German city has an efficient expert at the head of the building department. It is not a question of the fire department at all. They build their buildings so that the fire can't get from one story to another.

Now, we could save in that way something like $200,000,000 a year in this country of ours if we had expert management and proper regulations enforced by our cities.

Well, I could go on thus from one department to another. Take the department of finance. There is nothing that requires more expert knowledge than the question of the best method of imposing city taxes. Expert knowledge is required for the purpose of having uniform systems of accounts that really tell something about a city's condition and an expert is necessary in regard to franchises. The public service corporations have experts of the very highest character, to whom they give very large salaries and the city generally has men who know very little about franchises and a few "weasel words" get into them and in the course of a few years the city is within the grip of the public service corporations. You need an expert there to take charge of the giving of franchises by a city.

Everywhere special knowledge is necessary. Now, how are you going to get it? You can't elect experts with our plan of an enormous ballot. Is there anybody that has ever cast that ballot here in Chicago who really knows the qualifications of one tenth of the parties upon it? You don't know and you can't know. If you have a good voters' league, that will tell you about some of them—you have to take what they say; but in most cities the voters' league doesn't exist. The short ballot is a necessity to good government; yet you can't have a short ballot if you are going to elect all your experts. How can you tell their qualifications? You can't tell the technical qualifications of any one man, let alone the dozens that will be up for election. So you can't elect the experts; that is impossible, and yet if you leave it to your council to choose the experts you have something that is just as bad. The council, if it were composed of disinterested and skillful men, might get a good expert; but in point of fact a council is nearly always a political body. There is a lot of log-rolling. "You vote for my man and I will vote for your man." The result is you get a bad lot of officials. There is only one way to get experts and that is by the competitive system. People used to say about the merit system, "It is all very well for clerks and stenographers and things of that kind, but when it comes to men with high technical skill and accomplishments you can't get them that way, they won't submit to examination"; and so there were a number of exceptions made in offices where special qualifications were required. These were left out of the civil service examinations. They are the very men whose qualifications can be tested best of all in that way. I suppose there was a time when it was true that physicians of great skill or lawyers of considerable ability and so on would not consent to take competitive examinations conducted by commissions that did not know anything of technical subjects. But conditions have entirely altered. The commissions don't profess, themselves, to prepare the questions or grade the papers, but they call in experts of the highest class in the particular profession for which an examination is to be held. In the examination held for librarian here in Chicago, the most skillful men in the country, Mr. Putnam of the congressional library in Washington, and other librarians, were called to prepare the papers and grade the candidates, and they succeeded in getting for the public library of your city one of the greatest librarians of our country.

We find that not only are chemists and engineers and men of that kind employed in this way, but even high administrative officers. For instance, the superintendent of the lighthouse service is so chosen; the chief of the fire department in New York city was so selected and superintendents of Indian reservations. Those are places that require large administrative ability. You say, "How are you going to examine these men and find out what their qualifications are?" Supposing you were the president of a railroad and wanted to get a man for a position, perhaps the superintendent of an important division, how would you go about it if you didn't happen to know a suitable man? What such a president would do would be this. He would go to those that have knowledge of the respective applicants (for instance, the men they had worked for), and he would inquire of each, "How long has he worked for you, how many men has he been in charge of, what has been his experience, what is his education, what are his qualifications, what can you say as to his honesty," and so forth. If he were a careful president, he would take all the precautions of that kind that he could and he would investigate all the references given. That is exactly what the examiners of the Civil Service Commission do in the examination, for instance, of a superintendent of Indian reservations. They don't bring the applicants all together and ask them a lot of questions and see who answers the greatest number of those questions,—not at all; but they require that each man shall give the name of ten persons and of those ten persons at least five must be men who have been his superiors or subordinates and they inquire of these men what kind of work he has done, how long he has worked at it, etc. They give this investigation a grading of four out of ten. Then they inquire of the applicant himself as to his business experience, what men he has had under him, where he has worked, what kind of work it was, etc. That is what a man does if he be a head of a great corporation and that is exactly what the examiners of the United States Civil Service Commission do. They require him also to write a thesis or article upon what he considers his duty—what he ought to do as superintendent, and in some cases they have also an oral examination in order that they may test the qualities of the man by means of a personal interview, just as the president of a railroad would call before him some of the applicants in order that he could see which of them appeared to be the most intelligent.

Now, that is the kind of an examination it is. Perhaps it ought not to be called an examination. I think I would rather call it a competitive investigation or competitive test. It is a non-assembled examination. In that way you get the highest kind of service. That is the only way to keep those places out of politics and to have them go really to those who are most competent to perform the duties.

APPENDIX X

According to the proposed model law the man managing a department or perhaps a whole city can *neither appoint, suspend, transfer, or remove a single one of his subordinates.* He has not the slightest power over any of them except the power which every citizen has of making complaint to the Commission.

What means are left to enforce his authority and command the respect and loyalty of his employees? What assurance is there that the Civil Service Commission will coöperate with department heads in carrying out their plans and enforcing their ideas of efficiency and loyal service? When a man whom the hea of a department knows is dishonest or insubordinate is retained by the Commission what is the department head to do? He has made his charges and he has been turned down. What is his authority over his own force thereafter?

The Commission is not to be elected by the people or even appointed directly by the people's representative, but chosen as the result of a competitive examination, and cannot be recalled or removed by the people nor by any superior officer whatever but only after trial by a tribunal specially organized for the purpose. The Commission is therefore responsible to no one for its decisions, yet it removes or retains employees for whose conduct another is responsible.

Let us take the city of Dayton as an illustration of removals by a civil service board. It is the largest city which has adopted the manager form of government. This city is governed by five city commissioners who have selected an expert from another city, Henry M. Waite, to administer their municipal affairs. In answer to my inquiry as to what the Dayton manager thought of this proposal and after showing him the provision of the "model law" affecting removals, he wrote, "Discipline could not be maintained. Your civil service board had better operate, your results would be more likely to attain success than under the proposed idea. I cannot see how any person who desired success could afford to attempt to operate under such a rule. Certainly I would not."

If a deliberate effort were made to checkmate the present course of

326

municipal progress in securing business management for cities it could not be done more effectually than by securing the passage of a "model law" taking from expert managing officers all power to control their subordinates.

The leaders of the movement for civil service reform have expressed the conviction that the power of the responsible superior officer to remove his subordinates ought not to be taken away. Over and over again did George William Curtis declare this principle. In his address before the American Social Science Association September 8, 1881, and again in his address at the fifth annual meeting of the National Civil Service Reform League, August 4, 1886, he said: "Removal for cause, if the cause were to be decided by *any authority but that of the superior officer*, instead of improving would swiftly and enormously enhance the cost, and ruin the efficiency of the public service by destroying subordination and making every lazy officer or clerk twice as lazy and incompetent as before."

Mr. Carl Schurz, in his discussion before that League at its Newport meeting in 1886, said: "I would leave to the appointing officer the entire discretion of removing subordinates, but I would oblige him in all cases to state the reasons. The reasons would fall under either misconduct or inefficiency."

Mr. Dorman B. Eaton thought that the League's condemnation of removals should be limited to removals for partisan reasons or for the purpose of making place for another, and accordingly the resolution of the League so provided (*Proceedings*, 1886, p. 32).

Two years later the League expressed officially in its formal resolutions, without dissent, the following principle (1888, p. 32): "An office-holding class and a permanent tenure are practically impossible *so long as the power of removal remains unimpaired.*"

In 1896, its resolutions declared: "The League fully recognizes the importance of *preserving to responsible superior officers the power of removal of their subordinates whenever in their judgment this power* should be exercised in the public interest."

What is a life tenure? It is not that the official or employee is absolutely irremovable. Federal judges are not irremovable, yet they have a life tenure. The essence of it is that they cannot be removed by the executive or by any superior officer but only after trial by some independent body and that they are therefore themselves independent. This would be true of employees in the civil service if the proposed law were enacted.

It is asked, "Why are you unwilling to take away the power of removals from heads of departments and yet insist that the power of appointment shall be taken away by competitive examinations?" The answer is that the latter is necessary to protect the service against political appointments while discipline can be maintained, no matter who makes the appointments, only so long as the power of removal remains unimpaired.

It is said the lack of permanency of tenure will discourage the best men from competing. Has it discouraged them? Are we not getting all over the country, men of higher and higher qualifications, who are quite satisfied with the same kind of permanency which exists in private corporations, where every applicant knows that his tenure depends on giving satisfaction to his employer?

The arguments in support of vesting the exclusive power of removal in the Civil Service Commission as urged by the advocates of this system were these:

I. It follows the system adopted in our great industrial organizations.

II. It is approved by our most eminent publicists and civil service reformers.

III. It is necessary to protect the service against the evils of a trial in court and it avoids expensive and dilatory legal procedure.

IV. It has been justified by twenty years of satisfactory experience in Chicago and Cook County and by a number of years of successful experience in the State service in Illinois.

I. As to the first claim that the proposed plan follows the methods adopted in our greatest and most progressive industrial organizations, we were referred to the great railways of the country, to Marshall Field & Co., and to the International Harvester Co.

As to the railways, the secretary of the National Civil Service Reform League wrote to the superintendent of employment of nine of the principal systems,[1] and found that in every case but one (the Pullman Co.) the managing officer had the final authority. I afterwards wrote to the Pullman Co., which answered, "While the dismissal or retention of an employee is ordinarily handled and controlled by a Central Agency, extraordinary conditions occasionally arise wherein the action of the Central Agency is overruled or set aside by our Executive and General Officers."

I also learned from a superintendent of the Pennsylvania lines west of Pittsburgh that the division superintendents had themselves the power of dismissal, subject to an appeal to higher operating officers and that the board which took cognizance of the matter *in aid* of the executive officials had itself no final authority.

In answer to an inquiry addressed to the president of Marshall Field & Co., I received the following. "Our practice in most cases is to place the power of removal with the *departmental managers*, the executive staff, however, having knowledge of such removals and the causes leading up to them. If a departmental head is to be held responsible for the efficiency of his organization he should have control, within certain limits, of the personnel of his staff and without the power of removal he could not assume such responsibilities successfully."

---

[1] Chicago, Milwaukee & St. Paul, Chicago, Burlington & Quincy, Lehigh Valley, New Haven, Baltimore & Ohio, Southern Pacific, Delaware, Lackawanna & Western, Delaware & Hudson, and the Pullman Co.

I inquired of Mr. George W. Perkins in regard to the International Harvester Co., and learned from him that the ultimate right to remove subordinates remained in the operating officers; that they could not conduct their business in any other way. He considered removals by an independent employment agency impracticable.

After all the instances of business management cited had shown exactly the reverse of what was claimed, another case was brought up, that of Wm. Filene Sons' Company in which it was urged that something resembling the proposed law was adopted.

It appears that this company put the decision as to all dismissals in the hands of an arbitration committee appointed by its employees, who might by a two-thirds vote reinstate any man dismissed. But at the close of the instructions given by the directors on November 1, 1912, authorizing this committee, was the following significant paragraph: "The above instructions are subject to amendment, alteration or repeal by the Board of Directors."

The Filene Company also allowed its employees four members in a directorate of eleven. Still the ultimate power remained in the directors who represented the stockholders. Four directors cannot outvote seven and if any obnoxious employee should be reinstated by the arbitration board a complete remedy was held in reserve, the directors could amend or repeal the instructions and abolish the arbitration committee.

The proposed model law was entirely different. The Civil Service Commissioner was to be appointed, not by employees, but by an independent mechanical device—a competitive examination—and could not be removed except by an independent tribunal. Neither the governor of the State nor the mayor, manager nor council of any city would have the reserve power so necessary to discipline, nor could the action of the Commission be controlled if it were to do the thing which would destroy all subordination in the service. If the Filene Co. had established a rule that they would reinstate any man whom some independent officer decided should be restored, and if they had taken away from their own directors all right to repeal or amend the power thus conferred upon this independent tribunal the analogy would be closer.

It is said that this proposed model law is in line with the discipline in the military and naval service, that an officer cannot dismiss a soldier or sailor, but must bring the case to the hearing of a court-martial. Yet the finding of a court-martial is always subject to the approval of a commanding officer. The ultimate authority rests with the executive official. Whatever the form that is the vital principle. It is the reserve power to make the final decision which is necessary to maintain proper discipline and subordination in the civil service just as in the army and navy.

II. It was claimed that this removal plan was approved by our most eminent publicists and civil service reformers. On the contrary their opinions were the other way. The declarations of George William Curtis, Carl Schurz, and Dorman B. Eaton have already been given. President Lowell of Harvard was referred to. He wrote me "In Section 48 of the Model Charter for Cities, we agreed that officers might be removed by the City Manager or head of the department and I do not believe that an administration could be made to work well otherwise."

Mr. Charles J. Bonaparte, who had been chairman of the Council of the League wrote me, November 16, 1915. "I am inflexibly opposed to anything amounting to a trial for a subordinate removed or disciplined by a superior unless the latter thinks something of the kind is needed to guide his own judgment."

The two men in America who have had the widest experience in the Federal service, President Roosevelt and President Taft are utterly opposed to this measure. President Taft wrote, "I am very much opposed to any civil service law which takes from the managing and operating officers the power of dismissing subordinates and gives it to an independent body."

President Roosevelt wrote, "I regard the proposed law as seeking to establish a condition much worse than the spoils system. If the proposal or any proposal resembling it is adopted I shall resign and shall state that nothing proposed by Tammany during my life-time has begun to approach in mischief this proposal. . . . Proposals such as this tend hopelessly to discredit the cause of civil service reform among sensible people and nothing more mischievous could be imagined."

Seth Low, former mayor of Brooklyn and afterwards of Greater New York, wrote, "I am unreservedly in sympathy with the objections you make to the proposed section of the model law which would transfer the question of the removal of employees in the public service from the responsible officials to a civil service commissioner or commissioners. No man who understands the first principles of sound administration would be willing to accept responsibility under such a system. Nothing can do the system as a whole so much injury as to have its friends stand for such a proposal."

General Winkler, the venerable president of the Wisconsin Civil Service Reform Association wrote, "If the League adopts the model law as its platform, I was going to say I should cease to be a civil service reformer, but I will only say that the very little I shall be able to do will be on the outside of its folds."

Moorfield Storey declared, "I feel it would be disastrous if the power of removal were left as it is in the proposed bill."

Mr. Henry F. Hunt, the reform mayor of Cincinnati writes, "In my opinion, to lodge such power anywhere other than in the person responsible for the efficiency of his division would be ruinous."

III. It is said that we must provide for removals by the Civil Service Commission in order to protect the service against the greater evil of legislation providing for removals by a trial in court. In some special places there may be danger of legislation granting such a trial. But this proposed model law was not a local or temporary concession of an evil thing in order to prevent a still greater evil (which might well be necessary at certain times or in certain places) it was proposed for acceptance and adoption everywhere as a thing right in itself, and ought not to contain things adapted only to special conditions.

If the argument were to be received, that trials by the Commission were to protect the service against something worse, then we ought to look at the other side of the picture and see what danger may follow if the power of removal is taken from operating officers. For years past civil service reformers have been fighting session after session against the enactment of laws fixing a definite term for places in the classified service. The argument has been, "Why provide for removals at the end of a fixed term when the superior officer has a right to remove subordinates at any time for proper cause?" The argument is unanswerable and it has prevailed. But if this power of removal be taken away, the chief defense against such injurious legislation will fall to the ground.

IV. The next claim is that the system of removal proposed has been justified by over twenty years' satisfactory experience with a similar rule in Chicago.

The answer to this is that in the first place the rule is not similar and in the second place the experience has not been satisfactory.

The rule is not similar in two vital particulars. In the first place the Chicago removals are made by a commission appointed and removable by the same authority as that which administers the various departments, to wit, by the mayor. He is the responsible head and can get rid of the commission when he will. The mayor is also the head of the administration and appoints and removes the heads of departments. But by the proposed law the power of removal is entrusted to an independent tribunal, neither appointed nor removed by the head of the administration. By the proposed system there is to be a two-headed administration in which mutual struggles would be inevitable and discipline impossible.

In the second place the Chicago rule left to the head of the office some remnant of the means of enforcing discipline but the proposed law would not do this.

The Chicago law gives to the head of departments the right to suspend any subordinate for thirty days without pay. This amounts of itself to the fine of a month's salary and is imposed as a direct punishment. But by the proposed model law a man could only be suspended as a precautionary measure for fifteen days. Then if the charges are not sustained he gets full pay. The head of the department has no power of punishment whatever.

But it is emphatically untrue that the Chicago rule has worked well during the last twenty years. It has worked to the satisfaction of only two classes, the commissioners who administer it and the classified employees who are protected by it. I found the commissioners unanimous in their belief that the removal rule was a good thing, just as we would find that an autocrat would believe that the divine right of kings was a good thing.

They know that they have administered the law well and have dismissed and retained just the right persons.

But even some of those connected with the trial boards, realize that the system is a bad one.   Thus Professor Fairlie, who was one of them wrote me:

" From observation and informal inquiry, I believe that the requirement for a formal investigation *does* cause the superior officers to feel hampered in their relations with their subordinates, and encourages the subordinate in laxity and careless work in minor matters which do not lend themselves easily to the presentation of formal charges.

" A civil service commission or investigating officer under the Illinois law could easily interfere with the control of superior officers over their subordinates."

I found also that the classified employees protected by the Chicago removal rule were very generally in favor of it.

But as to the heads of departments whose power of discipline was taken away, I found the feeling was quite different.

I went up and down the corridors of the City Hall, first to one office and then to another, and introduced myself and found that every head of a department that I interviewed opposed the rule.   One of them told me that although he had had no friction with the Commission himself, he greatly disapproved of the plan of taking this power from the head of the department.   He said that bad conduct often consisted in a succession of little things lasting for years and not provable before a commission, and he also gave me for illustration a case which had come to his knowledge in another department where the head had repeatedly tried in vain to discharge an intemperate employee.

In the Police Department I learned that a policeman had been dismissed on the charge of receiving money from prostitutes for protection, but had been restored by the commissioners while the General Superintendent of Police was absent and knew nothing about it.

I accordingly called upon Mr. Healey, the General Superintendent of Police, who said, "I decline to discuss the civil service provisions except in the presence of the Civil Service Commissioners themselves."   It seemed to me that this refusal was more eloquent than any affirmative expression. If he had really approved of the act of the Commission in reinstating the man there could have been no possible embarrassment in saying so, but if the Superintendent thought otherwise and yet realized the absolute power which the Civil Service Commission exercised over the whole personnel of his department, and if at the time this question was suddenly put to him, he was at the moment unwilling to express his approval of the reinstatement of such a man to the force of which he was the chief, his answer would have been exactly what it was.   No incident in Chicago impressed me so strongly as this with the immense power of the Commission for evil as well as for good and the manner in which that power could be abused.

It might be better to take back uncomplainingly even such a man than contest this power.

I called upon the telephone, Mr. Clayton Smith, Warden of the Cook County Hospital. He said he had had a number of cases turned down by the Civil Service Commission, and that it had impaired discipline among his subordinates so that he kept some whom he thought ought not to stay and brought no charges unless he felt sure he would win his case. He added, "They don't have their boss in fear any more. They put on an air indicating that they can get back through the trial board if they want to." He noticed that employees on probation behaved well while they were subject to dismissal at his will, but as soon as they received their definite appointment and were subject only to the trial board their conduct changed and they became difficult to deal with.

The Chicago Smoke Inspector said to me, October 11, 1915, "The department heads should have the power of dismissal because they are responsible."

In order not to limit my inquiries to the new heads of departments recently appointed, I visited John E. Traeger the Sheriff, who had formerly been Controller of the city under Mayor Harrison, where his force was under the competitive system.

He approved of the civil service law but not of the removal clause. I asked him whether in cases where the Commission refused to dismiss a man upon charges by the head of the department that impaired discipline, and he said "Absolutely," and he added later, "Don't make a Czar of your commissioner. He'll ruin the service." He also told me that men behaved better when on probation and subject to discharge by the head of the office than they did after they had received a regular appointment.

I also interviewed over the telephone, James Gleason, former Superintendent of Police, under Mayor Harrison. He said, "I have known of cases where men were reinstated who ought not to be."

I further found that the tendency of this removal rule was to make very few removals. It is almost inevitable that any trial based on a complaint made by an appointing officer should become really a trial of that officer himself as well as the subordinate complained of. Hence these officers were inclined to make very few complaints and permanent tenure of all employees, both good and bad, resulted. This permanency of tenure had become ingrained into the habits of thought of the community and was promoted by the decisions of the courts.

For in Illinois it has been held that a place on the eligible list when once posted becomes a property right which cannot be canceled for two years. How much more then is a position actually acquired to be deemed a vested interest!

It was stated by the advocates of the model law that the Chicago removal rule really brought about more dismissals than where such removals were made by appointing officers but that such removals were made for actual derelictions and not for personal or political reasons. Was the statement correct? It was said that in 1910 there were 203 removals by department heads, and in 1911, 467 by the trial board. Was this a fair average or was it the case of a new broom sweeping clean?

I inquired of Mr. Swanson, Secretary of the Chicago Civil Service Commission, and he told me that out of more than 20,000 employees during the whole year 1914 the trial board removed 73. Less than 16 per cent of those charged with offenses were removed; the total percentage of removals in proportion to the whole service was less than thirty-seven hundredths of 1 per cent. The average of removals under other systems is about 2 per cent, but under the trial board plan it is only about one sixth of that, so the Chicago removal rule has undoubtedly secured permanency for employees. It comes as near creating an actual life tenure as is humanly practicable. Does this work well in the long run? Can anyone pretend or imagine that the Chicago civil service is so good that only one in 300 needs to be separated from it during a whole year? The general reputation and known facts concerning this service will not justify this happy deduction.[1]

---

[1] It is said by advocates of the proposed model law that the serious evils in Chicago were due to the fact that the present Commission was a particularly bad one and that all went on very well during the golden age which preceded it.

One of the most serious charges against the Commission was that they allowed an excessive number of temporary appointments—some 9163 authorizations for such appointments being granted. This was indeed highly reprehensible. But Mr. Swanson, the Secretary of the Commission both before and after the change, in his report says: "During the first four months of last year 11,866 such appointments were authorized by the former Commission. During the next four months under the present Commission 9163 such authorities were granted, a reduction of 2703. No criticism was made of the record of the first four months but the record of the second four months was seized upon as a gross violation of the law. The inconsistency of the criticism was at once apparent."

He also said:

"The number of temporary authorities outstanding in the classified service at various periods is shown here: April 30, 1912, 497; June 30, 1913, 522; May 31, 1914, 815; Sept. 30, 1914, 780; Feb. 1, 1915, 708; April 1, 1915, 674; Aug. 15, 1915, 819; Dec. 1, 1915, 485.

"Laborers being seasonal employees do not form a comparison and are accordingly omitted from the above table. December 1, 1915, shows the lowest point recorded in more than three years."

So it appears that during all these years of excellent administration of the Chicago civil service law these excessive temporary appointments were a continuous feature of that administration!

If the greater permanency caused by the Chicago removal rule has worked so well why has the Chicago police force been one of the most corrupt and inefficient bodies in municipal history? Why is crime rampant?

At a meeting of the Chicago City Club in December, 1915, called to discuss the iniquities of the Civil Service Commission many spoke. On the third day of this discussion Professor Graham Taylor, president of the Chicago School of Ethics and Philanthropy and one of the editors of *The Survey*, said:

"Now, talking about driving the crooks out of Chicago; I would like to know when in this administration or any previous administration the crooks have been very much dispossessed, not only of their foothold but of their power over three police stations in this city. I would like to know who has been in command of the Desplaines Street Police Station. Never the captain to all appearances. Every better captain that has gone there has either gone to the bad and gone down to his ruin, or else he has been transferred 'for the good of the service.' . . .

"And how about the East Chicago Avenue Station and the Twenty-second Street Police Station? I tell you, men, if we want life and property safe in this city, that kind of farming out of the police power in this city has got to stop and the only way to stop it is by loyalty to this most fundamental of all bases for good government, the Civil Service Law of the State of Illinois. If it isn't satisfactory then let us make it so."

The Mayor of the city said (Chicago *Tribune*, December 19th):

"In Rogers Park alone I am informed there have been twenty first class crimes in the last few days."

The State Attorney, Mr. McClay Hoyne, declared that the police department was a den of thieves. The former Chief of Detectives, John J. Halpin, was charged with accepting bribes and was dismissed. The brutality of the police toward the poor women engaged in the garment makers' strike was a subject of public scandal and almost universal reprobation.

Mr. Catherwood at the annual meeting of the National Civil Service Reform League in 1911 (see Proceedings, p. 12) reported for Illinois that the Chief of Police, all the inspectors, and most of the captains, 150 in all, had been entangled with graft, vice, and special interests or were blind and incompetent.

Yet this is the result of twenty years of "successful" experience under the permanent tenure promoted by the Chicago removal rule!

In the State civil service also there has been trouble with the trial board system in regard to the Illinois State library. The following statement is copied from a periodical known as *Public Libraries* published in Chicago by the Library Bureau, the official organ of the American Library Association.

"In order to have a trained cataloguer, it was necessary to dismiss an attendant who was there by political appointment when the present administration came in, and not because of any preparation for the work.

Since the library is under the civil service law of the State, the dismissed attendant called on the Civil Service Commission to defend what she thought were her rights in the matter. The Commission therefore brought State Librarian Woods to trial to make him prove his charge of incompetency against the attendant.

"Those in charge of the library testified that the attendant in question could not perform the duties assigned her satisfactorily, was not acquainted with the methods of classification, cataloguing, etc., in general use, and that they considered her incompetent for the work. The civil service board, however, took the position that she was not more incompetent than she had ever been and that if she were incompetent the others there were incompetent from the civil service point of view also, and that she should therefore be reinstated and receive her salary for the two months of her exclusion." (*Public Libraries*, March, 1914.)

I inquired of Mr. George B. Uttley, Secretary of the American Library Association, who informed me that the foregoing facts were exactly true and that the acting librarian was the chief sufferer by this remarkable decision of the State Commission.

In the face of all this evidence who can say that the trial boards and the exclusive jurisdiction of the Commission over removals have promoted good administration?

INDEX

POLITICS AND PEOPLE

The Ordeal of Self-Government in America

An Arno Press Collection

Allen, Robert S., editor. **Our Fair City.** 1947

Belmont, Perry. **Return to Secret Party Funds:** Value of Reed Committee. 1927

Berge, George W. **The Free Pass Bribery System:** Showing How the Railroads, Through the Free Pass Bribery System, Procure the Government Away from the People. 1905

Billington, Ray Allen. **The Origins of Nativism in the United States, 1800-1844.** 1933

Black, Henry Campbell. **The Relation of the Executive Power to Legislation.** 1919

Boothe, Viva Belle. **The Political Party as a Social Process.** 1923

Breen, Matthew P. **Thirty Years of New York Politics, Up-to-Date.** 1899

Brooks, Robert C. **Corruption in American Politics and Life.** 1910

Brown, George Rothwell. **The Leadership of Congress.** 1922

Bryan, William Jennings. **A Tale of Two Conventions:** Being an Account of the Republican and Democratic National Conventions of June, 1912. 1912

The Caucus System in American Politics. 1974

Childs, Harwood Lawrence. **Labor and Capital in National Politics.** 1930

Clapper, Raymond. **Racketeering in Washington.** 1933

Crawford, Kenneth G. **The Pressure Boys:** The Inside Story of Lobbying in America. 1939

Dallinger, Frederick W. **Nominations for Elective Office in the United States.** 1897

Dunn, Arthur Wallace. **Gridiron Nights:** Humorous and Satirical Views of Politics and Statesmen as Presented by the Famous Dining Club. 1915

Ervin, Spencer. **Henry Ford vs. Truman H. Newberry:** The Famous Senate Election Contest. A Study in American Politics, Legislation and Justice. 1935

Ewing, Cortez A.M. and Royden J. Dangerfield. **Documentary Source Book in American Government and Politics.** 1931

Ford, Henry Jones. **The Cost of Our National Government:** A Study in Political Pathology. 1910

Foulke, William Dudley. **Fighting the Spoilsmen:** Reminiscences of the Civil Service Reform Movement. 1919

Fuller, Hubert Bruce. **The Speakers of the House.** 1909

Griffith, Elmer C. **The Rise and Development of the Gerrymander.** 1907

Hadley, Arthur Twining. **The Relations Between Freedom and Responsibility in the Evolution of Democratic Government.** 1903

Hart, Albert Bushnell. **Practical Essays on American Government.** 1893

Holcombe, Arthur N. **The Political Parties of To-Day:** A Study in Republican and Democratic Politics. 1924

Hughes, Charles Evans. **Conditions of Progress in Democratic Government.** 1910

Kales, Albert M. **Unpopular Government in the United States.** 1914

Kent, Frank R. **The Great Game of Politics.** 1930

Lynch, Denis Tilden. **"Boss" Tweed:** The Story of a Grim Generation. 1927

McCabe, James D., Jr. (Edward Winslow Martin, pseud.) **Behind the Scenes in Washington.** 1873

Macy, Jesse. **Party Organization and Machinery.** 1912

Macy, Jesse. **Political Parties in the United States, 1846-1861.** 1900

Moley, Raymond. **Politics and Criminal Prosecution.** 1929

Munro, William Bennett. **The Invisible Government** and **Personality in Politics:** A Study of Three Types in American Public Life. 1928/1934 Two volumes in one.

Myers, Gustavus. **History of Public Franchises in New York City,** Boroughs of Manhattan and the Bronx. (Reprinted from **Municipal Affairs,** March 1900) 1900

Odegard, Peter H. and E. Allen Helms. **American Politics:** A Study in Political Dynamics. 1938

Orth, Samuel P. **Five American Politicians:** A Study in the Evolution of American Politics. 1906

Ostrogorski, M[oisei I.] **Democracy and the Party System in the United States:** A Study in Extra-Constitutional Government. 1910

Overacker, Louise. **Money in Elections.** 1932

Overacker, Louise. **The Presidential Primary.** 1926

The Party Battle. 1974

Peel, Roy V. and Thomas C. Donnelly. **The 1928 Campaign:** An Analysis. 1931

Pepper, George Wharton. **In the Senate** and **Family Quarrels:** The President, The Senate, The House. 1930/1931. Two volumes in one

Platt, Thomas Collier. **The Autobiography of Thomas Collier Platt.** Compiled and edited by Louis J. Lang. 1910

Roosevelt, Theodore. **Social Justice and Popular Rule:** Essays, Addresses, and Public Statements Relating to the Progressive Movement, 1910-1916 (*The Works of Theodore Roosevelt,* Memorial Edition, Volume XIX) 1925

Root, Elihu. **The Citizen's Part in Government** and **Experiments in Government and the Essentials of the Constitution.** 1907/1913. Two volumes in one

Rosten, Leo C. **The Washington Correspondents.** 1937

Salter, J[ohn] T[homas]. **Boss Rule:** Portraits in City Politics. 1935

Schattschneider, E[lmer] E[ric]. **Politics, Pressures and the Tariff:** A Study of Free Private Enterprise in Pressure Politics, as Shown in the 1929-1930 Revision of the Tariff. 1935

Smith, T[homas] V. and Robert A. Taft. **Foundations of Democracy:** A Series of Debates. 1939

The Spoils System in New York. 1974

Stead, W[illiam] T. **Satan's Invisible World Displayed,** Or, Despairing Democracy. A Study of Greater New York (The Review of Reviews Annual) 1898

Van Devander, Charles W. **The Big Bosses.** 1944

Wallis, J[ames] H. **The Politician:** His Habits, Outcries and Protective Coloring. 1935

Werner, M[orris] R. **Privileged Characters.** 1935

White, William Allen. **Politics:** The Citizen's Business. 1924

Wooddy, Carroll Hill. **The Case of Frank L. Smith:** A Study in Representative Government. 1931

Wooddy, Carroll Hill. **The Chicago Primary of 1926:** A Study in Election Methods. 1926